★ ★ ★ ★ ★ ★ ★ ★ ★ ★ ★ ★ ★ ★ ★ ★ ★ ★
★ ★ ★ ★ ★ ★ ★ ★ ★ ★ ★ ★ ★ ★ ★ ★ ★ ★
★ ★ ★ ★ ★ ★ ★ ★ ★ ★ ★ ★ ★ ★ ★ ★ ★ ★
★ ★ ★ ★ ★ ★ ★ ★ ★ ★ ★ ★ ★ ★ ★ ★ ★ ★

TURNING RIGHT IN THE SIXTIES

★★★★★★★★★★★★★★★★★★★★★★★★
★★★★★★★★★★★★★★★★★★★★★★★★
★★★★★★★★★★★★★★★★★★★★★★★★
★★★★★★★★★★★★★★★★★★★★★★★★
★★★★★★★★★★★★★★★★★★★★★★★★
★★★★★★★★★★★★★★★★★★★★★★★★
★★★★★★★★★★★★★★★★★★★★★★★★
★★★★★★★★★★★★★★★★★★★★★★★★
★★★★★★★★★★★★★★★★★★★★★★★★
★★★★★★★★★★★★★★★★★★★★★★★★
★★★★★★★★★★★★★★★★★★★★★★★★
★★★★★★★★★★★★★★★★★★★★★★★★

TURNING

Right

IN THE SIXTIES

The Conservative Capture of the GOP

MARY C. BRENNAN

THE UNIVERSITY OF NORTH CAROLINA PRESS

Chapel Hill & London

Library of Congress Cataloging-in-Publication Data

Brennan, Mary C.

Turning right in the sixties : the conservative capture of
the GOP / by Mary C. Brennan.

p.   cm.

Includes bibliographical references and index.

ISBN 0-8078-2230-2 (cloth : alk. paper)

1. Conservatism—United States.   2. Republican Party
(U.S. : 1854–   )   3. United States—Politics and
government—1945–1989.   I. Title.

JC573.2.U6B74   1995

324.2734'09046—dc20   95-11799

CIP

99 98 97 96 95   5 4 3 2 1

Parts of chapters 1 and 2 appeared in a different form
in "A Step in the 'Right' Direction: Conservative
Republicans and the Election of 1960," *Presidential
Studies Quarterly* 22, no. 1 (Winter 1992): 73–87.
Permission granted by the Center for the Study of the
Presidency, publisher of *Presidential Studies Quarterly*.

FOR MY FATHER,

who told me anything was possible,

AND MY MOTHER,

who taught me how to make it happen.

Acknowledgments *ix*

Introduction *1*

1 An Uneasy Alliance *6*

2 Challenging the Politics of
Consensus: Conservative Republicans
and the Election of 1960 *19*

3 Problems and Solutions *39*

4 Seizing the Moment *60*

5 Baptism by Fire *82*

6 Biding Their Time *104*

7 Victory? *120*

Conclusion *138*

Notes *143*

Bibliography *195*

Index *205*

★ ★ ★ ★ ★ ★ ★ ★ ★ ★ ★ ★ ★ ★ ★ ★ ★ ★ ★

CONTENTS

★ ★ ★ ★ ★ ★ ★ ★ ★ ★ ★ ★ ★ ★ ★ ★ ★ ★ ★ ★

ACKNOWLEDGMENTS

Although writing a book is frequently a lonely task, it cannot be accomplished without a wide network of support. The financial assistance of the Department of History and the Graduate School of Miami University enabled me to complete the initial research and then to write full-time. Grants from the Gerald R. Ford Foundation and the John Fitzgerald Kennedy Library allowed me to complete additional research. The librarians and archivists at the various research facilities I visited were helpful and efficient, and all of them went out of their way to be kind to a stranger. In particular, I thank the archivists of the Arizona Historical Foundation, who granted me full access to their resources in spite of the reorganization they were undergoing. Similarly, the staff of the National Archives and Records Administration, both in Washington, D.C., and Laguna Niguel, exceeded the bounds of duty by offering transportation and refreshment, as well as use of the archives' wonderful resources. I am also grateful to the staff of the Dwight D. Eisenhower Library.

Throughout the book's development, I have benefited from the suggestions and critiques of numerous people. In the early stages, Allan Winkler encouraged, challenged, and cajoled me into greater productivity than I thought possible, never doubting my ability to complete this project. I also received generous help and advice from scholars such as Leo Ribuffo and Richard Fried, who read and commented on parts of the manuscript that were presented at various conferences. In addition, colleagues and friends at Southwest Texas State University provided a wonderfully supportive work atmosphere. They listened and encouraged but did not pressure. I am particularly grateful to Gregg Andrews, who read through the entire manuscript with a historian's vision and an editor's red pen. I also thank Frank de la Teja, who guided me through the sometimes murky waters of word processing and never lost patience.

I have been blessed with the opportunity to study and work with historians who have shaped my perspective on the world as well as my profession, beginning in graduate school with professors such as David Fahey, Michael J. Hogan, Jeffrey P. Kimball, and Jack T. Kirby. Charlotte Newman Goldy at Miami University and Vikki Bynum at Southwest Texas State University taught me essential techniques for survival in this profession. Friends like Jennifer Bosch, Greta Bucher, Mark Fernandez, Vista McCroskey, Margaret Paton Walsh, and Cindy Wilkey served as helpful sounding boards for ideas and offered encouragement. In particular, I thank Padma Manian and Kurt Schultz, who heard and read more about conservatives than they ever wanted to know.

In the publication of the book, I was ably assisted by the staff of the University of North Carolina Press, who answered my questions and put up with my just-met deadlines. I am especially grateful to Lewis Bateman, who maintained steadfast support for the manuscript even in its early, rough form. I also appreciate the efforts of Paula Wald, who brought enthusiasm, as well as professionalism, to her work as copyeditor.

Finally, I thank my friends and family in Cincinnati, who did not always understand what I was doing or why but remained interested and supportive. I am especially and deeply grateful to my mother, Charlotte, my sisters, Brigid and Patty, my brother-in-law, Jack, and my nephew, Jacob, who always believed I could do whatever I set my mind to and made me believe it too.

TURNING RIGHT IN THE SIXTIES

INTRODUCTION

During the 1960s, while the majority of Americans were contemplating the fortunes and misfortunes of liberalism, conservatives methodically, and somewhat surreptitiously, became a dominant force in national politics by gaining control of the Republican Party. Disorganized and divided in 1960, defeated spectacularly in 1964, the Right at first glance appeared to be as obsolete and ineffective as liberals claimed. Yet despite its seeming impotence, the Right evolved into a complex, organized, and effective political force that dominated the GOP by 1968 and eventually secured the election of a staunch conservative as president in 1980.

Beginning in the 1960s and continuing in the succeeding years, a one-dimensional view of the 1960s as a decade of radical movements drew the focus away from other important developments occurring during that time. Journalists and scholars, by spotlighting only the protesters, students, hippies, and demonstrators, ignored the action taking place at stage right and therefore presented a lopsided view of the decade. They spoke of political and social polarization but concentrated their attention and study on the Left. When observers did glance to their right, their gazes frequently riveted on the most extreme figures—flamboyant individuals and groups who invited ridicule.

Journalists happily promoted this interest in the extremes. Portraying the "nut cases" as representative of the entire right-wing movement, magazines such as *The Nation* easily dismissed what they labeled a "pseudoconservative revolt." While some commentators implied that the movement on the right did not exist, others downplayed its significance. *Nation* author Hans Engh reported that historian Richard Hofstadter claimed the right-wing movement had "passed its peak of influence in 1955." Arthur Schlesinger, Jr., remarked in his account of the Kennedy years that the press "reported much of this [activity on the right] with *surprising* solemnity" (emphasis added).[1] Thus, even what little attention the mainstream media paid to the conservatives undercut the importance of the movement to the general public.

Feeling isolated from mainstream society and ignored by the press and politicians, conservative Americans from different economic, educational, and social backgrounds resolved to make their voices heard by their party, their elected officials, and their country. They turned to an increasingly vocal conservative press for guidance and to an ever-growing number of right-wing politicians for action. This conservative coalition mounted one of the only true draft movements of the twentieth century. Building on the increased willingness of disparate conservative groups to work together as well as on the potential apparent in the short-lived presidential drive of Arizona senator Barry Goldwater in 1960, Republican conservatives F. Clifton White, John Ashbrook, and William Rusher began almost immediately after the 1960 election to organize support for the nomination of a conservative in 1964. Secretly and steadily they contacted like-minded people across the country, eventually gathering enough grassroots delegates to ensure Goldwater the Republican nomination. Liberal Republicans, caught off guard, failed to stop the Goldwater steamroller. Unfortunately for the conservative candidate, however, enthusiasm was no substitute for experience. Novices at running a national campaign, Goldwater and his staff were swept aside by the Lyndon B. Johnson tidal wave.

Conservatives' failure to elect their candidate obscured the more significant fact that they had wrested control of the Republican Party from the men and women who had dominated it for years. They did not stop there, however. In moves that the New Left never mastered, conservatives learned from their mistakes, compromised with their opponents, and adapted to the changing circumstances of the late 1960s. Realizing how much they had achieved as well as how much they still had to learn, conservatives spent the next four years securing control of the GOP by redefining their position and gaining new converts. By 1968, they dominated the Republican Party.

Understanding the achievements and failures of the Right in the 1960s requires an examination of several overlapping themes. Essential to the growth of conservatism was an emphasis on grassroots organization. Though a few powerful, influential men and women shaped and guided the movement, much of its political success resulted from the activities of a network of local groups who supplied the money, the volunteers, and, increasingly, the votes necessary to ensure the continuation and growth of the conservative cause. Like other movements of the decade, right-wingers succeeded by exploiting hitherto untapped sources of discontent. Moreover, building a political movement from the bottom up allowed conservatives to work within the party while avoiding the liberal-controlled national organization. Consequently, whereas liberals in the party discounted the frustrations of their grassroots constituents and underestimated the ability of right-wingers to appeal to and organize these voters, conservatives united them in an effective political network.

This network of local organizations would have amounted to little, however, without the guidance and vision of more politically experienced men and women. Frequently working from a base within the Republican Party, these politicians realized the potential inherent in grassroots groups and worked to harness their voices and votes. For their part, various apolitical conservative leaders recognized that the movement could have no impact on the national scene if it remained internally divided and isolated from mainstream politics. Only by joining forces with like-minded individuals could conservatives gain a wider national audience for their views.

Forging an alliance of ideological grassroots conservatives, intellectual right-wingers, and pragmatic right-leaning politicians was no easy task. In addition to the ideological, methodological, and socioeconomic differences among various factions on the right, an underlying conflict developed between those who were willing to compromise their principles in order to gain power and those who refused to sacrifice ideological purity simply for the sake of winning elections. Conservatives often found themselves working at cross-purposes with others on the right without realizing that they were undermining the stability of their own movement.

Further straining this budding conservative coalition was an intraparty power struggle in the GOP. The ideological disputes between conservatives and liberals complicated the relentless desire of politicians to control the party. Denied the presidential nomination in 1948 and 1952 and generally ignored by liberal Republicans who took the loyalty of conservatives for granted, right-wingers sought more influence on party policy because they believed that liberalism was destroying the country and that they had earned the privilege to affect policy through years of faithful party service. Jealousy and personality conflicts thus played an important role in Republican politics of the 1960s.

Liberals exacerbated tensions within the party by misrepresenting the right wing's philosophy. Refusing to distinguish extremist groups from those with more mainstream views, liberals ignored conservative demands for a voice in party matters. The arrogant attitude of the liberals left them vulnerable to the grassroots strategy executed by conservatives in the early 1960s. More importantly, by lumping all right-wingers together, liberal Republicans nurtured and perpetuated the extremist image of conservatism. They failed to realize that this growing perception would damage the reputation of the entire party.

The overall political climate of the 1960s intensified the struggles within the GOP. Americans across the entire ideological spectrum increasingly questioned the political, diplomatic, and sociological truths they had placidly accepted in the 1950s. Conservatives played as large a role in this polarization as did liberals and leftists. Dismissing conservatives as a mere fringe group within the GOP, liberals and moderates felt little need to compromise with them. This intransigent attitude pushed right-wingers into a similarly hard-line stance. Most importantly, it strengthened the Right's determination to succeed on the national level. Thus, the gap between the factions continued to widen.

In some ways, such an atmosphere made the Right's task easier. So much attention was paid to challengers from the Left that, except for a brief period of media scrutiny and a Kennedy administration investigation of right-wing activity in 1962–63, conservatives were overlooked as a significant threat by liberal Republicans and Democrats. Right-wing Republicans used this time to build their constituency at the state and local levels without any significant interference from liberals. Moreover, the escalating violence of the civil rights and student movements as well as growing protests against the Vietnam War made the conservative agenda acceptable to more people, especially after the 1964 election.

The story of the growth of a conservative movement in the 1960s is thus a tale of misperceptions, misunderstandings, and missed opportunities among all factions within the Republican Party. Conflicts among right-wingers proved almost as destructive as those between the Right and the Left. Intertwined with the tensions between ideological purists and political pragmatists, the specter of extremism haunted the burgeoning movement on all levels and constantly threatened to destroy what conservatives had worked so hard to create. It was, in fact, this very conflict that undermined the Goldwater campaign and prevented the Right from winning the presidency until 1980, despite the fact that it controlled the party. Only by exploring the circumstances and personalities instrumental in shaping the conservative movement during the 1960s can we better understand that turbulent and intriguing decade and its political legacy.

AN UNEASY ALLIANCE

The Republican Party, plagued by philosophical, geographical, and socioeconomic differences among its members, struggled through an identity crisis in the late 1950s and early 1960s that eventually shifted power internally from liberals to conservatives. The battle could not have been won, however, without the assistance of right-wingers outside the party structure. Uniting to form a more effective force, numerous conservative intellectuals, local groups, and journalists worked together to promote conservatives within the political system. Realizing that they needed each other to achieve power, right-wing politicians and ideologues formed an uneasy alliance based on political expediency.

This alliance created the potential for a vibrant conservative movement, but the new unity of the various strains of conservatism was tenuous at best. Traditionalists, libertarians, anticommunists, and right-wing politicians worked together when it suited their purposes but remained firmly committed to their individual agendas. In the 1950s and early 1960s, conservatives recognized the benefits of cooperation and joined forces to create a stronger conservative movement, but their lack of practical experience impeded their efforts. This explains, in part, why they did not gain power until well into the 1960s.

Ideological disputes had bitterly divided the Republican Party since the stock market crash of 1929. The Great Depression exposed the weaknesses of Republican "trickle-down" economics and the inflexibility of Herbert Hoover's philosophy and policies. It also cost the GOP its reputation and the presidency. More importantly, the 1932 election of Franklin D. Roosevelt placed in office a man who embodied all that conservatives despised. Using the Constitution as a guidebook rather than a bible, FDR revolutionized the presidency, laid the foundations of the welfare state, and introduced Keynesianism to the economy. Although many of his policies expanded programs developed by Republicans during the Progressive Era, appalled right-wingers tried desperately to block his initiatives. Just as conservatives of both parties had begun to form a solid bulwark against the New Deal, World War II broke out, halting further expansion of the Rooseveltian policies but ensuring the continuation of the Democratic administration.[1]

Republicans achieved more success in the postwar years. In 1946 they gained control of Congress and prevented FDR's successor, Harry Truman, from expanding the New Deal. They also discovered that anticommunism could unite their party and inspire voters. Crusaders against the "Red Menace" at home and abroad undermined the Democratic Party by charging that both the party and its platform were "soft on communism," thereby playing a role in the Republican capture of the White House in 1952. Seen by much of the public as a conservative victory, the election of Dwight Eisenhower appeared to quiet the disputes within the party and to herald a new era of bipartisanship.

Just as the consensus of the 1950s proved to be an illusion, however, so the surface tranquillity of the Republican Party hid intense factionalism. In part, this factionalism grew out of geographic and socioeconomic differences that, although not always openly acknowledged, divided Republicans. Throughout the postwar period, members of what conservatives labeled the "Eastern Establishment" dominated the party. These Republicans shared a common background of Ivy League educations, exclusive club memberships, and financial success. Operating many of the major corporations of the United States, they controlled the purse strings of the party and of any candidate who wanted to win on the national level. Although some members were from outside the Northeast, such as Thomas Dewey and Wendell Willkie, they had only succeeded after they moved to the East. Members of the "Establishment," assuming that they knew what was best for the entire country, held sway through their occupation of policy-making positions throughout the executive branch as well as their manipulation of the party machinery.[2]

By the 1950s, however, businesspeople and political leaders from the South and West increasingly challenged these power brokers within the GOP. Rich Texas oil tycoons and people who had profited from the postwar industrial boom in the Southwest demanded greater influence at the national level. They believed that the burgeoning population and economy of their region entitled them to play a more important role in the formulation of policy decisions. Joining with midwesterners who also felt excluded from the "Establishment," these southern and western men and women began to coalesce into what Arizona senator Barry Goldwater described as a new populist movement.[3]

The geographic and socioeconomic distinctions between the two groups contributed to their formation of different ideological and practical goals as well. Following in the tradition of Theodore Roosevelt's progressivism, many members of the wealthy "Eastern Establishment" embraced New Deal–style social and economic programs in the belief that such policies would alleviate class conflicts, lead to economic stability, and keep governmental control in their hands. They envisioned what historian Robert Griffith has called a "corporate commonwealth." Believing it necessary to "come to grips with the problems of twentieth-century life," these people "worked out a program" that was, according to Eisenhower supporter Paul Hoffman, "better than anything the Democrats could offer."[4] As a result, "liberal" and/or "moderate" Republicans accepted the framework of the New Deal, created some new programs, and strove to maintain and expand American economic involvement around the world.

This program appalled the growing number of conservatives in the Southwest who stressed individual initiative over welfare programs, preferred free enterprise rather than government regulation, and desired a return to local control over matters such as schools, taxes, and race relations. Fearing communism at home, they advocated all means of exposing and eliminating real or potential traitors. In their eagerness to uncover left-wing agents, some right-wingers shocked other party members with their willingness to violate civil rights and liberties.

Although most on the right supported this domestic agenda, conservatives tended to disagree on foreign policy. Some right-wingers advocated a kind of isolationist, "Fortress America" style of diplomacy, although they opposed the taxes and bureaucracy necessary to maintain such a defense. Others wanted the United States to move aggressively to destroy communism wherever it appeared. Many of these were "Asia-Firsters," who had traditional business or missionary ties to Asia and thus focused their attention on the Far East.[5] Despite such disagreements, conservative political leaders united whenever necessary to fight against liberal domination of the GOP.

The Right had attempted previously to gain control of the party. In both 1948 and 1952, Ohio senator Robert A. Taft, leader of the conservative faction in the GOP, had sought the presidential nomination. Poor planning, a "loser" image, and powerful opponents prevented him from gaining the prize, however, and left a lingering bitterness in the mouths of many conservatives. Taft's sudden death in 1953 further weakened the Right and left them temporarily leaderless and dispirited.[6]

As the right wing of the Republican Party struggled to survive in the 1950s, a conservative movement began to coalesce outside the political structure. Conservative intellectuals who had long disagreed with one another found common ground in the struggle against communism. While maintaining their loyalty to their own philosophies, these intellectuals recognized the importance of standing united against liberalism. Essential to the development of an effective political movement, these men and women provided the philosophical underpinnings of the new drive for conservatism. Their growing involvement in the political world offered other conservatives legitimacy and justification.

During the postwar era, American conservatives generally followed one of two strands of thought: traditionalism or classical liberalism. Throughout the early 1950s, conservatives of all varieties concentrated on their differences rather than their similarities and therefore limited their audience and impact. Members of each faction believed that only they truly understood the cause of the United States' grave troubles.

Traditionalists such as University of Chicago English professor Richard Weaver, sociologist Robert Nisbet, and *Freeman* founder Albert Jay Nock judged the modern Western world distasteful in many respects and criticized the cult of conformity and the emergence of what they labeled "mass man." Others, such as political philosopher Leo Strauss and political scientist John Hallowell, looked back fondly to a time when morality was the guiding principle of humanity's existence and such concepts as relativism, positivism, and totalitarianism were unknown. Although they often disagreed on how to rediscover this so-called golden age, they were certain that it had existed at some point and that the answers it provided would miraculously solve the world's problems. Historian Russell Kirk feared the growth of a "Big Brother" state, but like most traditionalists, he agreed with Edmund Burke that government played an important role in community life because in the end "political problems are religious and moral problems."[7]

Kirk's belief in an active government and his attempts to deemphasize the Cold War contrasted sharply with the views of classical liberals and libertarians such as *National Review* contributing editor Frank Meyer, Austrian economist Frederick A. Hayek, and creator of the Foundation for Economic Education Leonard E. Read. These men, through journals, books, and organizations, preached the gospel of laissez-faire economics and libertarianism. Their scholarly defense of limited government and a free-market economy effectively attacked the New Deal and redefined the postwar economic debate.[8]

In the early 1950s, intellectuals from both camps found common cause in their fear of the spread of communism abroad, particularly throughout Asia. The anticommunist movement manifested itself in numerous journal articles attacking the foreign policy of the Democrats as well as in the unofficial but powerful China Lobby, which supported the Nationalist Chinese. Nor did anticommunists approve of all of Eisenhower's foreign policy decisions. Although Eisenhower worked very hard to maintain their support, his attempts at arms reduction and his willingness to meet with Khrushchev undermined his credibility as an enemy of communism. Many conservatives felt that the president did not understand circumstances that seemed obvious to them—that, in James Burnham's words, the "third world war" had already begun.[9]

Extending this crusade onto the domestic front, anticommunists applauded members of the House Un-American Activities Committee and cheered the defeat of Alger Hiss and the success of Wisconsin senator Joseph R. McCarthy. Conservative journals featured stories of alleged communist infiltration of prominent institutions in American society, while right-wing authors and citizens scrutinized everyone from senators to school board officials, whether Democrat or Republican. Anyone with a questionable background became suspect; anyone who defended the United States and worked against the communists deserved support and praise.

The crusade against the "Red Menace" played an essential role in unifying disagreeing conservative intellectuals and building a grassroots constituency. No matter what they thought about the domestic situation, almost everyone on the right—indeed, most Americans—feared communism. Consequently, the anticommunist crusade created a broad spectrum of support and provided conservatives with heroes. Besides Senator McCarthy, whose sensational allegations often made newspaper headlines, Alger Hiss's nemesis Vice President Richard Nixon and ex-communist informant Whittaker Chambers became legends in the battle against the Left. They served as magnets drawing diverse conservative groups and individuals to the Republican banner.

Anticommunism was not the only factor contributing to the unification and politicization of conservative intellectuals during the mid- to late 1950s. Equally important were the efforts of the evolving conservative press. Realizing that the various strands of conservative thought could not be fused successfully, men such as *National Review* founders William F. Buckley, Jr., and Willi Schlamm encouraged right-wing factions to overlook their differences in order to consolidate their opposition to liberalism. Along with other conservative writers working for journals such as *Human Events*, the *Freeman*, and the *American Mercury*, the editors of the *National Review* helped acquaint the public with the philosophical and practical tenets of conservatism as well as with conservative politicians and platforms. In addition, these journalists gave voice to conservative intellectuals' frustration with what they perceived as liberal domination of academia, the arts, and philosophy. In the process, the right-wing press advertised and encouraged the resurgence on the right during the 1950s.[10]

Buckley's *National Review* was more than just a chronicler of contemporary events. It played a vital role in articulating conservative grievances and consciously arousing and uniting the various dissatisfied factions. A devout Catholic from a wealthy family, steeped in conservatism from childhood, Buckley saw himself as a rebel against the liberal status quo and a warrior in the struggle against Soviet aggression. He first attacked liberalism in 1951 in *God and Man at Yale*, in which he charged the Yale faculty with preaching socialism and atheism. A talented speaker and a brilliant debater, Buckley continued his verbal and published assaults on liberalism throughout his brief career with the Central Intelligence Agency (CIA) and his pursuit of other business ventures.[11]

Buckley's primary contribution to conservatism came in 1955 with the founding of the *National Review*. Bringing together men and women of widely divergent views, Buckley encouraged them to explain their positions and to debate the issues. According to publisher William Rusher, the editors strove to present "a world view, rather than merely a political philosophy or the theoretical underpinnings of an economic system."[12] Aimed at intellectuals and opinion-makers, the *National Review* also appealed to working-class conservatives. Despite financial difficulties in the early years, the *National Review* became the most important conservative magazine and Buckley the most widely recognized spokesperson of right-wing thought.

Buckley and other right-wing intellectuals were not the only rebellious conservatives. By the late 1950s, a right-wing youth movement was becoming noticeably more vocal. Some of the members of this movement had discovered conservatism through conservative journals, while others had joined organizations such as the Intercollegiate Society of Individualists and the Young Republican National Federation, both of which shifted dramatically to the right in the late 1950s. M. Stanton Evans, among those young people caught up in the rising tide on the right, explained in his book *Revolt on the Campus* that by 1960 "at least three bursts of rebellion" occurred against liberalism: "one funneled into the Republican Party, one into a premature effort at a new national organization, and one into the exotic recesses of Bohemia." While he admitted that "none did the job" of turning back the liberal orthodoxy, he believed that each signified youth's frustration "with the conformity of liberalism."[13]

Indeed, these organized young people, by supporting conservative candidates on a national level, spreading right-wing literature, and establishing groups such as the National Student Committee for the Loyalty Oath, provided an active, informed conservative constituency, particularly on college campuses, throughout the country.[14] By 1960, enough support existed to create a nationwide conservative youth organization "designed solely for political action." While this new group, Young Americans for Freedom, worked independently of partisan ties, the growing conservatism of the Young Republican organization significantly affected the national party. By 1959, according to active member William Rusher, the "biennial [Young Republican] national conventions were recognized as significant straws in the Republican wind, and there seemed no doubt that in 1959 the signal would be a shift to the right."[15]

Simultaneously, citizens across the country reacted against what they regarded as the "monolithic conformity of 'liberalism'" in culture and education as well as liberal politics and economics by forming local and national groups to combat whichever aspect of liberalism particularly offended or outraged them.[16] On a local level, antiintegrationist, antiblack, anti-Semitic, anti-Catholic, antifluoridation, and anticommunist as well as libertarian and free enterprise groups appeared.[17] Funded mostly by a few major contributors, many of the organizations also depended heavily on small donations from members.[18] Organizations concentrating on a particular aspect of a broader cause, such as the American Survival Party and the Committee to Warn of the Arrival of Communist Merchandise on the Local Business Scene, had only limited support and impact.[19]

Anticommunist clubs abounded, but single-cause groups had a broader appeal. Many published their own newsletters or journals in an attempt to spread their message, build support, and pressure legislators to stop the growth of liberalism. Although they often reported political events and usually encouraged political participation, most of these groups despaired over the lack of differentiation between the national parties. The Congress of Freedom explained the situation from a grassroots perspective: "running true to form," the Republicans tried "to emulate the Democratic Fakers" by enacting more legislation to "siphon off [the] money of its people to enslave them."[20]

Besides these local groups, a number of national committees and organizations formed during the late 1950s and early 1960s. Some, such as the Committee of One Million, focused solely on foreign policy issues. Fred C. Schwarz and others won thousands of converts by combining a hardline attitude toward communism with Christian fundamentalism, neatly packaged together for the consumer. Other groups were more concerned about curing domestic ills. The Foundation for Economic Education, the National Economic Council, and the National Educational Program concentrated on fighting against collectivism in the government and educating the American public in conservative economics. In fact, many conservatives considered the education of the American people "in the values of freedom [and] our American heritage" to be their primary function. Moreover, right-wing groups had a responsibility, according to the members of Constructive Action, to warn the public about "the dangers and evils inherent in all forms of socialism."[21]

The most significant of these national organizations was the John Birch Society, founded in 1958 by Robert Welch. The "twin centers" of the society's ideology were an antistatism that emphasized individualism and local government and a conspiracy theory warning that certain forces were attempting to take over the world. According to Welch, these "forces" or "Insiders" were a modern manifestation of the ancient Illuminati who wanted to institute worldwide communism.[22] Discounted as fanatics by many Democrats and Republicans, members of the society used slick propaganda techniques and publications, particularly *American Opinion*, to build up a significant following that would not be silenced and eventually could not be ignored.

In fact, conservatives of all varieties were increasingly determined to gain political power. Throughout the latter half of the 1950s, conservative writers emphasized the necessity of political action. *Human Events* author Congressman Howard Buffet asserted that the "transcendent political duty of the citizen" was "vigilance" and that this task should not be left to politicians. Philosopher Richard Weaver similarly warned of the consequences of relying on political leaders, who were too willing to compromise. Notre Dame dean and right-wing organizer Clarence Manion concluded that "the terrible tide" was "turning" and the "political shot-gun marriage that Ike performed" was going to be over by 1960.[23]

Worried that eight years of "Liberal Republican" control of the party had weakened the conservative movement, *National Review* editor Frank Meyer still found cause for hope in the new activity on the right, which was "creating a climate in which conservatism is on the verge of emerging as the only live option for the intelligent and the independent of the new generation." Accepting the challenge, the Intercollegiate Society of Individualists, the Young Republicans, and later the Young Americans for Freedom began organizing and lobbying for right-wing causes and candidates.[24]

By 1960, most of this activity focused on developing strength within the Republican Party. As journalist George Sokolsky pointed out, the GOP had to serve as a "rallying point" for the "angry men" of the country because there was "no other party." Although both parties were ideologically "confused," the Democratic Party was a "catchall on every phase of liberal, and even socialist," views. The Republican Party, on the other hand, had, according to *Human Events* author John J. Synon, "lent little aid and comfort to the collectivists." Conservatives had to build on this trend to ensure that the party did not slip into the wrong hands.[25]

For their part, Republican conservative politicians worked hard to take advantage of this sentiment. As Senate Campaign Committee chair, Arizona senator Barry Goldwater traveled across the country attempting to bring frustrated voters "back in the party" by convincing them "that their positions were not contrary to ours."[26] From the standpoint of conservatives, gaining such support would secure a national platform for achieving their goals. It would also serve the purposes of Republican conservatives who had been struggling to win control of their party.

Although these conservative organizations and individuals provided a natural constituency for the right wing of the GOP, their support created difficulties. Since they were not elected officials, grassroots conservatives did not always see the need for, or the wisdom of, compromise. They could afford to be relentless in their quest for conservative goals; office-holders could not. Lacking political experience, intellectuals and crusaders on the right demanded a high price for their support.

Moreover, the diversity of right-wing organizations proved problematical. How could conservative leaders maintain unity among people with different goals and backgrounds? For example, although atheist Max Eastman agreed with Buckley politically, Eastman withdrew his name from the masthead of the *National Review* because he found the magazine too "christian." The widely distributed, oversimplified international communist conspiracy theory of Robert Welch and his followers created even greater difficulties. Many people associated with the *National Review* disagreed with important parts of the Birchite philosophy. Whereas Welch blamed communist conspirators for "delivering" Americans to their "doom," Buckley attributed the dangerous situation to anticommunists who "tragically misunder[stood] the nature of the crisis" Americans faced.[27]

The fact that the editors of the *National Review* worried more than the average midwestern or southwestern American about these intellectual subtleties created an additional obstacle to conservative unity. Farmers in the heartland, oilmen in Texas, academics in Chicago, and a journalist in New York City might all share the same basic philosophy but interpret that perspective very differently because of their distinct social and educational backgrounds. Conservatives had to treat these socioeconomic differences with care to prevent charges of elitism from undermining their cause. Surface unity existed by the early 1960s, but underlying theoretical and practical disagreements continually threatened to disrupt the calm.

Discord was particularly apparent in the political arena. Conservative Republicans united in opposition to liberal threats but squabbled endlessly when it came to advancing their own conservative agendas. Power struggles between strong personalities limited conservative unity, the most obvious example taking place in California. Both Vice President Richard Nixon and Senator William Knowland, Republican minority leader, saw themselves as the spokesperson for the California GOP. Never forgetting that Knowland had not supported him in his first campaign, Nixon denied the senator's claim to leadership in the Golden State. This rivalry continued throughout the 1950s until Knowland lost his gubernatorial bid and his power in 1958.[28]

Even those not directly involved in government recognized the danger of such infighting. Both W. Henry McFarland of the American Flag Committee and L. Brent Bozell of the *National Review* implored their readers to join forces with others on the right in order to increase their power. These calls for unity continued throughout the 1950s.[29]

Of more consequence than disunity was the taint of extremism associated with groups such as the John Birch Society. With their conspiracy theories and wild assertions that Eisenhower was a communist agent, Welch and his organization reinforced the view of many moderates and liberals that everyone on the right was a lunatic. This tendency to view all conservative thought as extremist developed during the postwar period for several reasons. Some scholars argued that the United States' lack of a feudal past had prevented the development of an indigenous conservative movement. Therefore, as many liberal commentators pointed out at that time, to be a conservative in the United States was an impossibility because it would mean "conserving" liberalism. Others, pointing to the "intellectual flabbiness" of American conservatism, portrayed right-wingers as liberals with an attitude problem. According to this theory, these men and women zeroed in on the parts of liberal philosophy that they opposed and ignored the rest.[30] Such viewpoints led to the conviction that in the United States conservatism amounted to little more than the desire of businesspeople and the upper classes to maintain the status quo.

Reflecting a second aspect of this argument, others acknowledged the existence of a conservative faction but defined it solely by its radical elements. Respected journals such as the *New Republic* described Goldwater as "the 'white hope' of America's thinning Neanderthal ranks" and his fellow conservatives as members of the "radical right" and "the crackpot fringe." Historian Arthur Schlesinger, Jr., also associated the Right with a single segment of society. In his discussion of "the failure of the right" in *The Vital Center*, Schlesinger examined only the business community, thus excluding all other conservative elements. When he spoke of radicalism, he associated it with a "confused and frightened business community" susceptible to fascism rather than rampaging anticommunists or ax-wielding moralists.[31]

The Right also was forced to pay for its support of McCarthy's crusade against the "Red Menace." Daniel Bell, Seymour Lipset, and other commentators emphasized the irrationality of the McCarthyites' response to threats from abroad. Most Republicans had applauded the Wisconsin senator's early attacks on communism in government. When he continued his investigations during a Republican administration, however, some began to question his reliability and usefulness.[32] Moderate Republicans believed that McCarthy's willingness to violate the civil rights of suspects and his abuse of senatorial privileges undermined the legitimacy of anticommunism and threatened the reputation of the GOP. Thus, the man who had made a name for himself fighting alleged radicals came to be perceived by many Republicans as an extremist who had to be eliminated before he irreparably damaged the crusade against communism. Censured, McCarthy lost power, but not until he had introduced an extremist dynamic within the GOP.

Obviously, part of the problem conservatives faced in establishing themselves within the GOP and the country was one of definition. Most Republicans supported a basic platform that stressed local government, reduced spending, and anticommunism. As a result, ideological differences among party members became matters of degree; conservatives wanted greater local responsibility for government, less spending, and a stronger stand against communism than did party moderates or liberals. By these criteria from the moderate perspective, someone who articulated different political or more far-reaching goals or who wanted to enact the platform more quickly or more thoroughly would be an extremist and could be legitimately ignored.

Conservatives realized the danger of being labeled "extremist" and worked to counteract such a perception. Throughout the late 1950s and early 1960s, various right-wing journalists warned that anti-Semitic and racist remarks by conservatives undermined their cause. Offering a strategy for increasing conservative ranks, author Elizabeth Churchill Brown encouraged *Human Events* readers to avoid associating with racists and anti-Semites. Similarly, Buckley cautioned independent publishers that "racists and crackpots" "discredited" the movement. He also attempted to convince such fanatics as Nazi George Lincoln Rockwell to give up their more excessive ideas. In 1960 Buckley denounced the *American Mercury* for its anti-Semitic posture, which he feared would "gravely damage the cause of true conservatism." Welch's ideas, however, presented a dilemma. While Buckley rejected Welch's hypothesis that Eisenhower was a communist agent, he considered the John Birch Society a worthy organization, maintained a friendly correspondence with Welch, and supported his publication, *American Opinion*, from its beginnings in 1958 into the early 1960s.[33]

Building on a widespread but unarticulated public dissatisfaction with government and society, a resurgent intellectual movement, and a mushrooming network of grassroots groups, conservative Republican politicians began to develop their own organization within the party. Unlike Taft, who had scorned the conservative intellectuals, the New Right enjoyed intimate financial and personal ties with these savants, as well as with the burgeoning conservative press. The resulting interaction gave voice to long-standing but previously inchoate sentiments. Conservatives soon discovered that they were not alone, but they confronted a wide range of opinion on the right. It was their willingness, albeit grudging at times, to tolerate the breadth of the developing movement that helped to unify the factions in their assault on the liberal "Eastern Establishment."

This trend toward unity is one of the most important events in the early development of the conservative movement. The integration of various right-wing groups during the late 1950s occurred on several levels. Philosophically, intellectuals with diverse beliefs realized the value of concentrating on their similarities rather than their differences in the common fight against liberals. Politically, conservatives of all stripes and socioeconomic backgrounds rallied around the cause of anticommunism, willingly overlooking their disagreements in their desire to support McCarthy.

The alliance between conservative intellectuals, grassroots groups, and right-wing politicians was extremely significant in the long-term development of the conservative movement. The anger and frustration of citizens created a substantial bloc of votes and money; the theoreticians and the press channeled those votes toward support of conservative politicians. By offering intellectual justifications, thinkers such as Frank Meyer, James Burnham, and Russell Kirk gave the developing movement the legitimacy necessary to challenge liberal control of the party.

2

CHALLENGING THE
POLITICS OF CONSENSUS
CONSERVATIVE REPUBLICANS AND
THE ELECTION OF 1960

As Barry Goldwater withdrew his name from nomination in the midst of the hoopla of the 1960 Republican National Convention, he issued a prophetic call and a subtle warning. The call challenged conservatives to "grow up" and work to take control of their party. The warning, unspoken but clear, advised liberal Republicans not to take the loyalty of the right wing for granted. As Senator Goldwater finished his speech, the audience applauded—liberals, because he had promised to support Nixon, and conservatives, because they accepted the challenge and the man who issued it. After a decade of disunity, the right wing of the Republican Party entered the 1960s energized and ready to fight for its cause.

The presidential election campaign of 1960 was a watershed in the development of American conservatism and the history of the Republican Party. While contemporaries contrasted the apparent complacency of the

Eisenhower administration with the youthful energy of Democrat John F. Kennedy and historians studied the implications of Kennedy's narrow victory over Richard M. Nixon, few took note of the emergence of a more organized and determined conservative movement. By 1960, a vocal right-wing constituency strengthened the resolve of conservative party leaders who were unhappy with the "modern Republicanism" of the Eisenhower administration, frustrated by the "Eastern Establishment's" domination of their party, and embittered by the loss of the presidential nomination in 1948 and 1952. Increasing the underlying tension was the tendency of party liberals to underestimate conservative strength and to misunderstand, or ignore, the real differences dividing one wing of the party from the other. The 1960 campaign provided an opportunity for the political and intellectual Right to cement their relationship and for conservatives to galvanize into a coordinated drive to seize control of the party.

The politics of consensus in the 1950s, embraced by many scholars and politicians and much of the public, undermined conservatives' efforts to voice their dissatisfaction with the Eisenhower administration and liberalism in general. Rejecting the emphasis on conflict as the guiding principle of human affairs, scholars such as Richard Hofstadter and Louis Hartz saw American history as a continuum. According to Hartz, since the United States lacked a feudal tradition and had no true Left or Right in the European sense, the major political parties shared more ideals than they realized. Moreover, whatever radicalism had been evident in the United States had dissipated. According to sociologist Daniel Bell, "Ideology, which once was a road to action, has come to a dead end." He argued that Western nations had achieved a "rough consensus among intellectuals on political issues: the acceptance of a Welfare State; the desirability of decentralized power; a system of mixed economy and of political pluralism."[1] In his view, this meant that politicians no longer argued over issues, only over the degree to which policies should be implemented.

These intellectual arguments were less significant to the American public than the economic boom of the postwar era that underlay the consensus Bell had touted.[2] The wages of industrial workers increased substantially between 1945 and 1960. New technologies developed during World War II led to increased industrial output, jobs, profits, and consumer goods. Through the education and loan provisions of the GI Bill, expansion of minimum wage eligibility, increases in defense spending, and the Federal Highway Act, the government attempted to ensure that returning veterans of all classes shared in the growing wealth. Enjoying their economic security after years of deprivation, many formerly working-class adults eagerly outfitted themselves for their new and hard-won status by buying houses in the suburbs. Everyone, it seemed, was middle class.

Just as Americans' financial troubles appeared to have ended, the problems of a war-torn world seemed less immediately threatening to those safely ensconced in the suburbs. After taking office, Eisenhower quickly ended the Korean stalemate and brought U.S. soldiers home. Then he kept Americans out of war despite many opportunities presented by various conflicts throughout the world. The president achieved this feat through a combination of restraint—sending troops into Lebanon for only a limited time and refusing to bail out the French militarily in Indochina—and intimidation—threatening nuclear retaliation against the Soviets, as a general policy, and the People's Republic of China for their attacks on Formosa. When all else failed, he sent in the CIA, as he did in Guatemala and Iran, where agents orchestrated successful coups. The surface calm lulled Americans into believing that major conflicts could and should be avoided.

Who could be better suited to ensure that Americans continued to enjoy peace and prosperity than a former five-star general with a kindly grandfather's smile? Dwight Eisenhower reassured a public tired of upheaval. Although some complained that he did not know what he was doing, that he was not in control of his administration, and that he played too much golf, many were satisfied that he was keeping the country on track and out of trouble. A few voices claimed that the president knew more than he let on, but, by and large, perhaps most regarded Eisenhower as a bumbling figurehead but a great guy who would not rock the boat.

Since Eisenhower was the first Republican president in twenty years, some of his fellow party members, especially those on the right, hoped that he would reverse the trend toward increased government spending and bureaucratic growth begun under Roosevelt. To conservatives' dismay, however, Eisenhower's administration epitomized the "Eastern Establishment" approach to politics. Practicing a "holding the line" policy, which meant increasing benefits for recipients of social security and unemployment compensation, Eisenhower did not attempt to dismantle the New Deal but only to forestall further expansion. That view, which he reluctantly shared with many liberal Republicans, was labeled "New Republicanism" by Arthur Larson in his election-year book, *A Republican Looks at His Party*. According to Larson, the new policy was a compromise between "the standpattism of the earlier GOP and the extreme welfare statism of the New Deal and Fair Deal." Eisenhower defined his approach as "the political philosophy that recognizes clearly the responsibility of the Federal Government to take the lead in making certain that the productivity of our great economic machine is distributed so that no one will suffer disaster, privation, through no fault of his own."[3] By accepting an active, enlarged federal government, "new" or "modern" Republicanism allowed for a moderate continuation of the New Deal.

In foreign policy, Eisenhower practiced Roosevelt-Truman internationalism. Although he encouraged Secretary of State John Foster Dulles to "talk tough" about "brinkmanship," "massive retaliation," and "liberation," when push came to shove in Hungary, he practiced containment. Although Eisenhower sympathized with the Hungarians' rebellion against Soviet control, he refused to risk a superpower confrontation and sent the rebels only spiritual support. Moreover, Eisenhower's desire to limit the arms race for fiscal and ethical reasons led to attempts at negotiation with the communists. Unsuccessful and at times halfhearted, Eisenhower's overtures to the Soviets did little but upset the conservatives, who increasingly believed he was all talk and no action.

Despite their disagreements, both the president and those on the Right realized that public bickering undermined the effectiveness of the Republican Party. As a result, particularly in Eisenhower's first term, they made an effort to cooperate. Eisenhower cultivated Senator Robert Taft's support, refrained from attacking extremist members of the party, and worked to gain the backing of those who did not agree with him. For their part, conservative Republicans agreed to give the president a chance. Although they disliked some of his policies and worked vigorously against him on others, by and large, party members gave Eisenhower solid support during his first term. This helped to create the illusion, articulated by Republican National Committee chair Meade Alcorn, that any ideological conflict within the party "was more mythical than real."[4]

Alcorn's statement was an oversimplification. Although ideological differences might have been relative, they were real. Moreover, regional and personal rivalries among the various factions led many to emphasize and exaggerate their differences.[5] After all, these people were politicians who sought power and influence. They had to distinguish themselves from one another or risk being lost in the crowd. Moreover, many sincerely believed that the best way to save the country was for them to win office.

The rivalry within the GOP explains, at least in part, the increasing internecine fighting within the party after Eisenhower's reelection in 1956.

Neither side seemed as willing to compromise or as eager to present a unified front to the public. Preoccupied with his attempts to cut defense spending and open a dialogue with the Soviets, Eisenhower did not believe that he had time to build coalitions. The Right regarded his commitment to these goals as an indication that he had moved to the left. Whether this was really the case did not matter. Right-wingers believed that Eisenhower was either showing his true colors or allowing himself to be duped by his advisers into making very bad decisions.

Foreign policy increasingly proved problematical. Eisenhower's failure to follow through with his "liberation" policy in Hungary and Poland disappointed conservatives who had applauded his campaign promises to free "captive nations." Determined to promote disarmament, to increase foreign aid to developing countries, and to open a constructive dialogue with the Soviets, Eisenhower frequently angered the Right. Moreover, after the Soviets' successful launching of *Sputnik I* in 1957, some Republicans joined Democrats in complaining about the purported "missile gap" between the United States and the Soviet Union.

Such squabbles paled in comparison with the major break over domestic issues, however, especially Eisenhower's 1957 budget plan. Conservatives' pent-up frustration over Eisenhower's inability to cut New Deal programs exploded after word of the president's budget plan was leaked. Attacked even before it was presented to Congress, the budget was roundly condemned by the Right for its huge deficit. Senate minority leader William Knowland called for $3 billion in cuts. In his first public criticism of the Eisenhower administration, Arizona senator Barry Goldwater chastised the president for his "abominably high budget," which countered everything he had promised in the 1956 campaign.[6]

Conservatives never understood the irony of this debate. Eisenhower also advocated a balanced budget but found himself hampered by rising military costs. Members of the Right refused to see the connection between their insistence on an ever stronger defense and the rising deficit. It was far simpler to blame the president. Similarly, many conservatives held Eisenhower accountable for the defeat of right-wingers such as William Knowland and John Bricker in the 1958 election. Both senators had supported state legislation to eliminate compulsory union membership in labor contracts, commonly known as right-to-work laws. The president refused to take a firm stand on this issue and thus, according to the Right, undermined support for these right-wing stalwarts.[7]

As a result, conservatives challenged the president more frequently and vehemently during his second term. Senator Goldwater, soon to emerge as the conservatives' new spokesperson, took the lead in voicing the Right's disapproval of Eisenhower's philosophy of government and the "faulty premises" of modern Republicanism. Although he blamed Eisenhower's staff rather than the president himself, Goldwater could "detect no evidence of [Eisenhower's] interest in politics, or . . . in the future of the party." In fact, by early 1960, Goldwater accused the administration of practicing "dime-store New Dealism" and publicly advocated a much tougher foreign policy than that of the president. Senator John Bricker of Ohio agreed with this analysis. He felt that the country was "in worse shape today than at the depths of the New Deal." New Hamsphire senator Styles Bridges denounced the president's policy on *Meet the Press*, and even former president Herbert Hoover felt compelled to protest the infection of the Eisenhower administration with the "Karl Marx virus."[8]

Besides criticizing his ideological weaknesses, conservative Republicans accused Eisenhower of failing to develop the party sufficiently to ensure continued GOP control on the national level. To support their claim, right-wingers pointed to a report by the Republican Senate Campaign Committee in March 1959 indicating that 8 million voters had abandoned the party between 1954 and 1958. Since liberals dominated the party during those years, conservatives interpreted the decline in membership as the voters' repudiation of modern Republicanism and as a reflection of their desire for a change in leadership. Finally, in spite of Eisenhower's major victories in the presidential elections of 1952 and 1956, he was not able to carry the rest of the Republican slate with him. The disastrous results of the off-year elections in 1958 suggested the limits of the Eisenhower magic as Democrats racked up significant majorities in both houses of Congress. In addition, GOP governors served in only fourteen states. Moreover, the only place Republicans gained congressional seats between 1958 and 1960 was in the Midwest—a conservative stronghold.[9]

The right wing of the GOP received encouragement and support for its attacks on the Eisenhower administration from the increasingly active conservative press. Serving as a forum for discussion and criticism of presidential policies, the conservative press played an extremely important role in focusing and communicating the frustrations of the right-wing intellectual, grassroots, and youth movements. The editors of the *National Review* sarcastically called the president the Republican Party's "Pride and Joy" and complained that his administration baffled "intellectually-minded folks." In the same magazine, ex-radical Max Eastman accused

Eisenhower of not knowing "anything about the principles upon which our government was founded." *Human Events* recorded the growing disgust and distrust that resulted from "Ike's" golfing while the government took care of itself.[10] Countless articles in conservative journals examined Eisenhower Republicanism from every conceivable angle. Perhaps more importantly, the letters to the editor section provided the public with an outlet for their frustrations with the status quo.

Conservatives were not the only disgruntled Americans in the late 1950s. Even the prosperous and secure sensed that "something" was not right. This vaguely discernible frustration and anxiety permeated all aspects of society in the 1950s. While Eisenhower attempted to contain Soviet communism, Americans tried to maintain their financial security and mental stability by conforming to "society's" standards. If reality did not measure up to the ideal, they told themselves that the problem was within themselves and pretended that their lives were wonderful.

Intellectuals, corporate executives, and government officials anxious to maintain the myth of a contented population enjoying the fruits of an expanding economy and a stable political system reinforced such notions. They dismissed the discontent as deviance and urged greater participation in the consumer culture as a cure. The problem, these "experts" assured, was not rooted in society but in the individual. Consequently, the dissatisfaction remained undefined and thus difficult to articulate. The contradiction between image and reality resulted in an epidemic of stress-related illnesses among both men and women, the widespread pursuit of psychological and/or psychiatric counseling, and a younger generation determined not to repeat the mistakes of their parents.[11]

In the late 1950s, however, several developments contradicted the myth of consensus. Black Americans increasingly challenged the established patterns of race relations as well as deeply held beliefs about the structure of society. Many white southerners responded angrily as the civil rights movement exposed the reality of life below the Mason-Dixon line. Startled by the furor created by the 1954 *Brown v. Board of Education of Topeka* decision, the 1956 Montgomery bus boycott, and the 1957 Little Rock school desegregation battle, white northerners observed the unfolding drama in the South with a mixture of fear, self-righteous indignation, and racism. Northerners' outrage only increased southerners' resentment and strengthened their determination to maintain control of race relations.

Events around the world also seemed to be increasingly out of control. The American public expected threats from the Soviets concerning Berlin

and from Communist China concerning Formosa, but they were less prepared for the rise of Arab nationalism, which they mistook for communism, in Egypt, Iraq, and Lebanon. A civil war in the former Belgian
Congo revealed that Africa was a hotbed of radicalism and nationalism.
More frightening, however, was the situation in South America, where
citizens of Venezuela and Peru showed their hostility toward the United
States by attacking Vice President and Mrs. Nixon during their goodwill
tour in 1958.[12]

The situation in Cuba undermined American confidence even further.
Fidel Castro seized control of the island in 1959 and implemented reforms
that the State Department considered communistic. As American businesspeople lost their influence, and property, and stories of military-style
trials were reported by exiles, Americans worried that the "Red Menace"
was thriving in their own backyard. The Eisenhower administration's inability to prevent Castro's consolidation of power seemed to indicate that
the United States was losing the Cold War.[13]

Sputnik I provided more compelling proof that the United States was
falling behind the Soviet Union. Launched by the Soviets in October
1957, the satellite shattered Americans' belief in their technological superiority and ignited a firestorm of debate concerning everything from defense to education. Americans wondered how the president could have
allowed the Soviets to gain the upper hand. They questioned whether
material success had made them weak; they sought easy answers by de-
manding more missiles and increased funding for education.[14]

If *Sputnik I* caught Americans by surprise, the 1960 U-2 incident fur-
ther undermined American confidence. While Eisenhower prepared for a
Paris summit meeting with Khrushchev, Harold Macmillan from Great
Britain, Charles de Gaulle from France, and Konrad Adenauer from West
Germany, the Soviets shot down an American U-2 spy plane over Soviet
territory. Eisenhower at first denied knowledge of the plane, but when the
Soviets produced both the plane and the pilot, he admitted that the plane
had been on a reconnaissance mission. Caught in a lie, Eisenhower went to
Paris for the meeting anyway. The Soviets, however, were in no mood to
talk, and after one tense session, the meeting was canceled.[15]

A sluggish economy deepened the public's dissatisfaction. Americans
had grown accustomed to an ever-expanding economy and therefore were
shocked by the onset of a recession in 1957. Industrial production declined by 14 percent, while unemployment rose by 7 percent. Eisenhower's approval rating took a nosedive, dropping to 49 percent in April 1958.

The public remained concerned about the economy for the rest of Eisenhower's term, despite assurances from the administration that the economy had recovered.[16]

Taken altogether, the events of the late 1950s created a crisis of confidence for the American people. In fact, journalists and politicians spent much of their time discussing the American purpose. "Something" seemed to have gone wrong, but nobody knew what that "something" was.[17] Eisenhower remained extremely popular, but many Americans felt the need for some sort of change.

Although they had problems of their own and were as divided as the Republicans, the Democrats believed that they could make a difference. Serving as a kind of umbrella organization, the Democratic Party consisted of a coalition of contentious groups: white-supremacist southerners, civil rights activists, labor leaders, machine politicians, liberal reformers, farmers, and second- and third-generation immigrants. This uneasy alliance, constructed during the Roosevelt era, had suffered serious defections in the 1950s. Believing in some cases that Republicans could better protect peace and prosperity and maintain the status quo, southerners, the newly secure working class, and various ethnic groups split their tickets and thus disrupted their traditional voting patterns. The Supreme Court's banning of the all-white primary in *Smith v. Allwright* in 1944 injured the party. Democratic candidates thus found that they had to walk a narrow line to avoid offending members of their coalition and losing elections.[18]

Despite these difficulties, the Democratic Party concluded that the final years of the Eisenhower administration had weakened the president's influence enough to open the door for serious opposition in 1960. The battle for the nomination began early, some candidates setting up organizations in 1958. Perennial candidate Adlai Stevenson ambivalently joined more enthusiastic and marketable challengers such as Hubert Humphrey, Stuart Symington, Lyndon Johnson, and John Kennedy. Throughout the primary campaign, as the contenders fought for delegates, they laid the groundwork for the more important struggle against their Republican adversaries. Citing economic problems and foreign policy mistakes, Democratic candidates focused on the lack of direction emanating from the Republican White House. Kennedy, a forty-three-year-old Catholic, overcame the initial handicap of his youth and religion to secure the nomination. His organization, his family's wealth, and, most importantly, his public image made him a formidable foe.

Republicans of various ideological stripes were ready for the challenge.

The front-runner was Eisenhower's vice president and heir apparent, Richard M. Nixon, a fiercely independent and sensitive man who was eager to establish his own identity as a contender.[19] In some ways, Nixon was the perfect candidate. His years as vice president pointed up JFK's lack of experience, and his acceptance by both liberals and conservatives made him a good compromise candidate for the Republicans. As a member of Eisenhower's administration, Nixon had supported many aspects of modern Republicanism, including the expansion of social security, foreign aid projects, and Eisenhower's "road of peace, prosperity and progress." The vice president's civil rights stance had earned him the enmity of many southerners and the early support of both Martin Luther King, Jr., and Jackie Robinson. He considered it a "privilege to participate in the great decisions of [Eisenhower's] administration."[20]

On the other hand, Nixon was not a member of the eastern elite, he had first been elected to the Senate as a rabid anticommunist, and he won national acclaim for his role in the Alger Hiss trial. Indeed, according to James Hagerty, Eisenhower's press secretary, Nixon's involvement in the Alger Hiss incident had been partly responsible for his choice as Eisenhower's running mate in 1952. Furthermore, Nixon had added to his conservative laurels and enhanced his national reputation for being an experienced, tough diplomat when he courageously faced anti-American mobs in South America and stood up to Nikita Khrushchev in Moscow in the televised "kitchen debate" over the merits of American materialism.[21]

Nixon considered himself a conservative in 1960. "I carried the banner of constructive postwar Republicanism," he would write later in his memoirs, "bred of conservative beliefs that a healthy private sector and individual initiative set the best pace for prosperity and progress." He later also maintained that the ideal ticket to compete against JFK and LBJ—a liberal and a conservative—would have been Nixon and Rockefeller—a conservative and a liberal.[22]

Nixon's mixed political legacy led most conservatives to question which perspective controlled his "political soul." Barry Goldwater regarded him as "basically conservative" but still felt compelled to lecture him in a 1958 letter on why the party would need to move to the right in 1960. Prominent conservative Alfred Kohlberg worried in 1957 that the favorable publicity about Nixon in the liberal press might alienate Nixon's "natural supporters." By 1960, he warned the vice president that his support for administration policies had generated a "lack of enthusiasm for you" among conservative Republicans. Ronald Reagan, still a registered Democrat but increasingly drawn to Republican politics, expressed concern that Nixon might commit a "fatal" mistake by accepting the advice of those who wanted to "outliberal" Kennedy.[23]

The conservative press reported the ambiguity surrounding Nixon's conservatism. By 1960, *Human Events* editors, who had warmly supported the "new Nixon" of 1958, questioned the depth of his commitment. A *National Review* reader warned Nixon that "genuine conservatives are weary of false or unlettered promises in the language of conservatism." L. Brent Bozell, William Buckley's brother-in-law, advised conservatives to stop waiting for Nixon to show his "true conservative colors." They were further discouraged because Nixon was apparently ignoring their warnings of a conservative boycott and continuing his "soft-shoe" march toward the "excluded middle." Even the editors of smaller publications such as *Closer Up* warned that Nixon was an "unpredictable opportunist" who would be "hard to control."[24]

The confusion surrounding Nixon's political ideology resulted in part from a deliberate policy implemented by the candidate himself. At heart a centrist, Nixon usually occupied the middle ground. In the area of civil rights, for example, the vice president supported policies that did not please or alienate either black or white southerners but were acceptable to both. As a government official, Nixon believed in finding workable solutions, a practice that generally required compromise and concession. As a politician, he followed the path that would gain him the most votes.[25] The result was that Nixon frequently advocated conservative means to achieve liberal ends. Right-wingers' ambivalence was thus understandable.

In addition, a mythical Nixon, the product of a reputation gained early in his career, obscured the real man. Nixon, so the story went, was a strident anticommunist and ruthless politician who would use any means at his disposal to destroy anyone who blocked his way. His successful prosecution of Alger Hiss and his "Pink Lady" campaign against Helen Gahagan Douglas laid the foundations for this reputation.[26] His role as liaison between the administration and the McCarthyites during his vice presidential years as well as his attacks on Democrats enhanced this reputation, as did his personality. A loner who was closemouthed about his actual feelings and beliefs, he lacked the charisma to engage people. The public saw the man with the heavy jowls and dark beard as "Tricky Dick." How could anyone believe anything he said?

Conservatives did not risk accepting Nixon at face value because they had finally found a national conservative role model in Barry Goldwater.

Neither a lawyer nor a member of a political family, Goldwater epitomized the successful southwestern businessperson, community leader, and right-wing activist. Elected to the Senate in 1952, he made his name as a conservative by voting against the censure of Senator Joe McCarthy and, as he recalled, by "consistently voting against spending programs" and criticizing the administration's budget policy. His service on the Senate Labor Committee pitted him against labor leaders, especially Walter Reuther, who, according to Goldwater, actively campaigned against him in 1958. Goldwater's reelection by a majority of 35,000 votes, despite intense union opposition, as well as national press coverage of "flamboyant events" in the campaign, increased his support around the country. According to Goldwater, the most famous incident involved the distribution of an unendorsed pamphlet stating that Stalin would approve of Goldwater. The circumstances surrounding this incident, including the supposed investigation by the Senate Select Committee on Elections and Privileges, were never fully explained, but the story made many of the national papers.[27]

After the election, *Human Events* declared Goldwater the "Man of the Hour" and welcomed the return of conservative leadership to Washington. Following his reelection, he appeared in almost every issue of that journal through 1960. Goldwater bolstered his national reputation by criticizing Eisenhower's policies and by writing "How Do You Stand, Sir?," a syndicated column in 140 newspapers. As chair of the Senate Campaign Committee, he was able "to visit every state in the union, almost every district and precinct, not once, but many, many times," strengthening his national reputation and his relationship with party workers.[28]

Goldwater's work with the committee solidified his position within the party machinery, but he leapt to the forefront of the conservative movement with the publication of his book, *The Conscience of a Conservative*. With the help of L. Brent Bozell, he drew on many of his earlier speeches to set forth a credo that redefined conservatism in twentieth-century terms. According to a review in *Human Events*, Goldwater's book succeeded because it provided "humanitarian reasons for following policies which usually have been associated with a mere lust for gain." Rejecting the common misconception that conservatism concentrated solely on economic theory, he insisted instead that conservatism "puts material things in their proper place." A true conservative, according to Goldwater, "believes that man is in part, an economic, an animal creature; but that he is also a spiritual creature with spiritual desires." Although conservatives emphasized freedom, Goldwater explained, they also realized that "the practice of freedom requires the establishment of order." The necessity for order, however, posed the twin dangers of excessive governmental control and the use of that power for illicit purposes. In addition to domestic concerns, Goldwater pointed out the dangers of Soviet aggression, urged the withdrawal of U.S. recognition from *all* communist countries, and advocated the use of nuclear weapons to liberate "captive nations."[29]

Goldwater repeated the same points in speeches across the country. Holmes Alexander, who found him the "frankest political speaker who has ever gone the rounds," echoed the opinion of many on the right when he asked in disbelief: "Was there ever such a politician as this?" South Carolinian Roger Milliken was equally impressed. He argued that Goldwater "most truly" represented the "thinking of conservative people in South Carolina and, indeed, of the nation." Thus, from Old Guard Republicans to the new conservative youth, people across the nation paid increasing attention to the senator from Arizona.[30]

In many ways, Goldwater was the heir to Ohio senator Robert Taft that conservatives had been searching for since Taft's death in 1953. Like Taft, Goldwater's straightforward language attracted a broad range of conservatives who previously had no voice in Republican councils. In addition, he influenced many people in search of a philosophy to express their discontent, and he inspired numerous young people with his sincerity.[31] Both men believed deeply in the right of all people to control their incomes, properties, and destinies. Similarly, both feared the growth of the federal government because they believed that most issues could be resolved more efficiently and effectively on the state or local level.

Key differences separated the two men and their movements, however. Perhaps the most important distinction in the domestic arena was the flexibility of Taft's views on certain social welfare issues. Although he had voted against federal intervention in education throughout most of his career, Taft altered his thinking after World War II. A visit to Puerto Rico forced him to see the connection between substandard education and poverty. This illuminating experience combined with his dedication to the principle of equal educational opportunity led him to introduce a bill to authorize federal aid to education.

In the area of public housing, Taft also proved flexible. He dropped his knee-jerk opposition to all federally funded housing programs after he heard of and witnessed the difficulties that returning veterans and many others faced in finding shelter of any kind. Again, the underlying principle of the importance of the proper family environment in promoting equal opportunity took precedence over the issue of federal interference. Despite opposition from fellow conservatives and the real estate lobby, Taft cosponsored a public-housing bill. He believed that these bills, although they seemed to violate his conservative views concerning the growth of the federal government, remained true to the more fundamental principle of promoting equal opportunity.[32]

To Goldwater, on the other hand, the most important underlying issue was the growth of the government. Convinced that the escalating federal bureaucracy threatened basic freedoms, Goldwater would not support federal aid to education or housing programs. In addition, his devotion to states' rights reinforced his determination to eliminate federal interference whenever possible.

Goldwater and Taft disagreed most dramatically in the area of foreign policy. Though not quite as isolationist as he was generally perceived, Taft strongly insisted that the United States must limit its military commitments abroad. Too many entanglements would overburden the budget and create economic havoc. Taft believed that Americans had to rid themselves of the false notion that they could solve all the world's problems. Disputing the conventional wisdom of his day, Taft insisted that the Chinese communists were the more dangerous threat and downplayed the Soviets' aggressive nature.[33]

Goldwater disagreed, arguing that the United States was engaged in a life-or-death battle with the Soviets for control of the world. He thus advocated a strong stand around the globe, and he accepted the necessity of maintaining far-flung military alliances in order to contain communism. As the only nation that could challenge the "Red Menace," the United States had a duty to protect Western civilization. This more activist, internationalist foreign policy would not have been acceptable to Taft.

Thus, Goldwater built on the legacy of Taft without directly following his lead. The Arizona senator confronted different world problems and therefore had to come up with new solutions. He also faced a different political situation. He benefited from developments within the conservative intellectual community and among the grass roots. With a larger, more organized network, conservatives were now ready for the right person to come along.

Goldwater fit the bill perfectly. Capable, photogenic, and dedicated, he also seemed to be a resourceful politician. Here, at last, was an electable conservative Republican. Gradually, right-wing journals began to note the endorsement of Goldwater for vice president by numerous Young Republican and College Republican groups, a trend that adults increasingly joined throughout the summer of 1960. Ronald Reagan "respectfully" urged Nixon to consider Goldwater as his running mate. At one point, Goldwater said that he would accept the vice presidential nomination, but neither he nor any of his or Nixon's political advisers seriously considered it.[34]

Meanwhile, the first Goldwater for President groups appeared in the spring of 1960. The movement scored a stunning success when the South Carolina Republican convention "pledged its delegates to the nomination of Barry Goldwater for President in 1960." Although Goldwater claimed that he did not want the nomination, state chair G. D. Shorey refused to disband the group. Instead, Shorey continued to seek votes and by 11 July was able to inform Goldwater that at least sixty-three delegates had pledged support for his nomination. Trying to make the best of a delicate situation, Goldwater then convinced the Arizona delegation to nominate him as a favorite son. He intended to withdraw his name before the nominations were made, hoping that the threat of his nomination would convince the Platform Committee that grassroots Republicans "were not particularly happy with Richard Nixon."[35]

By the summer of 1960, Goldwater for President groups had surfaced throughout the country. Shorey encouraged Goldwater to tie them all together into "a real campaign organization and staff." These organizations generally originated in Arizona but allegedly had established branches in a number of states. Their leaders urged volunteers to circulate petitions, write to Nixon and the Republican National Committee to express their opinions, and attend the national convention in Chicago. Although Goldwater had not authorized the use of his name or the formation of such organizations, these groups believed that if they spoke "loud enough," Goldwater could be nominated.[36]

Neither Nixon nor subsequent historians attached much significance to the Goldwater boomlet that developed and grew after March 1960. By ignoring these grassroots organizations, leaders of the Republican Party displayed their tendency to discount the power and potential of citizens' groups and demonstrated their unwillingness to recognize conservatives as legitimate members of the party. Ironically, F. Clifton White, who headed "Volunteers for Nixon-Lodge" and who was a catalyst in the later Draft Goldwater movement, recognized this shortcoming and encouraged Nixon to take "full advantage of citizens' and volunteer groups."[37]

Had Nixon and others paid more attention to these groups, they might have been able to integrate conservatives into the party instead of alienating them. They also might have saved their party the disastrous election of 1964.

In 1960, however, Nixon was more concerned with the divisive threat mounted from the left wing of his party by Nelson Rockefeller, governor of New York. A popular figure from a wealthy and well-connected family, Rockefeller crushed Nixon's dream of a united Republican Party. To conservatives, Rockefeller's willingness to implement New Deal–style programs, his ardent advocacy of civil rights, and his upper-class, northeastern background epitomized the "Eastern Establishment." According to right-wing thinker Richard Whalen, Rockefeller's "obvious grand strategy" was "to wreck Richard Nixon and, if need be, the Republican party itself" in order to "remake the Grand Old Party in his own liberal image."[38] In the melodrama of conservative politics in the 1960s, Rockefeller would play the role of the dastardly archenemy.

The irony of that bit of casting was that Rockefeller espoused few programs or policies that were actually liberal. Shrouded in almost as much myth as Nixon, Rockefeller earned his liberal credentials by his willingness to circumvent normal party procedures, by his tendency to overlook professional politicians in making official appointments, and by his civil rights stance. The fact that he had urged Eisenhower to increase defense spending, had disregarded the civil liberties of convicted criminals, and had become a primary sponsor of fallout shelters did little to alter the public's perception of the governor's ideology. Rockefeller's family background, incredible wealth, and "noblesse oblige" instincts only seemed to confirm the validity of the image. This willingness on the part of the public to rely on images indicated their desire to find a simple solution for increasingly complex political problems.

Rockefeller's presence complicated matters for the GOP even further by exposing disagreements within the Republican liberal wing. Although generally united in their opposition to conservatism, liberals and moderates argued over how far to take their reforms and how quickly they should be enacted. With the first real conservative attack in almost a decade looming, liberals thus began bickering, following Rockefeller's lead. Rockefeller, although philosophically akin to Eisenhower, in the late 1950s became increasingly critical of the Republican administration and, by implication, of Vice President Nixon. The president's brother, Milton Eisenhower, later claimed that Rockefeller had voiced criticisms "in order to forward his candidacy, to take positions different from those of the Vice President." Rockefeller particularly upset many staunch Eisenhower backers when he demanded increased defense spending, a position Nixon supported but could not openly advocate without angering Eisenhower.[39]

After testing the primary waters, which were decidedly chilly, Rockefeller announced on 26 December 1959 that he would not be a candidate for either the presidency or the vice presidency. He explained that he could not abandon his responsibilities as governor of New York to run a campaign, and he stressed that the "great majority of those who will control the Republican Convention, stand opposed to any contest for the nomination." Conservative Republicans took him at his word but were dismayed that Nixon would have no competition for the nomination. They underestimated Rockefeller. Despite his formal declaration of non-candidacy, he continued to make statements and to act in ways that made it look as though he awaited a draft. On 9 June 1960, he released a statement criticizing both the Eisenhower administration and the "leading Republican candidate" for their failure "to make clear where this Party is heading," and he enumerated the problems that he emphasized should be addressed. Two days later, when he tried to gain Eisenhower's endorsement to reenter the race, he received a lecture from the president on the dangers of calling for too much defense spending and an assessment that his prospects were not very good.[40]

Even though his nomination was nearly assured, Nixon tried to woo the Rockefeller wing by convincing Rockefeller to sign on as his running mate. Rockefeller resisted all such suggestions, however, and Nixon realized that he would have to court the governor. The meeting took place in Rockefeller's home on the very day that the press reported Rockefeller's dissatisfaction with the platform and his threat to "take a walk" and "just be Governor of New York" during the Nixon campaign. In a long meeting, the two men worked out a mutually acceptable statement concerning the contents of the platform. Whether one man compromised more than the other was of little importance in the long run; both claimed victory.[41]

Nixon's gesture in making concessions to Rockefeller sent shock waves throughout the rest of the party. Insulted by the apparent repudiation of his policies, Eisenhower angrily telephoned Nixon, who agreed to change the language in the offending planks, especially the statement on defense policies, making it general enough to suit both Rockefeller and Eisenhower. The Platform Committee, which had almost completed its work, was similarly displeased. It took all of Nixon's diplomatic skills, as well as some arm-twisting by Platform Committee members Melvin Laird and Charles Percy, to convince the committee to accept the changes.[42]

The loudest protest, however, came from the conservatives, who saw the Rockefeller-Nixon pact as a "surrender." Feeling that conservatives had been deceived, Goldwater blasted the meeting and the resulting agreement as the "Munich of the Republican Party." If liberal Republicans "alienate the Conservatives—as the party is now in the process of doing," Goldwater warned, "the handful of Liberal militants that are seeking to take control over the Republican Party will inherit a mess of pottage." The announcement of the Nixon-Rockefeller pact strengthened the resolve of those Republican delegates already committed to Goldwater and prompted many others to see him as "the only legitimate spokesman among National Republican leaders for true Republican principles." Finally, it convinced Goldwater to allow his name to be placed in nomination.[43]

Arizona governor Paul Fannin's nominating speech contained the usual political rhetoric except for his remark that he was making the nomination against the wishes of the candidate. In his memoirs, Goldwater explained that this was a deliberate subterfuge to give him the opportunity to make a speech withdrawing his name. Goldwater's speech was remarkable in at least two respects. Considering the anger that he felt toward Nixon, he was generous in encouraging conservatives to work for the vice president's election. He followed his own advice tirelessly, making 126 speeches in 26 states during the campaign. Although he was not happy with Nixon's performance at the convention, Goldwater nonetheless urged conservatives to support Nixon because the Democratic alternative was unacceptable, because Nixon was a conservative on foreign affairs, and because once he became president, Nixon's underlying conservatism would re-emerge.[44]

More importantly, Goldwater used the speech to issue a future challenge to conservatives: to "grow up" and work to set the party back on track. Nixon considered it a "particularly effective speech" but missed the significance of Goldwater's challenge. He and other Republicans assumed that the conservative wing of the party would simply fall in line as it always had.[45]

To some extent, as Goldwater's behavior proved, they were right. The senator was an important asset in convincing right-wingers to vote for Nixon. By painting a frightening portrait of JFK, Goldwater warned conservatives that they could not afford to remain neutral because the "hour of decision," "armageddon," had arrived. In less dramatic fashion, much of the conservative press agreed. The editors of *Human Events* had doubts about Nixon but made it clear that they preferred him over Kennedy. The editors of the *National Review* found it more difficult to endorse the Republican candidate. Emphasizing that the GOP was not the "proper instrument" for furthering the conservative cause, publisher William Rusher argued against supporting Nixon. Buckley thought for a time that staying out of the race would give conservatives more leverage but eventually decided to endorse Nixon.[46]

Goldwater's challenge, however, did not go entirely unnoticed. The *New York Times* commented on the depth of support he had generated at the convention. More importantly, young conservatives joined together not long after the convention to form the Young Americans for Freedom, and shortly after the election, a group of conservatives met to discuss the future of conservatism within the party. Six months later, political manager F. Clifton White, *National Review* publisher William Rusher, and Ohio congressman John Ashbrook formed a committee to work for the nomination of a true conservative in 1964.[47]

These developments were overlooked in the initial flush of excitement that followed Nixon's nomination and the beginning of an intense campaign. Running neck and neck in the polls, the two candidates worked diligently to overcome their weaknesses. Kennedy attempted to dispel doubts about his Catholicism and his inexperience; Nixon tried to shake off his reputation as an insincere "hatchet man." In addition, Nixon had to distance himself from the Eisenhower administration without losing the support of the president or his backers. Both men succeeded, to some extent, in eliminating their liabilities, but neither managed to gain a commanding lead. Even the famous television debates, in which Kennedy appeared much stronger than Nixon, did not take the pressure off the candidates. In fact, by election eve the race was too close to call.[48]

Exhausted, the candidates watched the results seesaw back and forth until Nixon finally conceded defeat. The results were so close, however, that charges of fraud immediately arose. Nixon, placing the welfare of the country above personal concerns, refused to demand a recount and allowed Kennedy to take office. The New Frontier was thus launched with only a limited mandate.[49] As Camelot liberalism took shape, conservatism was forgotten by all but the conservatives, who began to work slowly, and often secretly, toward their goal of capturing the White House.

The year 1960 proved to be pivotal in the conservative effort to develop an effective political movement. Strengthened by the activism of intellectual and grassroots conservatives, Republican right-wingers began to challenge liberal control of the GOP. Earlier tentative criticisms of Eisenhower's policies gave way to more forceful denunciations as conservative politicians measured the depth of right-wing support. To their delight, Republicans found conservative numbers growing. Moreover, many borderline conservatives were frightened into a more open espousal of right-wing views by the increasingly visible civil rights movement and the successes of the Soviets in the space and arms races, in addition to their dissatisfaction with Eisenhower's "stop-go" economy, continuation of New Deal "handouts," and failure to follow a hard-line foreign policy. Helping to articulate these vague feelings of discontent, right-wing journals such as the *National Review* provided their audiences with specific arguments and causes, in the process creating an image of conservatism that was neither stodgy nor old-fashioned but witty, bold, and attractive.

Eventually Goldwater came to represent such an image. He appealed to many members of the middle class who viewed him as a champion of hard-working businesspeople frustrated by governmental controls, parents concerned about their children's education, and patriots worried by the spread of communist ideology at home and abroad. Even those who found him intellectually limited and oratorically crude regarded him as the first attractive and popular right-wing Republican in the postwar era. He excited people in a way that Robert Taft had not and did not suffer from a loser's image. Goldwater's performance at the 1960 convention inspired conservative faith and raised hopes for the future.

The 1960s thus held promise for conservatives. After years of frustration as members of a minority faction that was ignored and abused within the party, conservatives were determined to heed Goldwater's advice and seize control of their party. Liberal and moderate Republicans, like the rest of the country at that time and like historians ever since, continued to view conservatives in a one-dimensional mold. Despite Goldwater's popularity, the rise of a successful conservative press, and the right-wing takeover of the Young Republicans, the party majority continued to discount the growing conservative challenge. Consequently, while Nixon and liberal Republicans ignored conservatives' complaints and assumed the cooperation of the right wing, conservatives were left alone to start building support within the party structure and among the voting public. Their efforts in 1960, although unsuccessful, were a prelude to the conservative takeover of the party four years later.

3

★ ★ ★ ★ ★ ★ ★ ★ ★ ★ ★ ★ ★ ★ ★ ★
★ ★ ★ ★ ★ ★ ★ ★ ★ ★ ★ ★ ★ ★ ★ ★
★ ★ ★ ★ ★ ★ ★ ★ ★ ★ ★ ★ ★ ★ ★ ★
★ ★ ★ ★ ★ ★ ★ ★ ★ ★ ★ ★ ★ ★ ★ ★

PROBLEMS AND SOLUTIONS

Conservatives, frustrated by Nixon's narrow defeat in the election of 1960 and still angry at what they saw as his turn toward liberalism, lashed out. In a letter to the *National Review*, a reader voiced his disgust that Nixon had given up his advantages by trying simply to outpromise Kennedy. The journal's editors agreed that Nixon had surrendered the ideological high ground to appear more like his opponent and chastised him for leaving behind no legacy but merely the memory of his defeat. Nixon's refusal to heed advice during the campaign similarly disenchanted conservative senator Styles Bridges of New Hampshire. Chronicler Theodore White, in his book written immediately after the election, argued that Nixon's lack of a campaign strategy left him helpless to deal with the problems he faced. According to L. Brent Bozell, the Democrats "intimidated" Nixon, who after first trying to "hammer away" at his opponents, later "obliged" them when he gave up the "Old Nixon" style and "surrendered his one chance of decisively breaking through party barriers and creating a 'swing vote' favorable to him."[1]

Although conservative criticism did sting Nixon, he and many others dismissed the specific remarks as insignificant. After all, he believed that voters had regarded him as the more conservative of the two candidates anyway, so a change in tone would have made little difference. Nixon attributed the tendency of critics to engage in second-guessing to the narrowness of the defeat rather than to their having legitimate complaints. "When a shift of ten or twelve thousand votes in three or four key states would have overturned the result," he wrote, observers could assert that the defeat was a result of the candidate's failure to follow advice. Nixon claimed that although he had fought a good fight, he had lost the battle of the image in the press and on television. Most importantly, despite conservatives' harsh words during and after the campaign, the election returns indicated that many right-wingers had voted for Nixon anyway. To most liberals, the continuing loyalty of the right wing seemed to be a safe bet.[2]

Liberals overlooked the threat from the Right, but they could not ignore the divisions that had surfaced within their own wing of the party during the campaign. Eisenhower's comments during the campaign had contributed to these divisions. Once when asked by a reporter what Nixon had added to his administration, he replied that he needed a week to think about it. He was slow to campaign for Nixon but drew large crowds when he did hit the campaign trail. Nelson Rockefeller, according to some New Yorkers, likewise failed to support Nixon fully. In fact, so much postelection gossip criticized Rockefeller for his lack of support that the New York state Republican chair issued a statement that the governor had done everything he could for Nixon.[3]

The external factors that led to the defeat concerned the liberals more than did the divisions within the GOP. Thruston Morton, Republican National Committee (RNC) chair, complained that the party had "paid too little attention to specific segments of the electorate—such as the Negro vote" and had not fought "hard enough in the centers of mass population." The statistics bore out his assertion, for Democrats outpolled Republicans in cities by almost 3 million votes. Nixon aide Charles Lichenstein blamed the problem on weak state-level party organizations and the declining number of registered members. As a result, Nixon had been compelled to build his own nationwide organization "from scratch."[4] By focusing on blaming defeat on the failure to attract special-interest groups, liberal Republicans overlooked the fact that the weakness of the state organizations created a strategic opportunity for the Right. Conservatives, however, did not.

Republicans, including conservatives, tried to put the defeat in the best possible light. Thruston Morton insisted that the GOP had not suffered a "repudiation of its record." In fact, he argued, the election had "shattered the hopes of the Democrats for a clear-cut mandate from the American electorate." William Miller, who succeeded Morton as RNC chair, was encouraged by the party's ability to carry more states in the election than had the Democrats. Rank-and-file Republicans seemed to share that optimism. Stephen Shadegg, a close political associate of Barry Goldwater's, did not "regard the 1960 campaign as a defeat." In his view, the results proved that the GOP was "a national party" and that "millions of Americans prefer a conservative philosophy of government." Even *National Review* readers, although generally disappointed with the election results, found some cause for hope. One reader, in a letter to the editor, pointed out that "this country is about to enjoy what it hasn't had for eight crucial years: an organized opposition to the Liberal domination of public affairs." This opposition would be intensified, conservative Republicans believed, by the election of the "Young Fogies," a group of forty freshmen congressmen from small towns and rural areas who preached a conservative line.[5]

Perhaps the most significant glimmer of hope was the apparent revitalization of the GOP in the South. Although Nixon won in only three southern states, in several others his tallies exceeded those of Eisenhower four years earlier, and in some his numbers matched Eisenhower's. Moreover, Nixon's victories in Arizona, California, Florida, Oklahoma, and Tennessee as well as his narrow defeats in Arkansas, Louisiana, New Mexico, and Texas indicated the widening cracks in the "Solid South" and emerging voting trends in the Southwest. In fact, even Nixon's nomination revealed the increasing influence of the Southern Rim in Republican Party politics, since his poor, small-town background and aggressive, ambitious personality identified him as a southwestern "cowboy" politician and set him apart from northeastern types who had been nominated for years.[6]

This revitalization was the product of developments that had taken place over the previous forty years. The Republican Party had made significant inroads into the "Solid South" during the 1920s and, despite a setback during the New Deal, had gradually built a viable party there, particularly in the upper South. Working from this base, the GOP then reaped the benefits of the socioeconomic transformation of the South following World War II. The development of a significant number of defense industries throughout the South and Southwest during the war provided steady employment for many unskilled and semiskilled workers who had been forced off their farms during the Depression or mechanized out of agriculture. After the war, industrialization lifted many southern whites out of poverty for the first time and into the working and middle classes. In addition, promises of jobs and the demand for middle-level managers lured many nonsoutherners below the Mason-Dixon line.[7]

This growth transformed the southern economy and had far-reaching sociopolitical implications. Transplanted Yankees usually lacked southerners' diehard loyalty to the Democratic Party; in fact, many were Republicans. Moreover, many southern whites whose economic status had improved as a result of the industrial transformation now paid taxes for the first time instead of receiving federally sponsored benefits as many had during the Depression. They greatly resented welfare programs and became susceptible to Republican rhetoric. By the late 1950s, this newly urbanized, increasingly educated middle class began to challenge the traditional political leadership of the South.[8]

One of the institutions the new middle class found wanting was the Democratic Party. Since 1876, the Democratic Party had served the political needs of white southerners by upholding segregation and, in times of economic distress, by providing federal assistance to the needy. The situation began to change, however, during World War II. Despite the moderation of the Roosevelt administration, federal assistance had often introduced federal interference in local affairs. For many of the newly prosperous, this trend established a dangerous precedent. Moreover, as their economic status improved in the 1950s, numerous white southerners began to question the need for governmental "giveaway" programs. Perhaps even more importantly, some white southerners started to doubt the ability or willingness of national Democratic leaders to help safeguard the Jim Crow system. As a result of President Harry Truman's support of the 1948 platform, which included a civil rights plank, southerners became increasingly wary of the national party. Northern Democratic victories in the late 1950s and early 1960s strengthened the liberal wing of the party and gave southerners more cause for concern.[9]

As a result, Republicans found southerners in the postwar period much more politically hospitable. In fact, beginning with Eisenhower's 1952 campaign, Republican presidential candidates had made significant gains throughout the South. Many white southerners called themselves Democrats but increasingly voted Republican in national elections. This encouraged Republicans to intensify their efforts to find viable candidates. These tendencies explain, at least in part, Nixon's gains in the South in 1960;

Senator John Tower's victory in Texas in 1961; the closely contested 1962 Senate races in South Carolina and Alabama; and the addition of four new Republican representatives in 1962 from North Carolina, Florida, Texas, and Tennessee. Although personalities and intrastate politicking played a role in these races, Republicans emphasized ideology as they proudly defended their wins.[10]

The revitalization of the GOP in the South strengthened the conservative wing of the party. Aside from the racists and other extremists who disliked the liberalism of the national Democratic Party, many southerners who joined the GOP embraced the classical liberal ideals embodied in the Republican Party's opposition to high taxes, federal spending, and government centralization. Hooverian "rugged individualists," they were often "neobourbons" who clung to their rural values while practicing corporate capitalism. Southern culture revolved around a dedication to family, God, and country—values that echoed northern right-wing ideals. As a result, many of the new conservative Republican officeholders represented southern and southwestern states.[11]

The failure of liberals to understand the implications of the dawning Republicanism of the South did not mean that they were totally unaware of the divisions that existed within the party. In early 1961, a group of liberal Republicans founded a new magazine, *Advance*, to promote a future vision for the party. *Advance* frequently took note of the conservatives but usually only to castigate them and explain why no serious Republican should agree with them. Calling for a "definite, positive" program, the editors of *Advance* believed that the GOP could become the majority party by combining its traditions with a progressive stance on civil rights and social welfare. Although the publication received support from such noteworthy Republicans as Nixon, Republican author Arthur Larson, and California senator Thomas Kuchel, it folded after two years.[12]

Most Republicans did not believe that internal ideological differences constituted a significant threat to the status quo within the party. According to most moderates, conservatives represented only a fanatical "lunatic fringe" that no one should take seriously. Moreover, liberals allowed conservatives to voice their opinions as long as they did not challenge liberal control of the party. Rockefeller, emphasizing the importance of a unified party image, nevertheless maintained that it would be a "tragedy to have a monolithic Republican Party" and that the party was "fortunate to have these variations." At the same time, he deemphasized the liberal-conservative split, arguing that this division had lost its meaning "in the evolution from the New Deal days." He preferred to concentrate on the differences between the two parties. On the other hand, RNC chair William Miller acknowledged a rising conservative trend in the nation, especially as manifested by Tower's election, but he noted that it was "difficult to assess the proportion of it or the importance of it to people running on a national basis."[13]

Only conservatives underscored the intraparty differences. As the only members to challenge the party's established power structure, they became keenly aware of the areas of conflict. Conservatives were more concerned with ideology than liberal Republicans; liberals who chastised them for not backing all Republican candidates missed the essential point that many right-wingers were conservatives first and Republicans second. This led liberals consistently to misunderstand and to underestimate the conservative challenge from within the party.[14]

More than anything else, Republicans had to devise an effective strategy for criticizing the image and often contradictory reality of the Kennedy administration. Kennedy appeared to be many things that he was not—a young family man in vigorous health, an intellectual, a war hero, and a traditional Democratic liberal. In reality, he carried on numerous extramarital affairs while in the White House, suffered from chronic back ailments and Addison's disease, read voraciously but preferred action to ideas, spouted Cold War rhetoric, practiced conservative fiscal policy, and moved with extreme caution in the areas of civil rights and social reform.[15]

Kennedy's relationship with liberals in his own party had been rocky since early in his career. His wealthy background, his father's reputation and tutelage, and his own ambivalent attitude toward Joe McCarthy created a divide between himself and the liberals that he made little effort to cross as a senator. After he decided to run for the presidency, however, he worked hard to woo the left wing of the party during the campaign. He met with various liberal leaders and intellectuals, delivered decidedly more "acceptable" speeches, and introduced legislation creating various social welfare programs.[16]

Although some intellectuals such as Arthur Schlesinger, Jr., and John Kenneth Galbraith moved into Kennedy's camp, others, including Eleanor Roosevelt and Alfred Kazin, regarded him with suspicion. Schlesinger dismissed such skeptics as "utopianists" who would never be satisfied. Once in the White House, JFK had to keep the liberals satisfied while he moved forward with his own cautious program. He was not always successful. As early as April 1961, the editors of *The Nation* noted that some of the press viewed Kennedy's programs as little more than "warmed over Eisenhower." By February 1963, they openly discussed "the liberal disillusionment with Kennedy."[17] Although JFK did not act as quickly or decisively as his rhetoric promised and the liberals desired, he did move cautiously to the left, and many liberal Democrats concluded that this was better than nothing.

Republicans thus found JFK a difficult target because of his liberal image and conservative policies. On the one hand, he talked like a traditional Democrat who accepted the New Deal framework. On the other hand, he embraced Cold War diplomacy and adopted a conservative approach to civil rights and government-business relations while taking care not to alienate his liberal constituents. This made it difficult for Republicans to criticize his administration effectively and widened the gaps between conservatives and the rest of the Republican Party by forcing their differences into the open.

Kennedy was a fiscal conservative who often told businesspeople that government and business were "necessary allies." From the early days of his administration, he worked to reassure businesspeople that he meant them no harm. By appointing Republicans like Douglas Dillon (Treasury) and Robert McNamara (Defense) to his cabinet, he hoped to assure Wall Street that he believed in sound economic policy.[18]

Kennedy followed through by introducing programs aimed specifically at benefiting the business community: a tax-credit plan, limited enforcement of antitrust laws, private ownership of the Communications Satellite Corporation, a trade expansion bill, and a 1963 tax bill that, according to *The Nation*, contained a "hidden tilt" favoring the few over the many. The liberal press noted with dismay his tendency to meet business "at least halfway." A later editorial in *The Nation* claimed that the relationship had extended much further: "The President has wooed business, flirted with it, proposed marriage, and curbed it only when it was a matter of desperate necessity."[19]

Many businesspeople, however, relied more on their traditional views of Democrats than on Kennedy's words. They rejected the president's outstretched hand for much of his tenure. Kennedy's heavy-handed response to the rise in steel prices in early 1962 reinforced their suspicions, and they felt perversely vindicated when a stock market slump followed.

Despite these tensions and Kennedy's eventual adoption of a more Keynesian economic approach, he managed to win over a significant portion of the business community. His relationship with business reflected not only his conservative tendencies but also the diversity of the business community. Since the early twentieth century, large capital-intensive multinational corporations had often shared few of the economic or political concerns of smaller labor-intensive firms that relied exclusively on national markets and could not compete with foreign rivals. As the disparity between these firms grew in the early 1900s, their needs often forced them to take opposite sides on political issues. In fact, according to political scientist Thomas Ferguson, this cleavage compelled multinational corporations to leave the Republican Party, their traditional home, to join other groups in a coalition that overwhelmingly elected Franklin Roosevelt in 1936. The "System of '36" proved powerful enough to sustain the liberals well into the 1960s. Even Republicans, Ferguson argued, did not dare alter the platform of "social welfare, trade unionism, minority rights, expanded popular participation in government, . . . a progressive income tax, and free trade" established by the Democrats. Liberal Republicans like Rockefeller enthusiastically supported these policies, but they could not convince conservative elements of their party to accept them.[20]

JFK's effective courtship of corporate liberals produced an important, though not immediately evident, change in the power structure of the GOP. Business contributions to the Democrats deprived liberal Republicans of funds at the same time that the growth of Southern Rim industries increased donations to conservatives. These circumstances helped conservative activists gain control of the Republican Party. By creating an alternative financial structure dependent on southwestern and rank-and-file money, conservative Republicans obviated liberal Republicans' reliance on corporate financing.[21] Conservative businesspeople complained about JFK, but in effect he was helping their cause.

Kennedy's position on civil rights, perhaps the most controversial issue of the 1960s, was also somewhat beneficial to the conservative cause. Ambivalence characterized his stance on the nonviolent protest movement seeking equality for black Americans that had evolved in the 1950s and gained added force in the early 1960s. On the one hand, Kennedy saw the problem simply as a technical matter that required delicate handling to ensure that vital southern votes were not lost. On the other hand, as the civil rights movement grew stronger, a kind of moral imperative and commitment to civil rights replaced his pragmatism.[22]

Kennedy thus sent mixed signals with regard to his position on civil rights. He had carefully cultivated his image as a liberal advocate of civil rights during the presidential nomination battle, and once he became president, he continued to nurture this image by making several dramatic but largely symbolic gestures. He signed executive orders prohibiting discrimination in new housing programs and creating the President's Committee on Equal Employment Opportunity. Even these gestures brought him criticism from within his own party: conservative Democrats attacked his use of executive orders as unconstitutional, while liberals complained that he was not doing enough. Civil rights leaders accused his administration of practicing "an essentially cautious and defensive" strategy and of letting tokenism serve as its policy. Meanwhile, civil rights workers in the field, through sit-ins and freedom rides, forced Kennedy to move more quickly than he preferred. By 1963, the escalation of violence and the flagrant southern disregard for federal law finally convinced JFK to risk sending to Congress the civil rights legislation he had promised three years earlier. The bill was still frozen there at the time of his death.[23]

Republicans, at least in theory, generally supported the principle of civil rights but were divided over how it should be implemented. Liberal Republicans like Nelson Rockefeller supported quick federal action to address the problem. As part of his "deal" with Nixon in 1960, Rockefeller had forced the inclusion of a plank in the 1960 Republican platform that called for " 'aggressive action' to abolish racial discrimination in all areas of life and explicitly endorsed the Negro sit-in demonstrations." In fact, *The Nation*'s editors believed that Rockefeller deserved "high commendation for his forthright endorsement of the President's program" on civil rights. They also noted with approval New York senator Jacob Javits's attempts to end segregation. The support of these liberal Republicans and others such as New York senator Kenneth Keating, California senator Thomas Kuchel, and Pennsylvania senator Hugh Scott was crucial to passage of the Civil Rights Act of 1964.[24]

On the other hand, conservative Republicans like Barry Goldwater expressed a commitment to equal rights but insisted that policies concerning race relations should be determined by the states. They pointed out the hypocrisy of northerners who wanted to force the South to change but refused to integrate their own communities first. Black and white southerners were very aware of the contradictions. Baseball player Jackie Robinson had warned Goldwater and his followers that Nixon's "southern strategy" of writing off the black vote had not worked in 1960 and would doom Goldwater in 1964. Meanwhile, some white southerners, vigorously opposed to the changes they believed inevitable under a Kennedy administration, had turned to the Republican Party. In addition, by 1963, a few journalists had begun to speak of a "white backlash" in the North. Although this may not have concerned Kennedy greatly, it had potential significance for conservative Republicans attempting to build a constituency.[25]

Kennedy's foreign policy further widened the splits within the Republican Party. In many ways a typical Cold Warrior, Kennedy believed that communism had to be stopped wherever it surfaced and that military action was the appropriate deterrent. Most Republicans and Democrats accepted this premise and encouraged the president to take a tough stand against the Soviets.[26] Less unity was exhibited however, when it came to assessing Kennedy's specific foreign policy actions. One of the first key foreign policy problems Kennedy was forced to tackle was the situation in Cuba. Fidel Castro, although hailed by the American press as a democratic reformer when he first seized control of the island in 1959, by 1960 symbolized the communist threat in the Western hemisphere. Many Americans refused to accept the existence of such a regime so close to the United States and demanded that the government remove Castro from power.

Thus, JFK's first opportunity to demonstrate his strong anticommunist credentials arose in the form of a CIA plan to help Cuban refugees stage a coup d'état against Castro. The failure of the Bay of Pigs invasion confirmed conservatives' worst fears about Kennedy. *National Review* editors described it as "a failure of will." Although Kennedy claimed full responsibility and apologized for the attack, he delivered a speech three days after the invasion reaffirming American determination to eradicate communism in Cuba. The editors of *The Nation* asserted that actions such as the invasion put Kennedy "in bed with" the lunatic fringe on the right, but conservatives insisted that the president acted too weakly in responding to the Soviet threat. Even when Kennedy reacted forcefully to the Berlin crisis in 1961 by increasing defense spending and calling up the Reserves and stood "eyeball to eyeball" with Khrushchev over the issue of Soviet missiles in Cuba in 1962, conservatives remained dissatisfied with his foreign policy. In addition, his willingness to rely on a quick military response disturbed some liberals who wondered why diplomacy had not been tried.[27]

Americans also increasingly worried about the revolutionary potential of emerging nations in Africa and Asia. Policy differences regarding these developing countries exacerbated the divisions within and between the political parties. The Kennedy administration, by supporting anticommunist leaders who, policy-makers believed, were strong enough to defeat the revolutionary forces, frequently ended up backing men who abused power and misused American aid. As a result, such policies often were not successful abroad or at home. The American-backed leaders in Laos, Vietnam, and Cuba were unable to maintain popular support, and both the Left and the Right criticized JFK's policies as ill-advised.[28]

Especially annoying to conservative Republicans was the foreign aid component of JFK's policy. While liberal Republicans such as Rockefeller and Javits accepted the necessity of such a program, Goldwater Republicans castigated foreign aid programs—including Eisenhower's—as "not only ill-administered, but ill-conceived" and unconstitutional. Moreover, whereas the Kennedy administration and some Republicans worked toward a bipartisan foreign policy, conservative Republicans continually disparaged what they regarded as the president's "no-win" strategy. Ironically, the analysis of foreign aid programs by conservatives like the *National Review*'s James Burnham paralleled the subsequent leftist critique of corporate liberalism's domination of foreign policy.[29]

The debates over Kennedy's foreign and domestic policies both grew out of and intensified changes in the political climate. Kennedy's pro-business economic policies, his reliance on military solutions to diplomatic problems, and his cautious approach to the civil rights movement elicited the suspicions and disappointment of many liberals. Increasingly, the nonpolitical Left—intellectuals, students, and civil rights workers—complained that Kennedy's willingness to compromise undermined his liberal credentials. If Kennedy and his supporters did not belong on the left, but in the center, where did that leave moderate Republicans who claimed that ground as their own? As the answer to that question became more apparent, the gulf between the branches of the GOP widened.

Some right-wingers reluctantly admitted that JFK was not the liberal they had expected him to be. In an interview published in the *National Review*, Goldwater observed that the president was "proceeding cautiously, and more conservatively than people expected him to." In a letter to the editor in the same issue, a reader commented that he could not "avoid noting" that although he was unhappy with some of Kennedy's cabinet choices, the situation had not "turned out that bad." Conservatives were not ready to abandon their view of JFK as a liberal, but even the editors of the *National Review* noted approvingly his growing caution as he entered his second year in office.[30]

Kennedy, by co-opting the corporate sponsors of the liberal Republicans, cleared the way for a change in the financial base of the Republican

Party. The full extent of this change would be apparent during Goldwater's 1964 campaign. By espousing civil rights, for whatever reason, he also drove the northern and southern opponents of the movement into the waiting arms of the Republican Party. The racist implications of this shift disturbed many moderate Republicans, separated them further from conservatives, and added another dimension to the developing extremist image of the Right. Conservative obsession with communism and fondness for military solutions further alienated many moderates. Kennedy's assassination in Dallas, an avowedly right-wing city, left the party more divided than ever.

Kennedy's concern about the apparent growth of the Radical Right throughout his presidential tenure had increased attention to the more extremist right-wingers, fueled the perception that all conservatives were dangerous, and further alienated conservative Republicans from moderate Republicans. Beginning in late 1961 and continuing throughout 1962, the media "discovered" the "ultra-right" in what became almost a national obsession. Private studies investigated the financing of extremist groups and the strength of their appeal. Numerous newspapers and journals devoted articles to the increasingly vocal conservatives. In early 1960, the *New Republic* warned that the "radical right" was "stirring again." Although they would almost totally ignore the Right in 1963, the editors of *The Nation* spent 1962 pointing out the growing number of right-wing groups and even published a special edition entitled "The Ultras: Aims, Affiliations, and Finances of the Radical Right." The *Journal of Social Issues* devoted an entire issue to the topic entitled "American Political Extremism in the 1960s" and focused exclusively on right-wing activities. Like moderate Republicans, the media labeled all varieties of conservatism as "extremist" and thus helped to create a fear of all right-wing ideas.[31]

Democrats also lumped all conservative groups together as they lamented the impact of the Right on the electorate. Providing "pat answers to . . . complex situations" and employing a grassroots campaign, the Right appeared to be gaining followers. In 1961 Wyoming senator Gale McGee warned the Kennedy administration that the "drift to the right" was "taking over the American mind almost by default." Even more concerned two years later, McGee submitted a detailed report to the White House staff, explaining that the right-wing strategy had been successful in the West and was now moving east. Texas congressman Wright Patman also warned that the Right was winning adherents by providing "poisonous food" for thought "for millions of Americans who hunger for political ideas and guidance." Blaming the proliferation of right-wing pamphlets for the defeat of the 1963 Foreign Aid Bill, Patman suggested that the Democratic National Committee should take action to counter the conservative activity.[32]

The Democrats believed that at least some of these right-wing groups had ties to the conservative branch of the Republican Party. McGee accused the GOP of "reviving the old cliches about the Democrats being 'soft on communism'" and of trying to create the impression that Republicans "somehow have a monopoly on concern about the ways and means of fighting the threat of both external and internal communism." In a series of confidential investigations authorized by the Kennedy administration, staff members closely monitored the activities of groups such as the John Birch Society, Young Americans for Freedom, and various Christian crusades, particularly with regard to their relationship with the GOP.[33] Democrats therefore intensified the fears of extremism while at the same time locating the source of the problem within the Republican Party. This only increased tensions within the GOP.

The lack of a viable national leader following the 1960 election further exacerbated divisions within the party. As Republicans regrouped for the 1964 campaign, several men—Richard Nixon, Nelson Rockefeller, and Barry Goldwater—were suggested as party leaders, yet none dominated the field. Rockefeller at least pretended that this was not a problem. "The real leadership of our Party," he explained at a press conference, "is in the Congress." Other observers also recognized the party's reliance on congressional leadership, but they questioned the effectiveness of leaders who spent most of their time on the defensive rather than the offensive.[34]

Nixon, of course, technically remained the obvious leader. As his party's presidential nominee in the previous election, he was the titular head of the organization. Unfortunately for him, for the first time in fourteen years he lacked a national platform. This did not stop him, however, from challenging the Kennedy administration. Through speaking engagements, letters to prominent Republicans, and the publication of his political memoir, *Six Crises*, Nixon played opposition leader to Kennedy while reminding everyone that he was still a viable political figure.[35]

The desire to remain in the public eye and to regain public office played a part in Nixon's decision to enter the California gubernatorial race in 1962. Both conservative senator John Bricker and Eisenhower suggested that by winning that contest he might have a better chance of winning the 1964 presidential sweepstakes. Nixon believed that he "should continue to write and speak on national and international issues" since those were his main areas of interest. In the end, however, despite his own reluctance, deep divisions within the California GOP, and the disapproval of his wife, he entered the race.[36]

After an intense primary battle in which Nixon condemned John Birch Society members for their extremist views about Eisenhower, he engaged in an uphill struggle against Democratic incumbent Pat Brown. Although he healed the wounds inflicted in the primary and won the support of many conservatives, Nixon lost the election by 297,000 votes. He blamed the defeat on the public's support of JFK's handling of the Cuban Missile Crisis.[37]

After suffering his second defeat in two years, Nixon lost control and almost ended his political career by bitterly telling a group of reporters, "You won't have Nixon to kick around anymore, because, gentlemen, this is my last press conference." After this outburst, many people agreed with *The Nation*'s assessment that Nixon was "an American tragedy in the classic pattern." Never one to let other people limit or label him, Nixon refused to stay in the background, however, and remained a visible and important figure as the party moved toward the election of 1964. Having failed in the West, he decided to move back East and accepted a position with a New York City law firm. His desertion of the California GOP upset party leaders who had hoped he would help unify the party. Goldwater believed that the move deprived Nixon of his power base. Neither the change in scenery nor the criticism from party members stopped Nixon from continuing, in a very subtle but deliberate manner, to build support for himself for 1964.[38]

One of Nixon's chief rivals for the leadership of the GOP remained New York governor Nelson Rockefeller. A "pragmatic liberal," Rockefeller resembled Kennedy in his activist managerial style of government. As a result, Rockefeller provided the Right with the "villain" necessary to mobilize the conservative faithful. His militant foreign policy could not excuse his willingness to accept and even exploit New Deal–style programs as governor, a fact that also infuriated the Kennedy administration. On the other hand, he recognized that he needed conservative support to win the nomination. Consequently, when the bitterness of the 1960 campaign died down, Rockefeller and his associates began meeting with Goldwater and his followers to discuss issues. According to Rockefeller, they found that they "were in agreement on the majority of the major issues."[39] Considering Rockefeller's pragmatism as well as his conservative foreign policy views, his assessment probably contained at least a grain of truth and was not simply political propaganda. Of more significance, Goldwater's willingness to see past the governor's liberal image hinted at the growing political maturity and savvy of the senator.

In the midst of this truce, however, Rockefeller divorced his wife and, in May 1963, married a recent divorcée with several small children. He suffered an immediate decline in popularity as the public questioned his morality. Rockefeller's honeymoon with conservatives gave way to bitter disputes. In a July 1963 press release, Rockefeller launched a withering attack on the "radical right," which he blamed for most of the accusations concerning his personal life. Warning that the party was in "real danger of subversion by a radical, well-financed, and highly disciplined minority," Rockefeller's message was a thinly disguised assault on Goldwater and his followers. He criticized conservatives' tactics and their philosophical commitment to states' rights.[40] Rockefeller thus fortified his claim to the nomination while alienating the conservative wing of the party. By doing this, he perpetuated the long-standing assumption of liberal Republicans that conservatives would always eventually fall in line.

The third potential Republican leader was Barry Goldwater, the "pinup boy" of the Republican Right. After his performance at the 1960 national convention and during the campaign, Goldwater received much adulation, respect, and support. General Douglas MacArthur wrote Goldwater that "a great vacuum exists which you can fill" and predicted that "dramatic and startling events lie just ahead." Many *National Review* readers, among others, were determined to make certain Goldwater took part in those events. A letter to the editor in December 1960 advised that "it is not a moment too early to put on our Goldwater buttons and set to work." Although Goldwater appreciated such support, at that time he was interested less in the presidential nomination than in fulfilling what he felt were his most important duties outside the Senate: helping candidates win elections and serving as responsible opposition to JFK. At the same time, he sought to refine Republican conservatism to enable it to fulfill its potential within the party.[41]

Nixon, Rockefeller, and Goldwater joined others, including Michigan governor George Romney, in vying for the Republican nomination in 1964. Although many had viewed JFK as unbeatable, all four were willing to challenge him. The ideological differences that separated the Republican contenders took on added importance as the candidates began to use them as weapons to attack each other. These "canabalistic [*sic*] instincts," in Nixon's words, further divided the party and cast the ideologies of the various factions of the party as rigidly exaggerated stereotypes that left little room for compromise or even intelligent self-definition.[42]

In addition, the GOP faced an ongoing image problem. Republicans knew that they had lost the 1960 election partly because they had not consciously built up a broader-based constituency. They made several attempts in the ensuing years to correct that oversight. Aware of the increasing impact of television and public relations on elections, Republicans began hiring advertising agencies to upgrade their image. They also tried to spruce up the party's image in Congress. Forty-seven-year-old Michigan representative Gerald Ford replaced Iowa representative Charles Hoeven, who was twenty years his senior, as chair of the House Republican Conference. This "minor upset" was symptomatic of the desire of the younger Republicans to make the GOP appear more dynamic as well as more moderate. Feeling pressure as a result of Kennedy's skillful use of the media, House minority leader Charles Halleck and Senate minority leader Everett Dirksen created their own television show "to rebut the president and present the GOP point of view." The venture, which became known as the "Ev and Charlie Show," pleased few Republicans. Although respected journals such as *Commonweal* mocked it, calling it a "turn of the century vaudeville act," and serious conservatives and moderates resented the way it turned the party and their beliefs into a joke, the show continued production until after the 1964 election.[43]

Charges of racism surfaced whenever the GOP mentioned its gains in the South, but the major image problem, of course, was the tinge of extremism that haunted conservative Republicans. Moderates within the party attempted not only to disassociate the party from more extreme views but to discredit the principle of extremism as well. Eisenhower complained about the "trends . . . developing in our body politic." "To try to make politics completely black or completely white," he warned, "is simply stupid." As he put it, "The extreme right is just as guilty as is the extreme left."[44]

Of most concern to Republicans from 1960 to 1964, however, was the John Birch Society. Robert Welch and his followers could not easily be ignored or silenced as their numbers and influence grew. By the early 1960s, two Republican congressmen—John Rousselot and Edgar Hiestand—admitted that they belonged to the society. During Nixon's tough primary fight against society member Joseph Shell for the California governorship, he finally felt compelled to "take on the lunatic fringe" and repudiate the organization. Nixon explained that "this statement of mine will undoubtedly cost some financial support and probably a few votes as well but in the end I think it is vitally important that the Republican party not carry the anchor of the reactionary right into our campaigns this Fall."[45]

If Nixon was somewhat immodest and self-righteous, he was also correct not to underestimate the power and influence of the society. Michigan governor George Romney persuaded the state Republican Party to disassociate itself from the actions of a Republican officeholder and John Birch Society member who had misrepresented himself to his constituents. With more unfortunate consequences, Leonard Finder, an Eisenhower associate who ran a large newspaper in California, discovered just how powerful and vindictive the John Birch Society could be after he printed a series of disparaging articles about the organization in his paper. The group organized a boycott of the paper, sent propaganda about him to his stockholders, and finally caused him to lose his position as publisher.[46]

Conservatives were especially concerned because Rockefeller and other liberal Republicans equated the John Birch Society and the extreme right wing with conservative Republicans. William Buckley, Barry Goldwater, and other conservative spokespersons attempted to differentiate between the two but achieved only limited success. The inability of liberals to distinguish between the Right and the Far Right blinded them to the true divisions that separated liberals and conservatives and led them to disregard all right-wing movements as merely the workings of the lunatic fringe. Moreover, attaching the extremist label to all conservatives served the useful political purpose of eliminating at least some of the competition. Moderate Republicans became very adept at using the extremist label as a tool, unaware that eventually it would come back to haunt them.

The problem of image only reinforced Republicans' efforts to broaden their base of support. Recognizing that Democrats consistently outpolled them in large urban areas, Republicans took the advice of political technicians such as Ray Bliss, state chair of Ohio, who created a "Big Cities" program to rebuild the party structure in urban areas. Modeled on Bliss's achievements in Ohio, the RNC applied a "Big Cities" plan to the nation as a whole in the ensuing years. Bliss further recommended that party members create "special activities" aimed at enticing various ethnic groups, women, blacks, and youth to join the GOP.[47]

In 1962 the creation of the All Republican Conference and its companion organization, the National Republican Citizens' Committee (RCC), typified moderate Republicans' assumptions about their party and exposed their greatest weaknesses. Instead of seriously investigating ideological or policy differences within the party, organizers hoped to build the party from the outside in the belief that internal difficulties would somehow take care of themselves. Ironically, members chose a format similar to that of the conservatives then working for Goldwater's election—a grassroots structure not limited to party membership—but they met with much less success.[48]

As early as March 1962, Eisenhower, who recognized the need to enlist nonprofessionals in support of political causes, expressed interest in the "projected Republican Committee," but little activity occurred for several months. In a letter sent to those invited to the All Republican Conference, William Miller explained that the conference would not decide policy but would provide a forum in which various dignitaries could discuss trends and political developments. Miller assured them that this free and open discussion would highlight "constructive Republican preoccupation with the major problems of our country" as well as demonstrate "the broad spectrum of able and attractive Republicans who give leadership in dealing with these problems." Although Miller pragmatically emphasized the public relations advantages of the conference, Eisenhower and Goldwater were more concerned that the conference issue a statement of basic principles "short and succinct" enough to inform voters of its objectives without boring, confusing, or antagonizing them.[49]

Despite these high-minded and practical goals, the All Republican Conference did not amount to much, but the other component of the plan enjoyed more success. At a Republican unity meeting in Gettysburg in July 1962, Eisenhower announced the formation of the National Republican Citizens' Committee, whose goals were similar to those of the All Republican Conference. The group was to serve as a "kind of bridge," in Eisenhower's words, "between the Republican Party and those people who now class themselves independents or unhappy democrats." Don Frey, one of the founders of the group, explained that the leadership of the RCC hoped "to encourage the participation of Republican-minded people, some of whom may not be aware of the fact that they *are* Republican-minded." The founders were particularly interested in organizing activities in large cities and metropolitan areas, where they could serve as a "magnet" to draw in "the 'mobile American.' "[50]

Leaders of the RCC intended to build this broader constituency by promoting a new type of "voluntary activity" that could marshal "the support and participation at the state level of business and professional people." They planned to achieve this goal by implementing Citizen Action Programs throughout the country. Under the guidance of Republican activist Tim Herrmann, who had established similar citizens' groups in several cities, local organizers could set up their own groups with the help of a manual and an organizing kit.[51]

Organizers hoped that the All Republican Conference and the RCC would help create a stronger, more unified party. New York senator Kenneth Keating was hopeful that the conference would result in greater unity, and Eisenhower strongly supported the RCC. The Organizing Committee, aware that the party's divisiveness could jeopardize its goals, decided that the RCC would have "no favorite candidate for nomination for any Federal office." It would support any Republican who sought help.[52]

Despite the broad goals of the RCC, it was not without its detractors. Perhaps the most significant, and loudest, critic was Barry Goldwater. Convinced that the committee was headed by the same group that had "contributed to the divisive tactics of the 1960 campaign," he predicted that it would engender "the same kind of confusion and distrust which cost us the presidency." Although angry at first, Eisenhower and other leaders of the RCC eventually concluded that they had made a mistake in not discussing the goals of the group with Goldwater. After meeting with representatives of the group, who explained that the RCC would not dictate policy to the RNC, Goldwater accepted the committee and its work.[53]

Others initially expressed misgivings. RNC chair William Miller disliked the idea of a separate volunteer association, particularly one under liberal control, and worked to ensure that the RCC "stressed organizational rather than ideological matters." F. Clifton White, an old hand at working with citizens' groups, insisted that a national group should not be able to impose its prerogatives on local committees. Others, like party regulars Charles White and Leonard Hall, agreed with the principle that lay behind the formation of the committee but pointed to flaws in the structure. White knew from experience that citizens' groups were resented by party regulars, who feared the competition for donations since both organizations would be targeting the same contributors. Hall complained to Eisenhower that the list of officers was a " 'Mayflower' group" that needed additional names for balance. Both party and committee members recognized that the new group must be careful not to attempt to set policy.[54]

Such a realization did not prevent the RCC from creating a Critical Issues Council "to conduct research, and articulate Republican-oriented positions on the great problems facing the people and government of the United States." Although Milton Eisenhower, chair of the council, explained that the positions taken by the council did not "represent official Republican policy," he later claimed that had a more liberal Republican been nominated in 1964, the policy papers of the council "could have been almost the campaign appeal."[55] Such a statement unconsciously exposed the deep divisions within the party and revealed the RCC's affiliation with the liberal faction. It further brought into question the committee's approach to unification. Its concept of unity, obviously, was that all factions should rally behind its liberal agenda.

As a political organization, the RCC was neither influential nor significant. Any impact it might have had was only temporary and had been erased before the 1964 primary campaign began. It was, however, an important mirror of the problems of the party. Frustrated and yet hopeful as a result of the 1960 election, Republicans searched for ways to strengthen their party from the outside in order to ensure victory in 1964. To change their image and broaden their constituency, they created programs aimed at urban areas and special-interest groups and established organizations such as the RCC. These efforts, however, could provide only a temporary solution to the party's dilemma—the absence of organized, unified, and sustained leadership. They were indicative mainly of the party leadership's inability and unwillingness to address the real internal problems.

The changes taking place in the country, while sometimes uniting Republicans in their criticism of the Kennedy administration, intensified the differences within the party. Republicans of various ideological stripes reacted in such divergent ways to Kennedy's admittedly limited social welfare programs and the increasingly militant civil rights movement that they ended up criticizing each other instead of the Democrats. Since some of this squabbling resulted from personality battles among those vying for the leadership of the party, the underlying ideological struggle over party policy was frequently ignored. In fact, liberal Republicans continued to overlook the increasing strength of the conservative wing. Whether the signs were not as clear then as they appear today, whether liberals assumed that conservatives would never gain the strength needed to take control of the party, or whether liberals arrogantly assumed conservatives would never attempt such a feat, liberal Republicans turned a blind eye to conservatives, except occasionally to disparage them as the "lunatic fringe." Conservatives, meanwhile, used these four years to consolidate their membership, to attempt to root out the more irrational extremist elements from their movement, and to build an organization to draft their own presidential candidate, Barry Goldwater.

4

SEIZING THE MOMENT

Conservatives, young and old, increasingly looked to politics in the early 1960s to solve America's problems. After years of frustration, right-wingers concluded that merely playing the role of an opposition party and serving as educator to the masses had failed to achieve their goals. They had to seize power. Winning the Republican presidential nomination in 1964 would provide them with control of party machinery and supply the most direct path to implementing their agenda. Prominent conservative politicians shared this objective with citizens who had little practical political experience and with conservative intellectuals who had formerly remained above the fray of campaign politics. Cooperative but still somewhat leery of one another, the various right-wing factions agreed that a conservative must be nominated in 1964.

Conservatives believed strongly that they could win control of the GOP because they viewed themselves as the only group addressing the needs of the American public. During the 1950s, liberals and conservatives had generally agreed on the problems Americans faced but had disagreed on the solutions. This situation changed after 1960. For a variety of reasons—

such as the growth of the civil rights movement, the refocused attention on poverty, and the conflict over the trouble in Vietnam—some politicians began to rethink and reject their old assumptions and ideals. Much of the American public, alienated and frightened by the changes, clung to old beliefs and continued to fight the old fights. At a time when civil rights, American imperialism, and poverty increasingly became part of the political dialogue, many looked to nostalgic conservatives as the only leaders who consistently used old clichés and conjured up comforting images by continuing to attack the New Deal, labor unions, and Soviet expansion.[1]

Liberals failed to discern this growing popular discontent with traditional liberal doctrine. Just as the Left's criticism of the liberalism of the Democratic Party would be written off as merely communist propaganda, so, too, did liberals dismiss right-wing frustration as simply the result of racism or extremism. Only conservative journals and newsletters catered to the "John and Mary Does" of the nation, who, tired of losing individual freedoms to bureaucratic controls, had created a "whirlwind" that the "would be master minds of the Republican party" would not be able to ignore. Columnist Alice Widenor, in the *ACA Newsletter*, asserted that the middle class disliked funding a government that gave them nothing in return. Emphasizing that the nation could not be "saved at Washington, but at home; not from the top down, but from the bottom up," conservative activists like Tom Anderson sought to funnel this middle-class dissatisfaction into an organized movement.[2]

Whether or not this middle-class restlessness was as widespread as some conservatives claimed, something mobilized right-wingers on the grassroots level to create more activist organizations. Many older organizations, such as the American Council of Christian Churches, the Freedoms Foundation, and the Foundation for Economic Education, joined forces with newer groups, such as Americans for Constitutional Action, Young Americans for Freedom, and the Liberty Lobby. Most of these organizations published their own newsletters, and many sold audiotapes or provided speakers. Some even produced movies.

Life Line Foundation, created in 1958 by Texan H. L. Hunt, exemplified this right-wing effort. In addition to a thrice-weekly newsletter, Life Line produced television programs and operated a book club. Its most pervasive influence was through radio. By the end of 1962, "Life Line's 15-minute radio program was being broadcast 343 times a day on approximately 300 radio stations in 42 states and the District of Columbia." In its first four years of existence, the foundation grossed $1,086,312.[3]

The increased visibility and variety of right-wing activities frightened liberals, especially since lunatic fringe groups seemed to be the most vocal. Convinced that a right-wing resurgence was under way, liberals assumed that extremists represented all right-wing organizations. They exploited such images for their own political purposes.[4]

The attention on right-wing extremism caused problems for more mainstream conservatives in their quest for political power. The Right's new determination to play a more prominent role in the GOP mandated that they cultivate a more respectable and reasonable image. Hence, conservatives intensified earlier efforts to distance themselves from the "lunatics" on the right.

Conservatives encountered the most difficulties in attempting to distance themselves from the John Birch Society, since many conservative politicians and activists agreed with significant elements of the society's philosophy. Early on, conservatives like William Buckley, Marvin Liebman, and Clarence Manion had supported the group even though they disagreed at times with Robert Welch. In 1961 Buckley commented in a letter to conservative activist Roger Milliken that the society fulfilled a necessary function by giving people something to do. Buckley was becoming "increasingly pessimistic," however, that Welch was spreading the right message.[5]

The John Birch Society could not simply be written off entirely. Although the number of members remained secret, the society's influence was felt in all fifty states. Organized by a full-time staff, members were zealous letter writers, demonstrators, and voters. Welch and his followers were becoming an entrenched organization with tremendous potential for power.

Liberals increasingly associated conservatism with the philosophy espoused by and the activities of the John Birch Society. As a result, the organization—and in particular, its controversial leader—polarized conservatives, including Buckley, who in early 1962 took a stand against the society. On 13 February, the *National Review* published its first explicitly critical essay accusing Welch of "damaging the conservative movement." Right-wing stalwart John Tower and newcomer Ronald Reagan agreed that Welch's charges that Eisenhower was a communist agent invited ridicule, and Barry Goldwater complained that the society "would be far more effective if its leaders were not making these intemperate statements."[6]

On the other hand, many conservatives continued to support Welch and to question the commitment to conservatism of those who criticized the society. The *National Review* and Buckley received countless letters chastising them for attacking fellow conservatives. Some even accused Buckley of trying to control the Right.[7]

Buckley's response to one such letter indicated that his reasons for the anti-Welch articles went beyond ideological disagreement. The movement, he explained, had to "expand by bringing into our ranks those people who are . . . on our immediate left—the moderate, wishy-washy conservatives." Leaderless, in a "tremendous vacuum," these people would never "join a movement whose leadership believes the drivel of Robert Welch." Instead, Buckley feared, they would walk past "crackpot alley" into the "warm embrace" of the Left.[8]

Although much of the controversy within the movement centered on the John Birch Society, other conservatives attempted to force a reexamination of the concept of extremism. Drawing attention to the evils of moderation, some pointed out that many "great men," including Moses, Paul, Martin Luther, and John Wesley, had been extremists. Others stressed that extremism was sometimes necessary to achieve an important goal. Many accused liberals of focusing on an exaggerated right-wing threat because of their fear of losing power instead of warning people about communism. To many conservatives, the only dangerous extremism existed on the left.[9]

Such arguments revealed the political naïveté of many conservatives. To gain public support, many on the right believed that all they had to do was deliver their message to the American people. This conviction inspired countless uncompromising political neophytes and spawned new organizations. For a time, these idealistic conservatives, many of whom belonged to such new organizations, joined forces with more pragmatically and politically oriented conservatives. Only later would the conflict between the goals of the two groups become apparent.

More than anything else, conservatives desired electoral success; the question was how best to bring it about. Party regulars like Richard Nixon encouraged the participation "on a permanent year-round basis [of] the thousands of volunteers who participated in the last campaign." Conservative organizer Marvin Liebman and others attempted in the early 1960s to found a national conservative forum to play a more important role in Republican Party operations and campaigns. Conservatives were determined to provide voters with a real political choice—a choice that in their view had not been available for thirty years.[10]

Activists on the right realized that their grassroots organizations provided a natural springboard for politics. Henry MacFarland of the American Flag Committee urged the Right to organize into "an effective political body for translating the principles which they support into the triumph of those principles at the polls." Political activist F. Clifton White agreed that conservatives throughout the country, "a large percentage of [whom] knew very little about politics," only needed to be provided with the "leadership and the techniques" in order to become effective political operatives.[11]

Some conservatives argued that the Right could fight better outside the GOP. Separatists triumphed in New York, Kansas, and California. In the Empire State, Conservative Party members ran in local elections. More importantly, in a direct challenge to Governor Nelson Rockefeller and the liberal wing of the GOP, the new party put forward a gubernatorial candidate in 1962, Syracuse businessman David Jaquith, who polled a solid 141,877 votes. Though not enough to win the election, Jaquith's showing guaranteed the Conservative Party a place on the ballot for the next four years and served notice that liberals would no longer have a free hand in the state.[12]

Other conservatives were not so willing to abandon their political home, preferring to remain in the Republican Party and attempt to guide it along a more conservative path. For some, loyalty played a key role in the decision to remain in the party; others had more practical reasons. Certainly conservatives stood a better chance at the polls with the GOP than with a third party, and they began to believe strategists who told them that they actually had a chance of winning the next election. William Rusher told readers of the National Review in 1963 that only a conservative could beat JFK in 1964.[13]

Conservative youths on college campuses manned one of the key battalions in the conservative war on the liberal leadership. Swept along to a certain extent by the same forces that created the New Left student movement, young people on the right set up chapters of such national organizations as the Young Republican National Federation, Young Americans for Freedom, and the Intercollegiate Society of Individualists. Dissatisfied with the status quo, students of all ideological persuasions at times found themselves on the same side. Mirroring later young leftist critiques of conservative professors, right-wing students complained about the liberal monopolization of education on most campuses and the resulting constraints on the academic freedom of conservative professors. In 1964 Youth for Goldwater members supported the initial efforts of civil rights activists and peace workers in Berkeley's free speech movement, which challenged the closing of the traditional public forum on campus.[14]

Common goals among students, however, were rare. More frequently, young right-wingers followed their adult counterparts in protesting Democrats' handling of foreign affairs and in attempting to define conservatism in terms that other young people could understand. Young conservatives attempted to hold their own in such left-leaning organizations as the National Student Association. To enlighten their fellow students and to present a forum for debate, many chapters published their own newsletters or magazines. With articles ranging from discussions of campus events to debates over foreign policy and ideology, these publications provided an opportunity for young people to question liberal assumptions and answer liberal charges.[15]

These young conservatives brought hope and encouragement to older members of the movement. Ohio congressman and Young Republican Donald Lukens explained that young people embraced conservative ideology for many of the same reasons that adults did. They did so out of a "religious or moral reaction to the growth of communism," out of a realization that the goals of the Roosevelt era had not been reached, or simply out of frustration with the apparent lack of political purpose and principle within the national parties. This support reinforced conservatives' commitment to their cause and ensured that there would be leaders for the Right for the next thirty or forty years.[16]

The participation of numerous former Young Republicans in the early Goldwater drive underscored the importance of youth. Conservatives thus made special efforts to capture and retain youthful converts. On the assumption that simply by reading the "truth," students would join the conservative movement, journals such as the *National Review* and *America's Future* offered special subscription rates to college students, while other organizations sent students free copies of conservative classics such as Goldwater's *The Conscience of a Conservative*, John A. Stormer's *None Dare Call It Treason*, and William F. Buckley, Jr.'s, *Up from Liberalism*.[17]

Others actively sought to enlist youth in the drive to nominate a conservative candidate in 1964. Both the party and the Draft Goldwater Committee acknowledged the value of youthful volunteers and encouraged their participation. Gaining control of the national Young Republican offices became an important step in winning the nomination. In fact, perhaps because they did not have enough experience to realize the odds against them, young conservatives were among the first and the most persistent advocates of Barry Goldwater's candidacy.[18]

After the 1960 election, adult conservatives increasingly joined their more youthful counterparts in believing that the senator from Arizona was the key to conservative victory in the GOP and at the polls. Organizations devoted to gaining Goldwater's nomination formed throughout the country, including Arizona's Goldwater for President, Chicago's Americans for Goldwater, and Valley Forge's Citizens for Goldwater.[19] These unrelated and dedicated grassroots organizations proved essential to winning Goldwater the nomination.

In the long run, most of these early organizations joined forces with the committee created by F. Clifton White, Ohio congressman John Ashbrook, and William Rusher in early 1961. Bringing together conservatives from across the country, White, Ashbrook, and Rusher hoped to secure the Republican Party as an effective conservative force. Their unspoken goal was the nomination of a conservative for president in the next election.[20] Loosely organized and meeting infrequently, members of the group maintained contact through White. Because their original meeting had taken place in Chicago, White referred to them as the "Chicago group."

A trained scholar with experience at all levels of politics, White held the committee together and turned it into a successful operation. Believing that he knew "more about how the Republican Party worked than anyone else in the country," White gradually enlisted a nationwide network of conservatives. Since he did not want the committee to be tied too early to any one candidate, he invited new members to discuss generally how conservatism could "best be promoted in 1964." He kept these activities under wraps until December 1962, when the press picked up the story.[21]

White's most important job during these years was to locate, organize, and teach conservatives throughout the country. In 1962 alone he traveled to twenty-eight states, met with governors, "state chairmen, national committeemen, county chairmen and some just plain dedicated folk," and made "contacts of varying degrees of effectiveness in 41 of the 50 states." Ignoring party "bigwigs" in the early stages, White concentrated on gaining influence with such vital organizations as the Young Republicans, the Federation of Republican Women, and the Republican National Committee. He reminded committee members that their "primary goal was to build delegate strength for the 1964 national convention" and to that end urged them to organize conservatives at the precinct, district, and state level. Encouraging regional chairpersons to learn their states' rules for deciding delegate election, White advocated working through party officials wherever possible and dealing with them "gently" if they proved uncooperative. Divisiveness was to be avoided. All of this time-consuming and essential work was carried out on a shoestring budget that almost snapped several times.[22]

Even though originally the group's primary purpose was to make the Republican Party more conservative, White and the other founders intended from the start to rally their cause around Goldwater. White claimed that they searched for other possible candidates but that since "conservatives weren't that popular," they found none more acceptable than the Arizona senator.[23]

In fact, Goldwater's popularity, especially with conservatives, continued to grow tremendously in the years between presidential elections. In addition to his continued work as chair of the Senate Campaign Committee, which helped him build "complete rapport with the party worker" and gave him the opportunity to spread his views by delivering after-dinner speeches, Goldwater continued to receive letters of support and congratulations for *The Conscience of a Conservative*. Invitations and offers for speaking engagements poured into his office in such quantity that he was compelled to hire a press secretary. In the meantime, in 1962 he published another popular book, *Why Not Victory?*, which drew on his foreign affairs speeches. This book and the publication of four favorable biographies about him kept Goldwater in the public eye.[24] Conservative journals encouraged Goldwater to campaign almost as soon as Kennedy took office. Advertisements for "Goldwater in '64" buttons appeared in the *National Review* almost continuously after January 1961.

Although White and his group felt that the upsurge of grassroots support justified their position that Goldwater could win the nomination as well as the election, they had difficulty convincing Goldwater that victory was possible. He first learned of the group's activities in November 1961, when William Rusher sent him a special-delivery letter informing him of "the beginning of the most serious professional effort in almost a decade to turn the Republican Party into a more conservative channel." With the understanding that the group's effort "was not necessarily for his candidacy," Goldwater enthusiastically expressed support. Throughout 1962, Goldwater tacitly backed White's quest for conservative delegates, and the group accepted and encouraged Goldwater's refusal to issue a public statement endorsing its activities.[25]

By late 1962, however, activists concluded, as Rusher explained to Goldwater, that they were "drawing to the end of the period within which it was possible to plan effectively and intelligently for 1964 without centering to some degree on a possible candidate." White's committee, unanimously agreeing that Goldwater was the conservatives' first choice, attempted to convince him not to destroy fifteen months of effort and demolish a carefully built organizational framework by repudiating the nomination. They assured him of the "tremendous support" he had "all across the country," warned him that his rejection would be "a deadly blow to the morale of everyone concerned," and emphatically asserted that he was the "only man" who could lead and "be the focus for this movement" and therefore had a "duty" to run for president in 1964.[26]

Goldwater and several of his close associates remained skeptical. A realistic politician, Goldwater recognized that he had only a slight chance of winning without the support of the large industrial states, where there appeared to be little interest in conservatism. Uncertain that anyone could beat JFK and unwilling to become, in his assistant Dean Burch's words, a "sacrificial pig," Goldwater denied that he had committed himself to seeking the nomination by encouraging White and praising the progress the group had made in spreading conservatism. Nor did Goldwater believe that he was the only person who could lead the movement. In fact, he saw himself as a "pusher" rather than a "leader" and hoped "fervently" that he would not have to trade the former role for the latter. On a practical level, he was unsure whether White's network would survive and feared the effect a failed presidential bid would have on his Senate race. He followed his "political instincts," which warned him against being identified with an effort that "was doomed to fail." Most importantly, as Goldwater told everyone who asked, because he doubted his ability to overcome the entrenched liberal bureaucracy and institute the kinds of changes he wanted and because he feared the impact the campaign would have on his personal life, he did not want the nomination.[27]

Goldwater's refusal to publicly endorse White's group turned into an adamant decision not to seek the nomination or accept a draft. That announcement, of course, produced a crisis for the members of White's committee, who had no other candidate in mind. They finally decided, in Indiana member Bob Hughes's words, to "draft the son of a bitch . . . anyway."[28] In a sense, they had operated under those conditions since the beginning. By concentrating on building delegate support for the conservative movement with Goldwater as its head rather than working to enlist the big names in the Republican Party, White had erected a framework within which grassroots groups could express their wishes and see them come to fruition. Goldwater's refusal to cooperate, then, did not destroy the work of White's committee.

Instead, White and his crew easily set up a new National Draft Goldwater Committee (NDGC) under the leadership of Texas state chair Peter
O'Donnell. Formally introducing the organization in April 1963, an
NDGC press release announced the committee's intention to "coordinate
this citizen's movement which is springing up all over the country and to
encourage and channel the efforts of all volunteers who want to help
Senator Goldwater." The NDGC continued to follow White's pattern by
setting up committees in each state, by organizing drives for signatures,
and by working for support from the National Federation of Women, the
Republican Governors, and the Young Republicans.[29]

A number of factors contributed to the long-term growth of the movement. The secret, deliberate method used by White and his Chicago
group to set up the organization had prompted little opposition at the early
stages of development when they would have had neither the funds nor the
support to withstand it. Their effort to build from the bottom up ensured
that conservatives could rely on a sturdy foundation of people throughout
the country actually running the party on the state and local levels. These
people would be ready with a supportive structure in place when a conservative coup occurred. In addition, Goldwater's reluctance to work for the
nomination and the ensuing draft left control of the movement divided
among a broad group rather than concentrated in Goldwater's hands. As a
result, his later presidential defeat did not cripple the movement as Taft's
defeat had. Moreover, the draft encouraged conservatives to believe that
they could have an impact on national politics and ensured that they
would continue rather than give up after 1964.

All of White's efforts would have been in vain, however, without Goldwater's willingness to seek election. To the relief of many, by the fall of
1963, the Arizona senator began to consider making the run. The amount
of support, both in money and in delegates, obtained by the committee
allayed some of his fears and doubts, while Rockefeller's bitter comments
accusing conservatives of undermining Republican principles and his
burgeoning campaign raised new concerns that the governor might win
the nomination. During the summer of 1963, Goldwater invited to Washington his most trusted Arizona friends and advisers: lawyer Denison
Kitchel, administrative assistant Dean Burch, the American Enterprise
Institute's William Baroody, and Washington lawyer Edward McCabe.
Called the "Arizona Mafia" because of their exclusive access to Goldwater, the group steered clear of the NDGC headquarters to avoid the impression that Goldwater was a serious candidate. "Mafia" members were
nevertheless very much aware of what was going on there.[30]

Goldwater's reluctance to announce his candidacy did not diminish the growing support for him throughout the country. In fact, the press touted him as the Republican frontrunner. By late autumn, Goldwater decided to enter the race. Although he may still have been uncertain of his decision, he was, according to his own recollection, looking forward to challenging Kennedy in an "old-fashioned, cross-country" campaign pitting liberalism against conservatism.[31]

President Kennedy also looked forward to running against the senator. Although the two men frequently opposed each other ideologically and politically, they maintained a mutual public respect. Kennedy told historian Arthur Schlesinger, Jr., that Goldwater "was a man of decency and character." Goldwater also recognized the president's abilities.[32]

This admiration did not blind either candidate to the other's faults. Goldwater complained that the president was indecisive, and Kennedy told one of his aides that the senator was "not very smart." In fact, as Kennedy surveyed the 1964 election from the perspective of 1963, he counted on Goldwater's lack of acumen to undermine Republican efforts. According to Robert Kennedy, the president believed the senator would "destroy himself" in the campaign. With this in mind, JFK concluded that Goldwater would be easier to beat than any of the other contenders despite Goldwater's attractiveness to a South disgruntled by the Civil Rights Act. Whatever votes the Democrats lost in the South would be made up for by the anti-Goldwater gains in the rest of the country. Moreover, although the Democratic National Committee and various Kennedy aides feared a right-wing candidate, Kennedy thought that Goldwater's campaign might, in fact, help to defeat extremism once and for all. As a result, Kennedy did whatever he could to encourage Goldwater's nomination.[33]

Kennedy's assassination changed everything. The tragic events of 22 November 1963 deeply affected Goldwater, who viewed JFK's death as "a great personal loss." Goldwater, again, reevaluated his decision to enter the race. Although some members of the NDGC believed that Kennedy's assassination had not substantially changed Goldwater's chances in the election, others, including Goldwater, concluded that the candidacy of Lyndon Johnson, a southerner with a conservative reputation, made Goldwater's bid more untenable. Complicating matters further, the fact that JFK's death occurred in Dallas, a conservative southern city, caused many people to blame the Right for the murder. In the end, however, Goldwater could not disappoint the thousands of people, especially the young, who had worked so hard for him. With extreme reluctance and a conviction that he could not win, Goldwater formally announced his candidacy on 3 January 1964 at his Arizona home.[34] Two weeks later, having completed its task, the NDGC was formally dissolved and members went to work for the Goldwater for President Committee.

Almost immediately, problems surfaced that plagued Goldwater even after his nomination and that eventually contributed to his defeat. The most obvious was Goldwater's extremist image, which led to a second major problem—the lack of party support for Goldwater. As Republicans argued the merits of the various candidates vying for the nomination, party factionalism intensified. Caused in part by Goldwater's intemperate remarks concerning social security and nuclear weapons, which reinforced his extremist image, the intraparty tension increased because liberals realized that a Goldwater victory would bring conservatism into its own in the party. Two other difficulties—tensions among members of Goldwater's staff and his own limitations as a candidate—appeared during the primary period but did not substantially affect the campaign until after the convention.[35]

Despite these obstacles, the Goldwater for President Committee, under the leadership of Denison Kitchel, Dean Burch, and Richard Kleindienst, another Arizona lawyer, and with the further guidance of Clifton White, worked to gain support for Goldwater and to increase his visibility and viability through holding rallies and fund-raisers and distributing propaganda. Constantly aware of the delegate count, White continued his emphasis on grassroots organization, encouraging groups of citizens to set up Goldwater Clubs throughout the country, to work with the party when possible, and to create their own structures when necessary. In addition to ensuring that Goldwater's name was placed on the ballot and that he then won the necessary delegates, these clubs taught thousands of political newcomers the techniques of winning a nomination. At the same time, the Goldwater for President Committee continued to target party affiliates such as the Young Republicans.[36]

The committee's fund-raising reflected the type of voter Goldwater attracted. Jewelry manufacturer Daniel C. Gainey, head of the preconvention fund drive, found that Goldwater received support from the "owner-operators of medium-sized businesses, in the $10-million and up bracket. These are men who have built up their own enterprise, who are strong on individual initiative." Some of these wealthy supporters made certain that their money went to the candidate of their choice by placing their donations into escrow accounts available only when, and if, Goldwater won.

Meanwhile, White and his crew encouraged and cultivated small contributors. One of their methods was a chain letter that suggested sending a dollar to Goldwater and a copy of the letter to five friends.[37]

The ultimate objective of these efforts was, of course, to win enough delegates in the primaries and caucuses to secure the nomination. First White and his early group and then the National Draft Goldwater Committee created a sturdy foundation on which the Goldwater for President Committee could build. As a result, Goldwater had a significant number of professed supporters by the time he announced his candidacy. In addition to those conservatives who had always seen him as the answer, right-wingers who were "not completely happy with Goldwater" agreed with columnist Tom Anderson that he was the "only electable conservative." Even third-party conservatives supported Goldwater once they were certain he agreed with their principles. As Texas editorialist Tom Martin pointed out, these people supported Goldwater "not as Republicans—but as Conservatives." On the other hand, some attacked Goldwater for not being conservative enough or for allowing himself to be used, as they saw it, by liberal forces.[38]

Goldwater enjoyed considerable Republican support. Both before and after his announcement, he had the backing of many party regulars, while the party leadership, if slow to extol his virtues, did not eliminate him from consideration. Former president Eisenhower believed that Republicans could carry no more than half the states "with this man" but still refused publicly to encourage any stop-Goldwater movement. He scrupulously maintained a neutral stance. Even Richard Nixon, who would have willingly thrown his own hat into the ring, stated in early June that he was "confident" that Goldwater would back a Republican Party platform agreeable to a majority of the delegates.[39] Such backhanded and half-hearted support did not fool Goldwater and other conservatives, who realized that most of their work would have to be done outside the party. While a certain amount of acrimony typified primary campaigns, liberal and moderate Republicans' realization that the nomination battle might shift control of the party to the right sharpened the debate.

The lack of a clear alternative candidate increased moderates' fears. Competition for the nomination included Democratic Alabama governor George Wallace, as well as Republicans Ambassador Henry Cabot Lodge and Michigan governor George Romney. Wallace withdrew from the campaign in July. The press reported that southern conservatives pressured the Alabama governor into withdrawing from the race in order to save those votes for Goldwater. Both Wallace and Goldwater denied this. Although a number of Republicans, including Eisenhower's good friend William Robinson, supported Lodge because they felt no one else was viable, Lodge never made a real attempt at gaining the nomination.[40]

Romney posed a more difficult problem. Having burst into the spotlight by spearheading the rewriting of the Michigan state constitution, the former American Motors president appeared to be the ideal Republican candidate. A deeply religious businessman who understood the need for change in the area of civil rights, Romney appealed to many factions within the GOP. "Delighted" to see a man "of obvious vitality, vigor, dedication and integrity" on the political scene, Eisenhower communicated with Romney fairly regularly after 1962. As a result, both the Goldwater and Kennedy campaign staffs saw Romney as a serious threat.[41]

Those fears went unfulfilled, however, as Romney's moment in the spotlight as a Goldwater rival proved brief. Emerging during the annual Conference of the Governors of the States of the Union in Cleveland in June 1964 as the most vehement opponent of Goldwater, Romney discussed the approaching campaign with Nixon at a breakfast meeting, after which he told the press that the vice president had encouraged him to run. Denying this, Nixon claimed that he had only suggested that someone should run against Goldwater to ensure that the issues were fully debated. In the face of the resulting embarrassment, Romney's candidacy never got off the ground.[42]

Most liberal Republican hopes centered on New York governor Nelson Rockefeller. Desperate for the presidency, Rockefeller lost his chance through arrogance, miscalculation, and bad luck as he continually underestimated the strength of the conservatives and overestimated his support within the party and throughout the nation. With only limited support from party regulars, Rockefeller's campaign plodded through the primaries toward the big California "winner-take-all" battle, where he hoped to show that he had more national support than Goldwater. Unfortunately for his campaign, his new wife delivered a son the day before the primary. This event revived the story of his remarriage, renewed doubts about his own personal ethics, and gave Goldwater the edge he needed to win the California delegation. Although Rockefeller continued to represent the recalcitrant Republicans after the primary, he never seriously threatened to steal the nomination from Goldwater.[43]

With Rockefeller out of the picture, liberal Republicans sensed that Goldwater might win the nomination. In fact, by early June, White's crew had already organized the party, state by state, and had almost enough delegates to secure victory. Moderate Republicans, fearing the implications of a Goldwater-controlled party, decided that something had to be done. No one could decide what that "something" was, however, and mass confusion resulted. Issuing Cassandralike prophesies, moderates waited for someone else to make the first move. Some recognized the strength of Goldwater's position and did not want to risk challenging it; others believed that he would never secure the nomination. Liberal and moderate Republicans took no action but instead, like petulant children, merely called the conservatives names, waiting for their elders to do the fighting.

Party leaders appeared similarly paralyzed. Richard Nixon epitomized this apparent paralysis. A man of intense political ambition, he entered 1964 an influential party leader, but one with a new political home and a losing record. His only chance was to play statesman, remain above the fray by avoiding obvious campaigning, and hope for a draft from the convention. In January 1964, Nixon announced that the "best way I could serve would be by not getting into the scramble myself but by talking about the great issues and attempting to give leadership." Nevertheless, he enlarged his staff and allowed his friend, former interior secretary Fred Seaton, to begin quietly to organize a campaign. That organization crumbled after news of a secret meeting with his advisers concerning the upcoming campaign leaked out, making Nixon, who had tried to be friendly to everyone in the California primary, suspect to all factions of the party. His only hope lay in the possibility that the convention would become deadlocked and would look to him for leadership. The chances of that option lessened considerably after the Romney episode at the 1964 governors' conference in Cleveland.[44]

Running out of solutions, everyone looked to Dwight Eisenhower for answers. As the most widely respected person in the party, the former president could have halted Goldwater's drive with a statement denouncing his candidacy. Eisenhower and his advisers realized that some party leaders wanted him to be the "hatchet man," a role that would have destroyed the image of the benign, apolitical statesman he had cultivated as president. Despite pressure from many of his political associates, Eisenhower refused to assume that role. In fact, Eisenhower was worried about Goldwater's abilities and disagreed with Goldwater on certain policy issues; he was also angered by conservative criticism of his administration. But still he withheld comment. The former president felt trapped. The only other viable candidate was Rockefeller, whom he disliked. In addition, Eisenhower realized that Goldwater had considerable support throughout the country and recognized that by deliberately depriving the senator of the nomination, he might split the party, perhaps irrevocably. Consequently, Eisenhower played statesman. As he explained to Walter Cronkite, he stayed out of the fracas to ensure that someone spoke for party harmony in the end.[45]

The conflict between Eisenhower's personal feelings and his professional instincts became most apparent during his discussions with Pennsylvania governor William Scranton concerning the latter's efforts to seek nomination. Although Eisenhower's appointment books reveal that he held a large number of conversations regarding Scranton and the presidential race, no evidence exists to support the idea that he told Scranton to run. He certainly encouraged him, but he never indicated that he would actively support Scranton over Goldwater, a fact that Scranton, basking in the glow of Eisenhower's encouragement, might have missed. Although in the end Eisenhower succeeded in saving himself for efforts to unify the party and kept his reputation untarnished by refusing to support a man who entered the race too late with too little, he earned the enmity of many moderates who felt that he had failed to do all he could to improve the situation.[46]

Ironically, if William Scranton had decided earlier to run, he might have been the perfect candidate. He possessed national political experience, a good record as governor of a large state, and moderate to conservative principles. Reluctant at first to commit himself to the race, he played, as Goldwater aide Travis Cross put it, "telephone tag" with Eisenhower until no one, including Scranton, was certain if he was running or not. In fact, when it appeared that Eisenhower would not support him, Scranton refused to make his scheduled announcement of candidacy only to reconsider his decision the following week when Goldwater voted against the Civil Rights Act. Goldwater's negative vote reinforced the racist image created by his opponents and compelled Scranton to declare himself the "progressive Republican" candidate.[47]

Scranton's five-week campaign typified the desperation of moderate Republicans as they tried frantically to prevent Goldwater's nomination. Refusing to recognize that Goldwater was the choice of much of the party at the precinct level, moderates continued throughout the convention and the campaign itself to commit partisan suicide by attempting to separate the Republican Party from Goldwater's supporters.

Eisenhower and Nixon were the only Republican leaders who appeared to realize the potential damage to the party. Despite pleas from all sides that he denounce Goldwater, including from his brother, Eisenhower insisted that his voice would not change the minds of the delegates and that he must be in a position to solidify the party following the convention. For his part, Nixon recognized that Goldwater had the nomination nearly locked up, and he hoped to do what he could to prevent further damage to the party. With his eye on 1968, Nixon again claimed the center as his own by maintaining friendly ties with all sides.[48]

Scranton's team obviously did not perceive the danger to the party. Despite claims that they were "dead-set against stopping anyone," Scranton's organization contacted Republican candidates for Congress and attempted to convince them that they would lose if Goldwater were the presidential nominee. Nelson Rockefeller wrote to Republican leaders around the country, urging them to support Scranton as the candidate dedicated to a "moderate, forward-looking platform." Realizing that "the hour is late," Rockefeller believed that the "moderate cause" could still be won if all "moderate mainstream" Republicans united under Scranton's banner.[49] These efforts only antagonized Goldwater, perpetuated the idea that a conservative could not win, and further split the party.

More importantly, Scranton's campaign reinforced the image of Goldwater as an extremist. Scranton continually evoked warmongering and racist images of Goldwater, at one point begging citizens to "send to the White House a man who thinks deeply, who is not impulsive." A letter sent to Goldwater by Scranton's campaign staff on the eve of the convention epitomized this strategy. Written and signed for Scranton by an aide, the letter, under the pretext of challenging him to a debate, instead accused him of standing for "a whole crazy-quilt collection of absurd and dangerous positions" and called his delegates "a flock of chickens whose necks will be wrung at will." Goldwater, though aware that Scranton had not written the letter, angrily distributed copies to the delegates. Thus, Scranton's strategy backfired, only increasing solidarity among those already committed to Goldwater and alienating some delegates who had been leaning toward Scranton. Moreover, by providing the Democrats with a ready-made campaign issue, the incident laid the groundwork for the destruction of the Goldwater campaign against Johnson.[50]

Ill feelings ran deep as Republicans prepared for their national convention. Although Goldwater and his crew had confidence in the strength and loyalty of their delegates, they spared no expense to keep track of them.

They even sent their state chairs a memo warning about "possible opposition tactics" as they sought "to prevent the kind of trouble Taft had in '52."[51]

Liberal Republicans, on the other hand, realizing that they needed a miracle to reverse the trend, searched for an issue to rally around. Finally concentrating on using the platform, they first attempted to convince Eisenhower to condemn Goldwater's nuclear policy, but at the last minute he refused. They settled instead on a plank repudiating extremism in general and the John Birch Society in particular. When Rockefeller spoke in favor of the plank at the convention and reminded delegates that he had warned everyone about the subversion of the party by a "minority wholly alien to the sound and honest conservatism" of Republicanism, the catcalls and boos drowned out his words. Considering that there were at least 100 Birchers among the delegates, their reaction as well as the defeat of that plank and the milder version proposed by Romney were not surprising. The incident merely increased the animosity and self-righteousness of each faction.[52]

On the whole, the platform reflected Goldwater's position, containing a weak civil rights plank and a hard line on foreign policy and defense. Conservatism had penetrated the Republican Party despite all efforts by moderates to block it. With the prize almost within their grasp, conservatives showed their lack of political maturity. The reaction to Rockefeller's address reflected their inability to curb the frustration and bitterness resulting from the campaign and to control their followers. The nomination of New Yorker William Miller as the vice presidential candidate indicated the narrowness of their thinking. Without consulting any of the party chieftains, Goldwater selected as his running mate Republican National Committee chair Miller, a harsh "hatchet man" with a rather dubious reputation resulting from his exposed lie that he had served as an assistant prosecutor at the Nuremberg Trials. Although Miller added geographic balance, his philosophy was too close to Goldwater's to add ideological equilibrium or to win liberal and moderate support for the ticket.[53]

Party leaders called for unity. Senator Everett Dirksen reminded delegates of Goldwater's call for support of all Republican candidates during the 1960 convention. Clare Booth Luce emphasized that "everywhere [Goldwater] has preached the doctrine that in unity . . . there is strength." In his introduction of Goldwater after his nomination, Nixon repeated Goldwater's words from 1960, urging all Republicans to work together for their candidate.[54]

Goldwater did not practice what he had preached. Instead, shocking the country, many Republicans, and even some of his aides, Goldwater gave a gutsy speech welcoming "anyone who joins us in all sincerity" but reading out of Republican "ranks" any "who do not care for our cause." In words that appeared to confirm the prophesies of the liberals, Goldwater lost his most important opportunity to unite the party by stating: "I would remind you that extremism in the defense of liberty is no vice. And let me remind you also that moderation in the pursuit of justice is no virtue."[55]

Perhaps no more extremist than JFK's inaugural promise to go anywhere and fight any fight for freedom, Goldwater's words were nevertheless incredibly naive, but they were consistent with the simplistic philosophy of his supporters. The defiance implicit in the use of the word "extremism" was as important as the meaning of the statement. Goldwater made it clear that conservatives had gained control of the party and that they intended to run things their own way. In the context of the delegates' response to Rockefeller, the speech appeared to be more than campaign rhetoric: it sounded a call to arms.

The speech caused an immediate uproar. Some conservatives admired Goldwater's willingness to hold his ground, and at least one aide felt it would have been "psychologically impossible" for Goldwater to have said anything else, but the tone of the speech shocked most people. A reporter remarked to writer Theodore White, "My God, he's going to run as Barry Goldwater." Richard Nixon, convinced that Goldwater lost the presidency with the address, felt "physically sick" as he heard it. Even Clifton White was "stunned" by the speech and felt it spelled "death" for the campaign. Eisenhower also was upset and demanded an explanation from Goldwater. Goldwater pointed out to him that leading the D-Day invasion made Eisenhower an extremist. Eisenhower accepted the vague response dubiously.[56]

In the end, the speech symbolized the convention and, in a broader sense, Goldwater's candidacy. The Democrats seized the opportunity to open their campaign by calling Goldwater an "extremist candidate," likening his supporters to fascists, and warning "responsible Republicans" to stay away from him. The press, despairing over the implications of Goldwater's nomination for the country, recognized the shift of power that had taken place within the party. As historian Allan Nevins pointed out at the time, "If the platform is upheld as written, and if Goldwater stands by his utterances, . . . there will be in effect a new conservative party."[57] He perhaps did not realize that such an organization was what the conservatives had been planning all along.

Now officially in control, Goldwater and his followers took over the national party apparatus. At an organizational meeting of the Republican National Committee, Goldwater and his newly appointed RNC chair, Dean Burch, assured committee members that they did not intend to read anyone out of the party and that they intended to run the campaign through the national committee.[58]

Ironically, even this straightforward meeting highlighted several problems Goldwater would experience during the campaign. First, many people, including Clifton White, had assumed that White would be named RNC chair. The failure to nominate White indicated Goldwater's lack of understanding of the reality of his political situation. Goldwater had not won the nomination himself; White and his group had gained it for him. By alienating these loyal workers, he deprived his campaign of the full support of skilled political technicians and concentrated attention on himself rather than on the movement.[59] Second, the division of control of the campaign between the RNC and the still-functioning Goldwater for President Committee wasted time and effort and kept Goldwater isolated from people and information.

Goldwater's major task, once he secured the nomination, was to unify his party, and he took several steps in that direction. In one letter of a series of public letters, he explained to a curious Nixon that his acceptance speech had been "an affirmation" of the "great principles" of the party and that people had taken the "extremism" lines out of context. He also worked to obtain Eisenhower's blessing and even traveled to Pennsylvania to meet with him in early August. Although he could not, in his own words, get his "enthusiasm out of my ankles," Eisenhower began to think that Goldwater was "really more attractive than his image."[60]

Goldwater's major unity effort consisted of holding a conference of Republican governors and gubernatorial candidates in Hershey, Pennsylvania, on 12 August. This "love feast," as Eisenhower called it, combined complimentary speeches by Goldwater, Eisenhower, and Nixon with intense, sometimes accusatory, private question-and-answer sessions.[61] Although all the participants happily agreed that Republicans could disagree among themselves and still present a unified front, many of those present expressed concern about Goldwater's position on various issues, particularly civil rights. Governors of large states like George Romney sought clarification of Goldwater's stance and reaffirmation of his commitment to enforcing the Civil Rights Act.

The most intense debate took place between Miller, Goldwater, and

Rockefeller over extremism. Criticizing Goldwater's failure to state that he would not accept the support of extremist groups, Rockefeller insinuated that Goldwater sympathized with their cause. Goldwater angrily denied this charge. Rockefeller countered that whether Goldwater actually backed extremists or not, his image as an extremist was hurting the entire party. Eisenhower played peacemaker by suggesting that everyone could help to correct that image by constantly reiterating the truth about Goldwater. More than a little fed up with all the talk about his weaknesses as a candidate, Goldwater defiantly stated the obvious: "You might not like us, but you're stuck with us, and we are Republicans."[62]

In the end, the conference, which Eisenhower regarded as about 85 percent effective, produced more discussion of Goldwater's poor image than it did practical ways to solve political difficulties.[63] The participants missed the irony of trying to solve a problem they had helped create—that is, Goldwater's extremist image—while ignoring the underlying difficulties of trying to reconcile their ideologies. They talked around their disagreements without actually discussing them and so missed a real opportunity for unity before the election. Perhaps some moderates secretly hoped that Goldwater would suffer a sound defeat that would destroy Republican conservatives forever, but they did not realize the depth of the conservative commitment or its hold on their party.

If the presidential campaign of 1960 saw the emergence of a revitalized political conservatism, the campaign for the Republican presidential nomination in 1964 witnessed the first major success in the conservative war against the predominant liberalism of the Republican Party. Right-wingers realized that they needed to "play the game" if they were going to succeed. As a result, many mainstream conservatives cut their ties to the extremists. Men such as Buckley and Goldwater paid a price, however, for severing their relationship with groups like the John Birch Society. At a time when they needed all the votes they could get, their movement was splintering.

Liberal Republicans, who concentrated only on the extremist elements of the conservative movement, had counted on party loyalty, but they ignored discontent at the grassroots level and discounted the emerging Goldwater candidacy. Assuming they were working within a framework that they knew and controlled, liberal Republicans refused to recognize that the context had changed. As a result, they did not know how to respond in June 1964 when it looked as though Goldwater's nomination was inevitable. Their disorganized reaction ensured Goldwater's triumph.

Moreover, by bitterly attacking conservatives during the preconvention campaigning, they not only provided the Democrats with a major campaign strategy but inflicted wounds that could not be easily healed.

Although Goldwater's nomination in and of itself marked a crucial milestone in the conservative takeover of the Republican Party, the process by which he won it had important long-term implications. By emphasizing grassroots activism, right-wing leaders significantly altered the relationship between the GOP and the conservative movement, ensured that the movement would outlast its candidate, and set important precedents for future campaigns.

Conservatives, unaccustomed to power, however, displayed an immaturity that plagued them throughout their campaign. By August 1964, they did not realize that although they had already won the war for control of the party, they were on their way to losing the November battle.

5

★ ★ ★ ★ ★ ★ ★ ★ ★ ★ ★ ★ ★ ★ ★ ★ ★
★ ★ ★ ★ ★ ★ ★ ★ ★ ★ ★ ★ ★ ★ ★ ★ ★
★ ★ ★ ★ ★ ★ ★ ★ ★ ★ ★ ★ ★ ★ ★ ★ ★
★ ★ ★ ★ ★ ★ ★ ★ ★ ★ ★ ★ ★ ★ ★ ★ ★

BAPTISM BY FIRE

Conservatives, with the nomination secure and control of the Republican Party machinery in their hands, began their campaign for the presidency. On a platform that Goldwater believed exposed the flawed policies of his opponent Lyndon Johnson, he built up considerable support by expanding on the grassroots organizations created during the draft stage. The campaign, however, turned into a disaster. The problems that plagued Goldwater throughout his primary battles intensified after July and finally destroyed the viability of his candidacy. The conservative movement was young, with untested policies and inexperienced personnel who often worked against, instead of with, one another. As a result, they failed to counter the negative image of themselves created by the liberals of both parties. Despite the problems they experienced, conservatives saw the 1964 campaign as an important learning experience and the beginning, rather than the end, of their domination of the Republican Party.

The power shift within the GOP mirrored the vast changes taking place in American society. Even as the Republicans crowned their new standard-bearers, racial rioting exploded in parts of New York and New Jersey.

Although not as prolonged or as widespread as in later years, the riots of the summer of 1964 exposed the divisions, limitations, and dangers inherent in the civil rights movement. Unlike the crusade in the South, which focused on ending codified discrimination and disenfranchisement, black protests in the North centered on economic issues that could not be solved simply by conducting sit-ins or enacting sweeping legislation. Young militant blacks in the North and South, frustrated by the lack of results from the use of nonviolent tactics, increasingly ignored established leaders as they moved toward the Black Power movement. Consequently, although civil rights leaders proclaimed a moratorium on demonstrations during the campaign and LBJ encouraged young protesters to cooperate, Democrats were unable to gain control of the younger militants in the Student Nonviolent Coordinating Committee and the Congress on Racial Equality.[1]

In addition to the obvious motive of seeking to prevent bloodshed and chaos, LBJ feared that any violence would result in the much discussed "white backlash." First coined by *New York Times* economic consultant Eliot Janeway, the term referred to white fear and resentment toward blacks as blacks moved up the economic ladder. The editors of *The Nation* found many "puzzl[ed]" "persons of goodwill who could not grasp why *northern* Negroes should riot."[2] The strong showing of Alabama's segregationist governor George Wallace in the Democratic primaries in Wisconsin, Maryland, and Indiana further proved the existence, if not the depth, of widespread racism. Johnson thus walked a tightrope as he tried to keep the movement from further alienating his white voters without losing his black constituency.

Goldwater had no desire to be the racist candidate and offered to keep the issue out of the campaign by avoiding direct discussion of it. Of course, his vote against the Civil Rights Act spoke volumes about his stand on the issue. In addition, by convincing Wallace to drop his third-party drive, Goldwater's followers in the South retained the backlash votes for their candidate.[3]

Simultaneously, the thrust of domestic policy shifted from the well-intentioned but restrained attempts of the Kennedy era to LBJ's all-out drive to create the Great Society. Using his legislative prowess, LBJ pressured and cajoled Congress into passing the Mass Transit Act, the Civilian Pay Raise Act, the Tax Bill, and the Economic Opportunity Act before it recessed for the summer.[4]

The Economic Opportunity Act most clearly demonstrated Johnson's intentions and the limitations of his philosophy. Based on the assumption that poverty was a sociological rather than an economic problem, an idea supported by intellectuals such as economist John Kenneth Galbraith and socialist Michael Harrington, the Economic Opportunity Act attempted to fight poverty through therapeutic intervention, rehabilitation, and re-training. LBJ's sincere empathy with the poor, the increasing violence of the civil rights movement, and his desire to leave his mark on the nation compelled him to push for swift passage of the bill. Epitomizing the liberal response to social welfare problems, the measure gave Americans a pre-view of Johnson's Great Society, provided conservatives with a concrete example to criticize, and ultimately lost the war on poverty.[5]

The war in Asia was not going well either. As governments rose and fell in Vietnam and the surrounding countries, Johnson vainly attempted to resolve the situation quickly. Tensions increased in August 1964 when the administration announced that North Vietnam had fired on two Ameri-can ships in the Gulf of Tonkin. Although LBJ knew that there were doubts about whether or not the attack had actually occurred, he used the incident to send Congress the Gulf of Tonkin Resolution, which approved American retaliation and authorized the president to do whatever was necessary to defend the United States. After a brief discussion during which important questions concerning the nature of the conflict and the administration's response went unanswered, Congress passed the resolu-tion with only two dissenting votes in the Senate. Johnson's swift response increased his popularity with the public, earned him the support of Re-publicans as well as Democrats, and "wrested the Vietnam issue from Senator Goldwater's grip." Only a few people on the left realized the impli-cations of the actions for the United States and Indochina. The issue faded into the background to be addressed only indirectly by the candidates.[6]

The presidential candidates in 1964 faced the challenge of providing alternative solutions among which the American people could choose. Unfortunately, because the media and the voting population demanded concise, easy answers and melodrama, the rivals rarely discussed impor-tant issues. Despite the speeches, press conferences, and appearances of Johnson and Goldwater, the campaign degenerated into a battle of images that the opponents encouraged in private but condemned in public.

Goldwater did make a concerted effort to convey his position through speeches and published statements, at least early in the campaign. He promised to "chart a new course of peace, freedom, morality, and consti-tutional order." Emphasizing that "progress comes from work, initiative and investment," he recommended expanding the free enterprise system by reducing taxes and balancing the budget. Highly critical of what he felt was the unnecessary expansion of the federal government into inappropriate areas, Goldwater advocated making many governmental programs, such as farm price supports and social security, voluntary and encouraged the development of individual initiative and corporate-sponsored programs. Goldwater was quick to assure people that he did not intend to destroy these programs and leave the needy stranded but that he believed an expanded economy and a strong dollar ultimately would prove more helpful than all the Democratic "give-away" programs.[7]

Goldwater believed the government, on the other hand, should be actively and enthusiastically involved in providing for the national defense. Promising to "take a firm stand against Communist aggression," he frequently stated his intention to follow Eisenhower's peace-through-strength defense policy by maintaining military superiority over the Soviets. Although he trusted military more than civilian authority in defense and security matters, he promised not to rely solely on "bombs and bullets" but instead to offer "freedom"—a term he only vaguely defined—to the world. Goldwater frequently chided Johnson for his lack of commitment to creating a free world.[8]

Goldwater's philosophy certainly offered Americans a change from Democratic policies, but the problems inherent in his proposals alienated voters. Although many Americans agreed that the federal government had become economically and bureaucratically bloated, they suspected that Goldwater's emphasis on military superiority would lead to increased governmental expansion and create a garrison state antithetical to his ideal of a free state. His oversimplified economic policies ignored the complexities of the world market and the power of the modern corporation and focused on a balanced budget as an economic cure-all. The emphasis on education and individual initiative as answers to the problems of the poor overlooked the realities of their lives and their place in the social hierarchy.

Goldwater's philosophy was marred by two major flaws. First, since he wanted to reduce the size of the federal government and dismantle the New Deal framework, most of his proposals were negative rather than positive. Many people cheered his promise to get "Big Brother" out of their lives but wondered what positive actions Goldwater would then take. Second, people often misinterpreted his intentions. The image of Goldwater created during the primary campaign and reinforced by his inclination to speak out at the wrong time and place led the press and the public to latch onto on a few key phrases from his speeches and ignore their contextual meaning. Because he wanted to change what people accepted and expected of the federal government, Goldwater sounded like a radical rather than a conservative. What he wanted to alter or how he intended to achieve these changes was not as important as the fact that he meant to modify the status quo.[9]

In fact, Goldwater *was* a "radical" in many ways. He advocated changing the political and economic structure of the country in very basic ways. He intended to dismantle the New Deal framework, reverse the Keynesian trend, and drastically reduce the size and responsibilities of the federal government. Because of his deep commitment to the free enterprise system, he would gladly have turned the clock back to the 1920s. As a practicing politician, however, Goldwater knew he would not be able to achieve any of these goals to the extent he desired.[10] His goal, rather, was to place ideas before the electorate so that they would know that alternatives existed. The public, however, did not realize this. The fact that Goldwater continued to preach these ideals despite their improbability only added to his radical image and frightened voters, who were used to more moderate campaign rhetoric.

Democrats encouraged voters' misunderstanding of and concern about Goldwater by emphasizing certain aspects of his policies to the exclusion of all others. They did this most successfully in challenging Goldwater's stand on social security, civil rights, and nuclear weapons. Believing in a sound economy, Goldwater objected to the social security system because he felt it was "actuarially unsound" and because he disliked the compulsory aspect of the tax. Never did he say that he intended to do away with it, however, as the Democrats claimed.[11] Similarly, Democrats charged Goldwater with racism. They based their accusation on his vote against the 1964 Civil Rights Act, which he had considered unconstitutional, and his outspoken espousal of states' rights. Fearing that he would benefit from a potential white backlash, the public and the press believed the Democratic accusations.

Goldwater's often reckless candor caused him problems with his defense policy. By endorsing the Eisenhower stance that North Atlantic Treaty Organization (NATO) commanders should have control of nuclear weapons, Goldwater proved his willingness to rely on military rather than civilian authority and aroused fears that he might be quick to use nuclear weapons.[12] By openly embracing a policy that frightened people but had been accepted by the government for years, he revealed that he was either politically naive or foolishly honest. Either way, the press and his opponents eagerly presented distorted fragments of his policy, causing voters to never seriously considered the alternative principles and policies he offered.

Goldwater still had a surprising measure of support, however, especially from the middle classes in the South and West. According to author Norman Mailer, these supporters believed that the "basic war was between Main Street and Wall Street" and willingly offered their time and energy in support of Goldwater by serving in numerous citizens' committees. Appointed national director of Citizens for Goldwater-Miller, F. Clifton White continued his grassroots work and built up a volunteer army to back the conservative cause as well as Goldwater. With chapters in every state, Citizens for Goldwater-Miller sought to mobilize those "who are not ordinarily politically active," to enlist "discerning Democrats and Independents who are disenchanted with the mess in Washington," and to "develop projects and special activities whereby people of allied interests and professions can join in a common effort." Citizens' committees cooperated with the party organization wherever possible but in some states ended up being the only dedicated and enthusiastic Goldwater organizations. In fact, some aides believed they must take a grassroots approach because the Republican Party was not solidly behind them.[13]

Citizens for Goldwater-Miller spawned and loosely coordinated various special-interest groups across the country that supported Goldwater. The conservative organizations that had boosted his candidacy from the beginning heeded the call of the *ACA Newsletter* headline: "Goldwater Wins! Now *We* Go to Work!" Members of Americans for Conservative Action, a grassroots organization headquartered in Indianapolis, sent out mailings in support of Goldwater using their Christmas card mailing list and announced new endorsements—such as that from the *Butler County American*, a black newspaper—in their newsletter. Captain Eddie Rickenbacker's Fighting Aces for Goldwater and Admiral Ben Moreel's Americans for Constitutional Action also offered their wholehearted support, but attempts to form a Democrats for Goldwater Committee met with only limited success.[14]

Goldwater's financial backing reflected his grassroots and regional support as well as the successful party effort to broaden its constituency by utilizing direct-mail techniques. Using lists gathered from conservative organizations, Goldwater's staff sent out frequent mailings requesting funds, providing information on campaign activities, and generally building a network of supporters. Continuing a trend that had begun during

Eisenhower's campaigns and had been encouraged by the development of the Republican Sustaining Fund, Goldwater's campaign received over a million contributions, many of which were from people who had never made a political donation before.[15]

White consciously sought to replace the party's reliance on large donations from eastern financial institutions with reliance on a wider constituency. He clearly succeeded since 72 percent of the Republican individual contributions were under $500. The tremendous increase in the number of contributions indicated that Goldwater appealed to many people who had failed to contribute to the Eisenhower and Nixon efforts. On the other hand, Goldwater also received significant donations from conservative eastern businesspeople such as the DuPonts and the Pews as well as from Texas oilmen and ranchers. Proving that a conservative would not necessarily alienate contributors, Goldwater raised $7 million more than Nixon had received in 1960 and ended his campaign with a surplus.[16]

Ironically, although Lyndon Johnson concluded his race with a deficit, he received a great deal of support. From the outset of the campaign, he was favored to win. The fact that he was the incumbent gave him the advantages and resources of his office, while his skillful and tactful handling of the difficult transition following Kennedy's assassination earned him the respect of a broad spectrum of the population. In addition, his reputation as a New Dealer and his ability to maneuver the Civil Rights Act through Congress characterized him as a traditional liberal. A man driven to prove himself by winning the presidency, Johnson possessed the political skills, acquired through long years in the Senate, to run an effective campaign. Heartened by the nomination of the avowedly conservative Goldwater and an almost certain victory, LBJ nevertheless insisted on conducting a full-blown campaign to ensure that instead of merely winning the election he would sweep the race by a greater margin than FDR had received in 1936.[17]

To gain the broadest support, Johnson followed a nonpartisan campaign strategy of running as "president of all the people." In fact, during the first weeks after his nomination at an LBJ-dominated convention, he did not campaign but instead concentrated on his suddenly more numerous and more public presidential duties. Constantly quoting statistics that proved the prosperity of the country, informing the public about the consensus that existed in political affairs, and making subtle insinuations about the extremist character of his opponent, LBJ traveled across the country, opening dams and airports, speaking at dinners, and visiting the scenes of natural disasters. His dedicated staff fed him information about Goldwater's proposals and strategies.[18]

The polls indicated that LBJ was ahead in both popular and electoral votes by a huge margin. Across the country, his support grew as national and local organizations sprang up to work for his election. Besides the national campaign committee and its state affiliates, Young Citizens for Johnson and Students for Johnson offered their support. Business leaders, including many traditionally Republican executives, rallied to Johnson's campaign and formed Businessmen for Johnson. His nonpartisan approach proved fruitful in gathering not only Independents, who formed the National Independent Committee for President Johnson and Senator Humphrey and the Independent Citizens for Johnson Committee, but also disenchanted Republicans.[19]

So many Republicans wrote to LBJ pledging their support that the president's advisers and friends encouraged him to publicize this fact in the campaign. Some suggested forming a group called Responsible Republicans for Johnson. Columnist Drew Pearson believed that even Eisenhower "might be induced to urge a bi-partisan policy for the Republicans." Minnesota senator Eugene McCarthy delivered campaign speeches portraying Goldwater and his followers as "radicals" who were not merely attacking Democrats but assaulting the "mainstream of American political life." Johnson was ambivalent about this support. Although he had been consciously campaigning as the president of everyone, he did not want to be elected merely because he was the lesser of two evils; he wanted to win for himself.[20]

Johnson's driving ambition and constant need to be reassured that he was liked often made him difficult to work with and for but did not detract from his generally favorable position. His image as the consummate political manipulator was, however, a more serious problem. Many people agreed with Goldwater that Johnson "used and abused . . . power . . . for his own personal political gain." Polls indicated that a large percentage of people who intended to vote for Johnson did not credit him with much integrity or honesty. Although Americans did not know it at the time, LBJ's exaggeration of the Gulf of Tonkin incident laid the groundwork for the "credibility gap" that would later plague him.[21]

In addition to Johnson's apparent lack of integrity, several episodes during the campaign raised questions about his choice of aides and associates. LBJ's connections to Senate aide Bobby Baker and real estate magnate Billie Sol Estes, both under investigation by the Justice Department for financial impropriety, undermined his credibility and refueled Goldwater's assault on immorality in Washington. The arrest of Johnson's aide and friend Walter Jenkins on a morals charge might have further supported Goldwater's accusations if it had not been forced out of the headlines by Soviet leader Nikita Khrushchev's resignation and mainland China's atomic bomb explosion. In addition, it was rumored that the White House pressured several defense industries to contribute heavily to LBJ's campaign or risk losing government contracts.[22]

LBJ and his aides also realized that Goldwater represented a considerable segment of the population. Even before the Republican convention took place, LBJ aide Henry Wilson warned that Johnson could lose the election because he was in a "situation brand new in American politics"; the opposition, Wilson explained, was "peddling three potent commodities": race prejudice, nationalism, and simple answers to complex questions. Economist and ambassador to India John Kenneth Galbraith advised LBJ to stay away from any liberal-conservative debate because such a contest would only "dignify Goldwater's position" and alienate the voters who did not want to be thought of as liberals. Editors of *The Nation* discounted what they labeled the "shoo-in fallacy" and urged Democrats to begin "running somewhat scared." Goldwater's grassroots organization, his dedicated followers, and the existence of an anxious and frustrated American public convinced the journalists that a Republican victory was not out of the question. Aware of these problems as the campaign moved into October, LBJ pulled out all the stops, traveling 60,000 miles and inviting millions to "the speakin'." He never let up, no matter how certain his victory appeared to be.[23]

As time went by, Goldwater's defeat seemed more and more inevitable, partly because of LBJ's advantages and political skills and partly because of the Republican's own problems. Both internal and external, these serious and interconnected problems—involving his organization, his image, the lack of united Republican support, and his deficiencies as a candidate—played as much a part in Goldwater's defeat as did Johnson's skills and outside circumstances.

Goldwater's campaign staff suffered from internal dissension and disorganization. Perhaps because of Goldwater's lack of experience and his insecurity about running for an office he felt incapable of handling, he did not take advantage of the wealth of political talent available to him in the committee that drafted him. In fact, he alienated many of those capable organizers by ignoring their skills and advice. Time and again, as he filled positions in his organizations, he passed over important men and women, such as Draft Goldwater Committee chair Peter O'Donnell and women's director Ione Harrington. Goldwater's controversial appointment of Dean Burch instead of Clifton White as chair of the Republican National Committee deprived the campaign of White's experience and prompted criticism that he preferred loyalty and friendship over competence.[24]

Internal squabbles and jealousies within the Goldwater committee took a heavy toll on the campaign. In state after state, loyal volunteers reported communication, managerial, and morale problems to White, who could do little but offer advice. Goldwater's failure to fully utilize these volunteers resulted in a staff crippled by tangled lines of communication and mixed loyalties. The overall goal remained Goldwater's election, but personal power struggles undercut the operation and led to hostility, name-calling, and ostracism.[25]

To make matters worse, rumors of incompetence haunted Goldwater's campaign staff, especially at the upper levels, throughout the campaign. Many conservative activists feared the consequences of relying on an inexperienced staff and resented being replaced by amateurs. In fact, few of the men and women serving as Goldwater's key advisers were party regulars. For example, Dean Burch was a lawyer whose only real political experience before he was appointed RNC chair was as Goldwater's administrative assistant. John Grenier impressed everyone with his effective campaign techniques in Alabama, but campaign leaders only reluctantly accepted his advice. William Baroody's influence with Goldwater distressed more politically minded conservatives who believed that Baroody was giving Goldwater bad advice and isolating him from his supporters. Stephen Shadegg, who had enjoyed a close relationship with Goldwater and had served as his Senate campaign manager, had more practical campaign experience than many of those over him in the hierarchy and was relegated to the position of regional head of the western district.[26] By the end of the campaign, everyone, both inside and outside the Goldwater hierarchy, was frustrated by speechwriter Karl Hess's tendency to isolate the candidate from everyone else on the campaign airplane. His sometimes childish behavior led one insider to describe him as the "court jester to his majesty, the candidate." Campaign manager Denison Kitchel, whose past association with the John Birch Society surprisingly never came to light, was criticized so much for mistakes made in the strategy and execution of the campaign that he felt compelled to defend his appointment and his commitment to the Republican Party.[27]

Much of the criticism of Kitchel resulted from the difficulty everyone had in ascertaining the chain of command connecting the campaign committee and the RNC. Following the advice of political theorist Raymond Moley, Goldwater had separated the political technicians who would run the campaign from the conservative ideologues who would control it. As a result, the two groups often contradicted each other.[28] Goldwater did create a campaign hierarchy, but this command system could not overcome the communications problems and did not prove conducive either to a smooth-running campaign or to harmony in the ranks.

The major problem was that no one could tell who was really in control. Burch claimed that Goldwater made his own decisions based on the "recommendations" of his advisers. Some members of the staff believed that Kitchel actually ran things; others, such as John Grenier, thought Kitchel shared power with William Baroody, who was "very influential." Clifton White agreed with head of field operations Richard Kleindienst, who claimed that the "real decisions were made at strategy sessions where only McCabe, Baroody, Kitchel and Goldwater were present." Kitchel believed that the problem resulted from the lack of clear understanding that Burch was the campaign manager and that Kitchel served as Goldwater's "representative to the campaign organization." This confusion meant that people working on separate parts of the campaign at various levels did not work effectively with the national committee.[29]

Goldwater's changes in the committee further alienated party workers. Seeking to implement a "thorough-going reform of Republican party programs and operations," Goldwater immediately restructured the RNC to ensure that the party remained in conservative hands no matter what happened in the election. This meant replacing key RNC personnel with people who agreed with his philosophy. As the press commented on the "upheaval," party regulars worried about the ultimate consequences as well as the valuable time being wasted.[30]

Others were far more concerned about the effect of the personnel problems on the overall campaign. Quite a few people, particularly old friends and associates, observed that Goldwater's new staff isolated him from people outside the inner circle. White, Shadegg, Rusher, and even Kleindienst noted that Goldwater allowed himself to be secluded from the people who could provide him with the information necessary for a successful campaign. One volunteer expressed the view of many workers at the grassroots level when he complained to California senator William Knowland that Goldwater appeared "to have withdrawn from the source of his main support." Another party regular later claimed that the "Mafia" had helped "to kill Barry with the conservatives" by neglecting "those of Barry's friends who brought him the nomination," by not heeding the warnings in campaign workers' letters, and by separating Goldwater physically and mentally from grassroots volunteers.[31]

Many workers were frustrated by the shabby treatment and lack of direction within the campaign organization. The seemingly arbitrary and unnecessary changes in scheduling delayed their access to necessary campaign materials. More importantly, time and again, the Goldwater high command ignored the advice of regional directors who knew the issues and the people most important to winning in their states.[32]

With no support from the national leadership, workers in some states where party regulars did not support Goldwater were left to suffer the consequences. In Michigan, for example, Goldwaterites endured the "attacks and smears" of the Romney Republicans without any support from the national Goldwater committee. "After getting NO cooperation, NO help, NO nothing but the cold shoulder" from official Goldwater organizations, many longtime conservatives, "overcome with a mood of dismay and depression," turned "sour" on the whole operation. They were not alone. The committee's high-handed and pompous methods cost Goldwater workers as well as votes.[33]

Goldwater's public image was a second major problem during the campaign. Because of his unabashedly conservative philosophy, the tenor of the times, and the beliefs of some of his supporters, it was easy for enemies to portray him as an extremist. After all, he did call for some measures, such as the elimination of the graduated income tax and its replacement with a flat tax, that were "radically" different. He did assert that communism must be confronted militarily at a time when people wanted peace, and he insisted that it was unconstitutional for the federal government to dictate civil rights policies to the states, a stance that signified racism to many people. Although he voiced these positions within generalized campaign rhetoric rather than specific policy proposals, his deviation from the consensus politics of post–New Deal presidents frightened many voters.

Adding to this extremist image, however, were the ideas and actions of many of Goldwater's supporters. In spite of the fact that Goldwater did not share the views of some conservative groups, their endorsement made him guilty by association, according to some opponents. Consequently, when the *National Chronicle* warned Americans that blacks and Asiatics were "mongrelizing" the United States, or the *American Capsule News* editor contended that Rockefeller had been involved in JFK's assassination, or the John Birch Society accused Eisenhower and almost everyone else of being communists, many voters assumed Goldwater held similar views. Even the fact that some extreme right-wing groups refused to support Goldwater did not erase his negative image as an extremist.[34]

Perhaps more significantly, Goldwater's Democratic opponent promoted perceptions of Goldwater as a dangerous radical. Johnson's staff members were encouraged by letters from concerned citizens, such as the man who called Goldwater "the most dangerous candidate for President that America has ever had." Consequently, they developed a conscious plan to exploit the extremist image of their opponent for all it was worth. Realizing that their "main strength" was "not so much in the FOR Johnson but in the AGAINST Goldwater," LBJ aide Jack Valenti warned the president that they could not afford to let the public think that they were treating Goldwater as a serious candidate. Valenti wanted voters to see Goldwater as "dangerous" and a "national joke." Democrats circulated material linking Goldwater to the extreme right-wing and reinforcing his image as a warmonger but skirting the race issue since that topic could possibly lose LBJ votes.[35]

Johnson's reelection staff used every conceivable means to challenge Goldwater's status as a legitimate candidate and to make voters fear him. The Democrats' advertising firm of Doyle, Dane, and Bernbach spread the extremist image through the media via several famous television commercials. The first and best-known commercial showed a little girl plucking petals from a daisy as a voice counted down; when the voice reached zero, the screen exploded into a mushroom cloud. No mention was made of Goldwater, but the implication was clear. The commercial was only aired once, but the outraged response from both Republicans and Democrats kept the image alive much longer.[36]

The second commercial focused on a pair of hands tearing a social security card in half, thus evoking fears that Goldwater would end that program. Such ruthless tactics sickened Goldwater and disturbed some older Democrats but successfully frightened many voters into the Democratic camp. Additionally, by publicizing reports of negative foreign reaction to Goldwater's positions, condemnations of Goldwater in leading Christian publications, and psychologists' testimony that Goldwater was not fit for office, LBJ and his staff demonstrated that a broad range of people viewed Goldwater as a radical.[37]

Their most effective weapon was humor. Cartoons and quips trivialized Goldwater and kept him on the defensive. Americans for Democratic Action circulated "Through a Looking Glass Darkly: A Political Fantasy," a farce featuring President Garry Boldwater and his aide Robert · Welch, secretary of defense Curtis LeMay, secretary of labor H. L. Hunt, and ambassador to Formosa, General Edwin Walker. In this satire, the United States had withdrawn from the United Nations and was preparing to sell the Tennessee Valley Authority; the number of State Department personnel had been cut in half and the top floors of the State Department building rented out to a major corporation. Democrats even mocked Goldwater's campaign slogan, "In your heart, you know he's right," by adding the threatening codicil, "Yes, extreme Right." Others were more irreverent, devising the slogan, "In your guts, you know he's nuts."[38]

Liberals both in and out of office joined the Johnson staff in characterizing Goldwater as a radical. Insisting on labeling the Arizona senator an extremist rather than a conservative, the editors of *The Nation* disclosed the "method in the apparent madness" of the Goldwater camp and pointed out the serious long-term implications of the nomination. "Goldwaterism," they warned, would outlast Goldwater. Arthur Schlesinger, Jr., and Robert Kennedy believed that only an overwhelming Democratic victory could repudiate Goldwater's attack on American institutions. Throughout the Democratic Party, staffers tried not to underestimate Goldwater and continued to exert pressure against him until election day.[39]

Goldwater's campaign staff was very much aware that they had to take the offensive, but they could not find an opening. Since, according to deputy director of research Charles Lichenstein, they were "always operating against yesterday's distortions," they did not have time to implement positive measures. They also found it necessary to explain Goldwater's positions to voters. Conservatives stressed that he was not as unpopular as the liberal press made him out to be, that he was frank because he assumed his audiences were intelligent, and that he had overreacted to the initial criticisms of his speeches. Nothing seemed to undo the damage done by his extremist image.[40]

Others blamed liberals and the press for misquoting and deliberately distorting everything Goldwater said. The misquoting of his statement on *Issues and Answers* about nuclear weapons serves as a good example. Goldwater stated that it had been suggested that the United States use low-yield atomic bombs to defoliate the jungles of Vietnam but that he did not support the suggestion. The first part of his statement was quickly publicized, but the last part was not. This nurtured Goldwater's image as a warmonger.[41]

The liberal press played a pivotal role in establishing the image of Goldwater as an extremist by almost continuously questioning his credentials and even his sanity. Only a handful of newspapers endorsed Goldwater, with an overwhelming majority supporting Johnson.[42] Goldwater was partly responsible for this lack of support from the media, however, since he made only a few real attempts to gain media backing and often treated the press as the enemy. The extremist image caused incalculable damage to Goldwater's campaign.

The label of radical also undermined Goldwater's standing with Republicans and accounted for his third major problem. Many moderate and liberal Republicans refused to support the national ticket. The split that resulted caused problems throughout the party structure. In some states, party regulars fought over whether or not to support the national ticket; in others, they simply refused to work for Goldwater.[43]

A desire to return control of the national party to the Center motivated Ohio Republican Charles P. Taft to form the Committee to Support Moderate Republicans. On the assumption that moderate Republicanism was "the most responsible force on the American political scene," Taft warned that the two-party system would be destroyed unless moderate Republicans were elected. Political correspondent Robert Spivak noted that many "homeless" Republicans concentrated on keeping the state platforms more in line with the moderate view and stayed out of the national contest. Even campaign contributors divided along ideological lines. Some gave only to state committees to ensure that they were not supporting the national committee, while others did the opposite.[44]

Goldwater made only a few halfhearted attempts to accommodate those in the center and then complained when he lost their support. He was not the only one who did not grasp the significance of moderate support. The newly powerful conservatives on the RNC circulated an advertisement for a "new parlor game" called "Moderately Yours." Players gained points for "casting authentic U.S. heroes—'extremists' to some—in more moderate roles." Such humor negated any attempts to woo the moderates of the party.[45]

Other Republicans abandoned party loyalties and publicly encouraged LBJ's election. To "save the GOP" by voting for LBJ, many of these dissatisfied Republicans joined numerous Republicans for Johnson committees that sprang up around the country. The endorsement of Republican author Arthur Larson and former Republican presidential candidates Thomas Dewey and Harold Stassen reinforced Johnson's image as a consensus president.[46]

More disturbing to Goldwater's staff was the lack of support from Republican governors Robert Smylie of Idaho, George Romney of Michigan, and Nelson Rockefeller of New York, who had tremendous influence on their state party organizations. Romney's handling of the situation was particularly galling to Goldwater and his staff. Although Romney "accepted" the decision of his party to nominate Goldwater and promised that the Michigan Republican Party at the state and local levels would work with Goldwater's campaign organization, he never offered his own help. In fact, he passed out campaign literature encouraging Michigan voters to "split the ticket" by voting for him as governor and LBJ as president.[47]

On the other hand, a number of Republicans put loyalty ahead of their personal disagreements with Goldwater's philosophy. They worked, if not for Goldwater, at least for the party. Representative Bob Wilson of California, chair of the Republican Congressional Committee, told an interviewer from the *Republican Congressional Committee Newsletter* that Goldwater's nomination would "enhance our opportunities to elect Republicans to the House." Pennsylvania governor William Scranton, perhaps thinking of the future or seeking to make up for his actions during the convention, refused to "join in any effort to divide" the party and worked hard for Goldwater in Pennsylvania and other states.[48]

Both Eisenhower and Nixon took to the campaign trail in 1964 and worked diligently, even if not enthusiastically. Eisenhower, in particular, did not want to campaign and realized that the party would be lucky to carry two or three states. Frustrated by Goldwater's lack of self-assurance and almost belligerent defensiveness, Eisenhower marveled at Goldwater's inability to say "anything appealing." At one point, he told Nixon that he thought Goldwater was "just plain dumb." On the other hand, despite the fact that Eisenhower did not believe that Goldwater would be able to unite the party leadership, he had unquestionable faith in Goldwater's "sincerity, honesty and innate decency." Eisenhower preferred Goldwater to Johnson. Additionally, Eisenhower felt that he had to campaign for Goldwater because, as he said in speeches and letters to citizens across the country, he was "a Republican who is loyal to his party and who is respectful of the decisions made by the Party in its county, state and national conventions." The good of the party was foremost in his mind.[49]

Concern for the future of the party also persuaded Nixon to carry out the "hopeless task" of stumping for an "inept" candidate. Throughout October, Nixon traveled 25,000 miles to 36 states, made 136 speeches, and held 103 press conferences. He also sent out an appeal for funds on behalf of Goldwater that met with only mixed results. Candidates of all ideologies asked Nixon to help drum up support for their campaigns in particular and for the party in general. Addressing the most pertinent issues in each city he visited, Nixon castigated Johnson for his lack of morality and integrity, and he attempted to dispel the Democratic-inspired fears and distortions concerning Goldwater's views on social security and nuclear weapons. In addition, Nixon hoped to persuade Republicans not to desert the party because of disagreements with Goldwater and to bring "back into the fold" those Republicans who had already left. Nixon worried that the mass departure threatened more than the Goldwater campaign; if the election swept away Goldwater and all other Republican candidates, it would signify the end of the GOP and the American political tradition.[50]

Goldwater's campaign, despite the help of a few party pros, contained serious technical flaws that often threatened to destroy it. Inextricably intertwined with other problems, these technical problems highlighted and intensified the campaign's weaknesses. The tensions between national campaign headquarters and the state and local organizations grew as the election neared and workers could not gain access to necessary campaign materials. Inexperienced members of the Goldwater staff alienated even loyal supporters with their disorganization. For example, plans for a live television broadcast of a Wisconsin Goldwater rally, funded by local supporters, were changed at the last minute by Kitchel, who decided to broadcast the rally over the radio instead, causing legal problems for the local organization and angering those who had supported plans for a television broadcast. A potential scandal occurred when John Grenier tried to stop leaks in the organization by buying information from a Democratic National Committee employee about a spy who supposedly had infiltrated Goldwater headquarters. The incident disappeared from the headlines, however, after only a few days.[51]

Goldwater and his supporters clashed over how to attack the Democrats. Although conservatives decided to emphasize questions about Johnson's morality, they could not agree on how to proceed with the assault. Goldwater refused to exploit events such as the arrest of Johnson's aide Walter Jenkins on a morals charge, causing his supporters to wonder what they could use against the president.

The best example of such differences over strategy was the furor that arose concerning the campaign film, *Choice*. Intended to develop the Republican theme of the Democrats' immorality, the film featured images of burning cities, rampaging criminals, junkies taking drugs, and dancing strippers in order to suggest what life would be like under continued Democratic leadership. The movie also contained shots of a speeding black limousine—an obvious reference to LBJ—and of Johnson's associates, suspected swindler Billie Sol Estes and con man Bobby Baker. Sponsored by Mothers for a Moral America, approved by White and his aide Rus Walton, but not viewed by Goldwater or any of his inner circle, the movie sparked controversy even before it was released. As the press speculated about the actual contents of the film, Goldwater and the "Arizona Mafia" decided it would be wise to avoid criticism by not releasing the film, and Kitchel ordered White to cancel the first showing the night before it was scheduled to be presented. Such an abrupt move led to further rumors of the movie's extremist content, especially after John Wayne, who had been slated to introduce it, was frightened away by the controversy.[52]

Many grassroots conservatives disagreed with the decision. A Goldwater campaign worker in Colorado complained to White that the cancellation caused people to question the commitment of party leaders, who obviously did not "have the courage to show the truth." Moreover, he continued, the press was portraying the citizens' committee as "some kind of an extreme group" that Goldwater was unable to control. These criticisms were disheartening to local branches of the committee.[53]

Goldwater, by his own admission, made serious campaign mistakes. Prone to speaking before thinking and quick to reduce complex ideas to simple terms, Goldwater often spoke in generalities when he should have addressed specific local issues. Some people, such as Shadegg, blamed these deficiencies on the failure of the "Arizona Mafia" to keep Goldwater informed. Others, such as the state chair of Pennsylvania, believed that Goldwater was "essentially a lightweight" who could be tripped up by the press because he spent his time on the plane "carousing" instead of "boning up" on the issues. Goldwater's loyalty to and reliance on inexperienced friends worried some supporters, who feared that his choices for national leadership would be no better.[54]

These problems ultimately led to Goldwater's overwhelming defeat. Although he garnered almost 27 million votes, he carried only Arizona and the five states of the Deep South. The rest of the party capsized along with him. The Democrats won a 68-to-32 majority in the Senate and a 295-to-140 majority in the House.

Republicans immediately searched for explanations for the devastating defeat. Liberals attributed the loss to Goldwater's conservatism, but conservatives offered other explanations. Many right-wingers, though acknowledging that they had not run the most efficient campaign, claimed that the political situation in 1964 made the defeat inevitable. RNC chair Dean Burch told the National Press Club that Goldwater had been running against the martyred JFK as well as against his successor LBJ. Goldwater concluded that the voters had not been "ready for three presidents in two and a half years." In addition to the "political honeymoon" resulting from lingering public guilt and sympathy following JFK's assassination, William Buckley attributed Johnson's victory partly to the fact that he had the advantage of the publicity, prestige, and power of the presidency behind his campaign. Moreover, Buckley continued, the president was "buoyed by the felicitous co-operation of the world around him" and was blessed with a "booming economy [and] a Communist world momentarily paralyzed by introversion."[55]

Conservatives postulated that Johnson was fortunate to run against an opponent with little experience, limited abilities, and an overwhelmingly flawed image, all of which made the president appear to be the only reasonable choice. Journalist John S. Knight argued that Americans were not certain "what they would get with Barry Goldwater in the White House" and did not want to risk finding out. The popularization of the extremist image of Goldwater by some Republicans and the refusal of others to support the national ticket ruptured the party and gave LBJ the further advantage of facing a divided opposition.[56]

Goldwater's conservative detractors were divided between those who accused him of not really wanting to win and therefore not participating wholeheartedly in the campaign and those who stressed the damage created by his "almost excessive candor" and often inflexible thinking. Goldwater accepted responsibility for the defeat but, rather self-righteously, asserted that what the "majority of criticism of the campaign on my part boils down to is that I was not dishonest enough" to win.[57]

The extent of the defeat clearly damaged Goldwater's career. No longer a member of the Senate, ignored by the Republican Party, and blamed by conservative as well as liberal Republicans for the defeat, he nevertheless continued to criticize the Democratic administration. His gradual ostracism began in early 1965 and was almost complete by June 1965, when he was the only prominent Republican not invited to speak at the Ohio jamboree celebrating the appointment of a new Republican National Committee chair. His ill treatment during the 1968 and 1972 national conventions proved that the taint of defeat lingered for years. Even more upsetting to him was the fact that some conservatives abandoned him in favor of more successful right-wing candidates. In later years, he discovered that some of his old supporters even questioned his conservatism.[58]

The defeat alone does not explain Goldwater's ostracism. Herbert Hoover and Thomas Dewey lost to Franklin Roosevelt but remained active in the GOP. Certainly the devastating nature of the loss played a part in Republicans' desire to distance themselves from Goldwater. Equally important, however, were memories of the bitterness of the primary and national campaigns, anger at Goldwater's inefficient organization of his staff, and resentment concerning the shift in power within the GOP from the Center to the Right. Many unleashed their lingering hostilities and frustrations on Goldwater in an attempt to force him out of the spotlight.

In 1964, however, Goldwater still represented the conservative movement, and his suggestion that the parties realign along ideological lines reflected the extent of the divisions within the GOP. As unrealistic as the idea might have been, the intensification of internecine bickering following the election as everyone scrambled to claim leadership of the party and as each side blamed the other for the defeat indicated that the party needed considerable help to heal the wounds of the campaign.[59]

The discord was even apparent in discussions concerning Republican gains in the South. Moderate Republicans claimed that the credit for organizing a southern Republican Party belonged to the Eisenhower team, which had made the first significant crack in the Solid South. Others insinuated that Goldwater's gains in the South were merely racist votes. Conservatives disagreed. Former Alabama state chair John Grenier argued that "history will not be concerned with motives of the Southern vote" but with the new reality of a viable two-party system below the Mason-Dixon line. Dean Burch agreed, reassuring southern Republican workers that their successes had not been "one-shot victories" and that the GOP was "now a feature of the whole Southern landscape."[60] The continuing vehemence of the dispute proved the new tenacity of conservatives, who simply refused to abandon their party to liberals as they had done in the past.

A few conservatives feared that 1964 signaled the end of their movement, but most right-wingers were pleased with the results of the campaign. Even journalist David Lawrence, who did not support Goldwater, disproved the notion that conservatism had suffered a "setback" by pointing out that LBJ was regarded by many as a conservative. In addition, the 27 million votes Goldwater received formed a large bloc of voters who could not simply be written off as a bunch of "kooks." Conservative journalist M. Stanton Evans touted 1964 as the year the "relatively young conservative movement in America flexed its muscles, achieved things the experts and oracles said could never happen, and moved part-way down the road toward political maturity." Emphasizing the developmental aspects of their movement, some conservatives believed that losing the 1964 election made them better prepared for the next one.[61]

It gradually became apparent that the campaign had left a greater impact on the country than first thought. Almost immediately after the election, Johnson aide Bob Hunter acknowledged that Goldwater's charges of immorality in the White House hurt the president "to an extent not revealed at the polls." More significantly, as LBJ escalated the war in Vietnam, the American press and public began to reexamine their assessment of him and to reconsider some of Goldwater's predictions.[62]

Conservatives also recognized the view illustrated by a *Washington Evening Star* cartoon depicting Goldwater and a woman, dressed as parents of the bride, waving good-bye to their daughter and consoling each other by saying, "Look at it this way. . . . We haven't lost a presidency! We've gained a party!" Within that party, they discovered a new star on whom to focus their attention and hope: Ronald Reagan. An actor turned political activist, Reagan had delivered a television address that for many was the highlight of the campaign. According to Nixon, in that address, Reagan demonstrated that he possessed what Goldwater lacked—"the ability to present his views in a reasonable and eloquent manner."[63]

The importance of the Goldwater candidacy to the rise of political conservatism was evident to everyone involved. Having finally gained a platform from which to present their philosophy and to outline policies, conservatives relished their newfound power. Unfortunately for the Right, however, the American people—comfortable, secure, and prosperous— were not yet receptive to conservative proposals. Nor were the conservatives themselves ready to defeat a man far more skilled than they in the art of political campaigning and manipulation. Lyndon Johnson's years of experience contrasted sharply with the conservatives' untested plans and ideals. Conservatives possessed workers, money, and enthusiasm, but they lacked organization and experience in national politics and therefore were thwarted in their attempts to control supporters, to refute the extremist image associated with their philosophy, and to maintain unity in their ranks.

Although Goldwater was thoroughly defeated, conservatism was not. Because of the immaturity of the campaign staff and the absence of a receptive national audience, conservatism as a philosophy was not even discussed during the campaign. Only the radical aspects of the movement received media attention, causing the American people, including many social conservatives, to reject all of conservatism. However, the organization that White and his crew built during the draft stage did not fall apart after the defeat. The volunteers formed a standing army, invigorated by their first taste of battle and ready for the next. Having learned the value of grassroots activism, conservatives continued to cultivate associates at that level by direct-mail techniques developed during the 1964 campaign. Because of the manner in which Goldwater's candidacy had emerged, the conservative crusade had always been bigger than the man, and so his defeat was merely a way station in the march of the overall movement. After their 1964 baptism by fire, conservatives were ready to regroup, solidify their holdings, and look to 1968.[64]

BIDING THEIR TIME

In November 1964, the future viability of the Republican Party seemed in doubt. Even before the final tallying of votes in the election, Republicans contemplated the future of their party. In fact, many moderates had been planning postelection rehabilitation since August and September. By late October, even Eisenhower was mulling over possibilities for the party after November. He eventually championed the idea of establishing an advisory council that would not be tied to the national committee or to any special-interest group. Both Michigan governor George Romney and House minority leader Charles Halleck agreed with Eisenhower that party members needed to examine what they stood for and where they were going.[1]

One of the main purposes of Eisenhower's proposed advisory council would be to redefine Republicanism in terms acceptable to most party members and understandable to the voting public. After the disastrous defeat, Eisenhower insisted, Republicans needed to correct "the false 'image' of Republicanism" created during the campaign. Goldwater, too, wanted the party to make its priorities clear, especially since he felt that many Americans had misunderstood his platform and therefore had rejected it outright. Nixon spoke for more Republicans when he told the press that the party had to move more toward the center and away from a far right position.[2]

Even as Republicans attempted to stabilize intraparty relations and preached party unity, the inevitable search for a scapegoat began. Perhaps because they could not excommunicate Goldwater without risking total destruction of the party, moderate and liberal Republicans focused their anger on the Goldwater-appointed RNC chair, Dean Burch. Idaho governor Robert Smylie, a moderate and chair of the newly formed Republican Governors' Association, believed that "even the senator himself was not well-served by the national committee." Smylie felt compelled to explain that he was not criticizing Goldwater by suggesting that a new chair be appointed.[3]

Others were more blunt. Pennsylvania governor William Scranton wrote Goldwater that "the exclusive policy of the National leadership is so imbedded in the minds of most people in the nation that I do not think it can be overcome unless there is a change of leadership to one which practices non-exclusion." Convinced that Burch was too closely associated with Goldwater to unite the party successfully, both Oregon governor Mark Hatfield and Michigan governor George Romney told Eisenhower that they felt Burch should resign. Although Eisenhower did not view the chairmanship as particularly important, he agreed that Burch and Goldwater had failed to disassociate themselves from the far right and therefore had damaged the party's image.[4]

Conservatives did not want to capitulate, although some agreed that Burch was not right for the job. Most feared that Burch's sudden resignation would be seen as a surrender to party liberals.[5] Others, including the editors of the *National Review*, hoped for a compromise candidate of Goldwater's choosing so that he could retain control while appearing flexible. Goldwater, however, understood that he himself was the moderates' actual target and refused to consider Burch's resignation. With his mentor's support, Burch attempted to divert attention from his position in the party to the problems of rebuilding. On 8 January 1965, in a speech before the National Press Club, he emphatically denied that he intended to resign. Consequently, when he and Goldwater announced on 12 January that his resignation would be forthcoming, many conservatives felt betrayed. Ex–Draft Goldwater Committee chair Peter O'Donnell complained that Goldwater had mishandled the situation. The editors of the *National Review* similarly criticized Goldwater for his initial inflexibility.[6]

The mysterious circumstances surrounding Burch's resignation provide insight into the structure of the Republican Party, the conservatives' position within the organization, and the growing maturity of the conservatives as political activists. Up until 11 January, Burch insisted that he would not resign. After a secret meeting with unnamed but powerful members of the party, however, Burch and Goldwater agreed that Burch would step down and be replaced by Ohio state chair Ray Bliss, who also attended the meeting. Presented with a fait accompli at the Republican National Committee meeting, several committee members, such as Texan Albert Fay, bitterly resented not being allowed to have a voice in the matter, but they had no choice but to accept the decision or risk further destruction of their party's image and morale.[7]

Goldwater accepted the inevitability of Burch's resignation only after he realized that if a vote of confidence in Burch was taken, he would win or lose by only two or three votes. Such a close margin would, according to Burch, be "extremely harmful" to a "party that can't sustain any more injuries." Believing that the GOP was "just barely in the ballgame," Burch and Goldwater hoped to "avoid any confrontation" that might cause permanent damage.[8]

The handling of the situation revealed the inexperience of some of the conservatives and the developing maturity of others. If Goldwater had appointed someone with more national and regular party connections, many of the problems could have been avoided in the first place. If he had not made Burch a symbol of his own power within the party, the battle might not have disintegrated into such a bitter struggle. And if he had consulted other conservatives, some of the strains within the movement could have been eliminated. On the other hand, a number of conservatives on the Republican National Committee realized that the movement was bigger than any one person and that they would have to compromise to retain power within the party. Burch admitted to the committee that he cooperated with the "forced resignation" because "a group of substantial, loyal, hard working members of this Committee . . . felt this change was inevitable."[9] Their cautious willingness to accept the new chair further indicated their recognition that they could cooperate with moderates without being disloyal to the conservative cause.

Ray Bliss was perhaps the only person who could have evoked such a response from all factions of the party. Most Republicans knew and respected him because of the effective programs he had created in Ohio and his efficient technical skills. In fact, Goldwater had recommended Bliss as

RNC chair in 1962 to replace Thruston Morton, but Bliss had declined the position at that time. When the suggestion was made again in 1965, he agreed to take on the job as long as he had Goldwater's "full support in building a strong organization capable of winning Republican victories." Goldwater pledged his cooperation and assured "the devoted Americans" who had followed him that Bliss had always consulted all factions of the party in Ohio and would continue the fight "for what we believe in." Dean Burch also facilitated the transition by offering helpful suggestions and recommendations, some of which Bliss utilized.[10]

When Bliss began his tenure, the committee was financially in the black. This allowed him to concentrate from the start on his main goal: winning elections. A "nuts and bolts" man, he set out to rebuild the party organization at the local level and to unite all factions of the party. To that end, he constantly encouraged Republicans to field local, state, and national candidates, and he conducted statewide workshops across the country to create "vigorous and effective" party organizations at every level of the party structure. Utilizing methods similar to White's, Bliss attempted to exploit the financial and electoral potential of Goldwater's grassroots support. By cultivating attractive, dynamic candidates, by exploiting the important issues of the day, and by defining Republicanism in terms broad enough to satisfy everyone, Bliss hoped to build up new constituencies and retain old ones.[11]

Bliss's most important and most difficult task was to stop the feuding that had plagued GOP politics for the past two decades. Republicans of all varieties agreed that the factionalism had to end. From the liberal Smylie, who believed that a "winning Republican Party must include" supporters of Eisenhower, Taft, Goldwater, and Nixon, to the conservative Goldwater, who described the party as "a great tent" with room enough for all interpretive variations of the basic Republican philosophy, Republicans realized the value of the image, if not always the reality, of unity. Eisenhower saw "no need for a hyphenated term to describe the political convictions of the party" to which he belonged. Admitting that disagreements existed within the GOP, Gerald Ford and George Romney preferred to deemphasize the "minor" arguments of their compatriots and concentrate on the differences between the parties.[12]

Even assuming that much of the talk of unity was merely political rhetoric packaged to sell a new image, the reality of the situation demanded that all Republicans make an effort to get along. No matter how liberals and conservatives felt about one another, they realized the price of factionalism. Liberals resented what they believed conservatives had done to their party but recognized that the power of the right-wing constituency could no longer be ignored. Conservatives, embarrassed by the defeat but determined to retain their new power and position, concluded that they would have to make some accommodation with liberals and moderates. Each faction still believed that it represented true Republicans and continued to work behind the scenes to enhance its position in the party. Opposing factions also realized, however, that the national viability of the GOP required at least an outward appearance of unity.

The creation of the Republican Coordinating Committee was an important practical manifestation of this emphasis on unity. The committee was composed of the eleven members of the Joint Senate-House Republican Leadership Committee, the five living nominees for president, five representatives of the Republican Governors' Association, and the chair of the RNC. Designed to foster communication between party members, the group set up task forces to outline a common policy for all Republicans to draw upon in challenging their Democratic opponents. Although Eisenhower thought the proposal had merit, others did not. RNC members feared this additional challenge to their power, while former presidential candidate Alf Landon criticized the assumption that the party could "furnish the leadership" the country needed with "new committees and new conventions." Landon felt that GOP policy should emerge naturally from Republican lawmakers.[13]

Republican governors agreed with Landon. Forming a Republican Governors' Association, they boldly claimed the right to influence party policy because, they believed, "political power in the United States is most enduringly built where it starts—at the Court House and City Hall level—and moves up through the State Houses and the Congress to the White House itself." Practicing what they preached, the governors played a significant role in the effort to replace Dean Burch and, over the next years, demanded still greater influence over party matters.[14]

While these state leaders tried to consolidate their power within the party, Republican senators and representatives worked to hold their own against the Democrats and to refurbish their party's image. Illinois representative Paul Findley reminded his colleagues that, as the "only Republicans in national elective office," they had the responsibility to work together to provide "constructive and effective opposition" to the Johnson administration. The time for laying blame was past; Republicans needed to prepare for the future.[15]

In an attempt to invigorate the party, Republicans replaced Indianan Charles Halleck with younger former Michigan football star Gerald Ford as House minority leader. Although Ford won the approval of many, including former Halleck supporters, both liberals and conservatives disputed his effectiveness.[16] The change was more than cosmetic. Halleck was an Old Guard right-winger whose presence harkened back to the days when Robert Taft, Kenneth Wherry, and Joseph Martin ran conservative politics and dominated Congress. Some Republicans hoped that replacing Halleck would remove one more conservative stain from the GOP. They did not understand, however, that Halleck was part of an older brand of conservatism. The Goldwaterites had moved beyond the Old Guard; therefore, replacing Halleck with Ford would not, in the long run, injure the Right in 1965. Ford might not have been a Goldwaterite, but he was certainly no liberal.

Other Republicans believed that the party's problems were more deeply ingrained. California congressman Edgar Hiestand felt that the GOP's "greatest weakness" was its inability to " 'sell' Republicanism to the nation." House minority leader Ford agreed. In his view, the problem grew out of a "widespread, but erroneous, impression that Republicans have no constructive ideas." He made it a priority to combat that perception. Goldwater argued that there was some truth in that impression, however, and he urged Republicans to develop more positive programs. Republicans, aware that part of their image problem resulted from their poor relations with the media, created Operation Enlightenment to promote effective press relations.[17]

Eliminating the extremist blemish on the party was central to the new image Republicans tried to create. As a first step in this process, Republicans of all ideologies repudiated extremist organizations such as the John Birch Society. Significantly, party members recognized the power of the conservative constituency by not labeling all conservatives "extremists." Richard Nixon claimed that right-wing radicals had penetrated only the fringes of the Republican Party, and he distinguished them from mainstream conservatives. In a press conference, Congressman Melvin Laird insisted, as had conservatives at the time, that conservative delegates had not been responsible for the rude treatment of Nelson Rockefeller during the 1964 convention.[18]

The new Republican Coordinating Committee endorsed Chairman Bliss's statement denouncing right-wing radicals but distinguishing them from "patriotic and conscientious conservatives." In defense of Bliss's statement, Ford emphasized that only Republicans should control the GOP and that no outside group or faction should "determine policies for the party." He made it quite clear, however, that he was "in much more agreement with the conservative forces" in the country than with the liberals. This support did not comfort the hundreds of people who were John Birch Society members or who saw Bliss's statement as a general attack on conservatism.[19]

Conservatives also attempted to disassociate themselves from extremism in general and the John Birch Society in particular. Goldwater staffers finally joined other prominent conservatives and Republicans in repudiating what Kitchel called the "pseudo-conservative organizations of which the John Birch Society is the prime example." The *National Review* renewed its denunciation of the society by publishing a special section explaining why the organization was not really conservative. Increasingly frustrated by the narrow vision of society members, Buckley explained to one member that he was "perturb[ed]" by "the downright lunatic nature of Welch's pronouncements."[20] Although such actions did not immediately erase the perception of a link between conservatives and extremists, it indicated a growing maturity and sophistication within the movement.

Further mirroring the GOP as a whole, conservative groups worked to redefine conservatism in terms more acceptable to the general public. Many right-wingers realized that some of the more sweeping tenets of their basic faith would have to be moderated if the American public was to be won over to conservatism. The conservative notion that if given a clear choice, Americans would choose the Right had been refuted on 3 November. Consequently, conservatives sought ways to present a more attractive and compelling image to American voters. Goldwater argued that conservatives should offer a platform promoting the enhancement of the power of the states instead of concentrating, as usual, on simply reducing the power of the federal government.[21]

Although liberal and conservative Republicans talked a great deal about unity, moderation, and foregoing ideological labels, many continued working to further their particular brand of Republicanism. Goldwater's overwhelming defeat reinforced the conviction of some liberal Republicans that they should control the party. Overlooking the fact that Goldwater had received 27 million votes and ignoring the shifting political situation, these men and women waged an uphill battle against conservative domination of the party.

Numerous extraparty organizations sprang up, proudly emphasizing their moderate/liberal ties. These sometimes short- lived groups included the Ripon Society, the Committee to Support Moderate Republicans, the Republican Negro Assembly, the Committee to Support Forward-Looking Republicans, Republicans for Progress, and the Committee of '68. The Republican Citizens' Committee, which had been formed to broaden the Republican constituency following the 1960 campaign, fell apart after the 1964 election. Although it had always been in a precarious economic position, its financial situation deteriorated significantly in 1965. More importantly, as committee officer Elmer Anderson explained to secretary Joan Nelson, the group was "not having too much success in getting a program pinned down."[22]

Conservatives also began to look to the future. Although they had been "hauled through the furnace" of the 1964 campaign, Donald Lukens, president of the Young Republicans that year, and other Goldwater workers believed they had witnessed the beginning of the end of liberalism.[23] Consequently, they concentrated on how much they had accomplished in their first run for the White House and examined the situation of their movement in general and its place within the Republican Party structure. Over the next four years, the Right sought ways to retain its constituency, gain new converts, and consolidate power within the national political system. Although right-wing elements sometimes seemed to disappear from the scene, their seeming absence often hid calculating attempts to gain power.

Most importantly, conservatives insisted on maintaining their influence in the Republican Party. Most, wedded firmly to the two-party system, thought it essential to offer American people a viable alternative to liberalism rather than merely a Republican adaptation of the Democratic platform. Many agreed with Denison Kitchel that the Republican Party was "obviously the proper vehicle for the continuation of [conservatism]." Moreover, most right-wingers felt that the party remained, at least tenuously, under their control despite Goldwater's loss and Burch's ouster. Years later, Clifton White explained that the "conservatives won control of the party in 1964 but it took them fifteen years to find out what the hell to do with it."[24]

Responsible conservatives understood that the continuation of right-wing control of the GOP required a flexible attitude, a willingness to work with all factions of the party, and a sharp eye on potential liberal usurpers. Goldwater, William Miller, and even the editors of the *National Review* actively promoted a unified party. Disagreeing with "hard shells" in the conservative camp, Ronald Reagan believed that tactical compromise with liberals was acceptable and would ultimately benefit the Right.[25]

Their adoption of a less rigid stance did not mean that conservatives dropped their guard against a liberal counterattack. Although Reagan saw the need to work with liberal Republicans, he resented their willingness to "kiss off" Goldwater supporters and their demands that the party be returned to the establishment wing. Political theorist William Rusher kept a sharp eye on the Left and warned those on the Right not to let unity talk and their growing influence blind them to the threat of a liberal resurgence within the party. The liberal "plot to steal the GOP," according to Rusher, consisted of an attack on the conservative control of the Young Republicans and the Federation of Republican Women, important and influential party subsidiaries. Representative John Ashbrook warned fellow conservative representatives that they could no longer remain "shrinking violets" and let liberal Republicans speak for the party. Grassroots conservatives complained vehemently about what they viewed as poor treatment accorded right-wing Republicans by the national committee.[26]

In particular, many on the right targeted Ray Bliss as the troublemaker. Acutely sensitive to any threat to their position, conservatives reacted immediately to any sign that the chair did not favor them. Although Rusher thought Bliss was doing a good job of remaining neutral, some conservatives, including Rusher's *National Review* editors, complained that Bliss leaned left rather than right. Donald Lukens accused Bliss of deliberately depriving conservative candidates of campaign funds. By June 1965, the *National Review* reported that Bliss had "discreetly purged every living, breathing Goldwaterite from Republican National Headquarters." According to the journal, he also attempted to lobby for the nonconservative candidate at the Young Republican National Convention. All of this indicated to the editors "a basic anti-conservatism in the supposedly nonideological Mr. Bliss." Prophesying that the RNC chair would either have to find a policy satisfactory to the Right or end up with an empty Republican headquarters, the *National Review* warned Bliss that many Republicans cared more for their conservative principles than for the party.[27]

Underscoring that point, some conservatives advocated making conservatism, rather than Republicanism, the top priority. Frank Meyer, an influential *National Review* editor and contributor, cautioned conservatives not to lose sight of their most important goal—protecting and improving Western civilization—in their quest for political power. Of more practical significance, the Conservative Party of New York grew impressively during these years. Founded in 1962 to offer, according to its original press release, an alternative to the state GOP, which had "abandoned" Republican principles, the Conservative Party had withstood ridicule and financial trouble. Party chair David Jaquith maintained that party members' "unremitting effort" paid off in 1966 when they outpolled the Liberal Party and gained a "decisive position of political leverage."[28]

Of particular interest was the 1965 New York City mayoral race between Republican John Lindsay and Conservative Party candidate William F. Buckley, Jr. Running as a Republican, but with the endorsement of the Liberal Party of New York, Lindsay readily admitted that he was closer philosophically to Democrats than to Republicans. Buckley, who was only half serious about making the race, campaigned as much to emphasize conservatives' dissatisfaction with the New York GOP as to gain votes. He constantly reiterated that he was forced into a third-party candidacy because the "Republican designation" was not "available nowadays to anyone in the mainstream of Republican opinion." Although Lindsay won handily, Buckley received 340,000 votes, triple the previous Conservative showing.[29] More significant than the numbers was the fact that a well-known and generally respected political activist had chosen ideology over party.

The continued right-wing domination of the Young Republican National Federation provided another sign of conservative influence in party affairs. If liberal Republicans had doubted that the Young Republicans could have much impact on the national political scene, they were proven wrong by the Young Republicans' dedicated work during Goldwater's campaign. The realization that the youths could work effectively, combined with the gradual but heartening increase in the number of Republican youth, led to a renewed emphasis on organizing and utilizing them.[30] Moderate Republicans made a concerted effort to liberalize the Young Republican hierarchy at their conventions; after they failed, they then tried to minimize the importance of the Young Republicans.[31] Meanwhile, the RNC continued its creative exploitation of the Young Republicans, the College Republicans, and even the Teenage Republicans in its attempts to rebuild the party. Bliss developed a "soft-sell program titled Opportunities Unlimited" to attract "serious minded college students" and convince them "to take an interest in the unglamorous job of Party organization activities."[32]

Conservatives in the post-1964 world concentrated on the missionary work of converting and organizing new recruits. *New York Times* correspondent Donald Janson noted the growth of right-wing groups following the 1964 election. Goldwater's supporters, determined to exploit the potential of the 27 million votes he had received, sought to continue the momentum from the campaign by enlisting and training new conservatives.[33] Former Young Americans for Freedom leader Richard Viguerie expanded the grassroots fund-raising technique utilized during the campaign. Collecting names from such varied organizations as the American Economic Foundation, the Committee of One Million, and the newly formed, intellectually oriented Philadelphia Society, he created the first mailing list "containing most of the active Conservatives in the U.S." With the help of these lists, right-wing organizations not only expanded their memberships but also raised considerable sums of money.[34]

Goldwater and members of his postconvention staff also made a bid for the leadership of the movement through their Free Society Association (FSA). Incorporated in May 1965, the FSA was officially "organized exclusively for research, literary and educational purposes" and was intended to enhance Americans' understanding of constitutional principles, analyze public policy issues, and "demonstrate the various methods and approaches for dealing with such issues." On a more practical level, as the *National Review* editors pointed out, the FSA provided an organizational base for Goldwater and his staff "to thumb their noses at Mr. Bliss," who appeared not to want them at Republican headquarters. Bliss had ambiguous feelings about the new organization. Although he claimed not to worry about the new group as long as it supported the party, he expressed concern that it might be disunifying. The association, however, did not last long enough to cause much trouble. Due to lack of financial support and the declining influence of its organizers, the FSA disbanded in 1968.[35]

The American Conservative Union (ACU), a more broad-based and successful conservative organization, was officially launched in January 1965. Grounded in grassroots political activity, the ACU counted a number of Draft Goldwater Committee organizers among its founders. Early fund-raising appeals were sent to Goldwater contributors, emphasizing the need to maintain conservative control of the party and elect conservative candidates.[36] Aware that they were under close scrutiny by liberals waiting to pounce on any sign of weakness, the members of the ACU carefully disassociated themselves from anything resembling extremism. In fact, the group debated whether or not to establish a relationship with the John Birch Society at its first meeting. After much discussion, members agreed to adopt an unstated policy barring society members from sitting on the ACU board, and they decided to issue a statement denying any connection between the two bodies.[37]

The ACU initially experienced some internal difficulties, but by 1969 it had expanded its operations to include not only its own publication, *Battle Line*, but also the Conservative Victory Fund to help finance conservative candidates, the ACU Education and Research Foundation, and the National Journalism Center.[38] Fulfilling both its educational and political missions, the ACU regularly published a statistical scorecard of legislators' conservative voting records, which kept the right-wing public informed about what was happening in Washington and reminded legislators of their conservative constituency.

Conservatives also worked hard to build a following among the nation's youth. Although they denounced the manners, clothing, and attitudes of student demonstrators, many right-wingers believed that most young people were clean-cut, moral, and patriotic Americans who disdained the riots that disrupted classes and campuses. According to conservatives, the liberal press ignored upstanding young people; the right-wing press, on the other hand, made every effort to publicize the activities of this segment of the nation's youth, especially those fighting in Vietnam, and to encourage the growth of nonliberal youth groups.[39]

Considering the tenor of the times, a significant number of young conservative groups existed. Besides the various local committees, several national organizations played an influential role in fostering conservatism. Young Americans for Freedom struggled to check the radical trend on college campuses by holding public rallies in favor of Vietnam and by utilizing radical methods for conservative ends. For example, they took over a Students for a Democratic Society office to protest the hypocrisy of the society in supporting candidates and working within the political system while at the same time threatening to overthrow it. The YAF also created a forum to answer liberal challenges. Another more specialized conservative group was the World Youth Crusade for Freedom, formed by YAF official Tom Huston under the guidance of Marvin Liebman and with the support of conservative stalwarts such as Goldwater and Congressman Walter Judd. Before financial, tax, and personnel troubles forced it to disband, the group sent nine volunteers to several Asian countries to preach the virtues of capitalism and democracy.[40]

Some young conservatives attempted to gain supporters by pointing out the similarities between the position of the demonstrators and right-wing thought. Students, rebelling against the liberal establishment and its all-engulfing bureaucracy, shared conservatives' fear of "Big Brother" government and echoed libertarians in their appeals to "do your own thing" and their warnings not to "fold, spindle or mutilate." Right-wing young people on many campuses advocated the termination of the draft and the legalization of marijuana. Although many on the right disagreed with such positions, the young conservatives as a tiny minority were entitled, according to William Rusher, "to stress the arguments that work."[41]

The complaints of conservatives about the ever-expanding number of right-wing groups further indicated the maturation of the movement. These numerous organizations competed with each other for the limited time and money of grassroots conservatives. William Rusher complained in early 1965 about the "alarming proliferation of conservative fund appeals." Rusher worried that this trend would end up "emptying" conservatives' pockets and "disillusioning contributors." In addition, some on the right feared that such a large number of groups divided right-wingers just when they most needed to be united.[42] Obviously these people missed the irony of the situation: ten years earlier, such problems were inconceivable because the groups did not exist. Conservatives were now grappling with problems that accompanied the maturation of their movement.

Conservatives did not want to be seen as the screaming naysayers of pre-1964 days. Many thoughtful right-wingers learned from experiences in the Goldwater trenches that they could not afford to be narrow-minded, rigid, and obnoxious. Although some on the right complained that the movement had become "quiescent," others saw this period as a time of transition during which "profound changes" were taking place in the United States. In the process, the composition of the Right was also changing. Frank Meyer pointed out to his fellow *National Review* editors that the journal's readership consisted of a "great many less Neanderthals" and an increasing number of "intelligent and troubled people of varied formal persuasions."[43] The metamorphosis on the right led many Americans to assume mistakenly that the conservative movement was dead.

The actions of the Johnson administration both reinforced and ultimately undermined that assumption. As hundreds of pieces of liberal legislation sped through Congress, it certainly appeared that the Republican Party in general and its conservative wing in particular could not mount an effective opposition, much less come up with their own program. Appearances, however, were deceiving. The torrent of Great Society legislation combined with the escalation of the war in Indochina and growing tensions over the civil rights movement ultimately challenged Americans' ideas about their society and caused them to see conservatism in a new light.

In early 1965, however, liberalism reigned and all eyes were on the White House. Johnson, realizing that he had only a limited time before his mandate ran out, bombarded Congress with legislation aimed at creating the Great Society. Medicare/Medicaid, federal aid to education, the Voting Rights Act, housing legislation, antipoverty and Appalachian development programs passed through Congress with little or no trouble. Although conservatives warned that these programs would result in inflation and an expanded federal bureaucracy, their pleas mainly fell on deaf ears. Republicans in Congress faltered in their efforts to slow the pace of liberal reform and either endorsed the programs or merely stood on the sidelines prophesying doom.[44]

Conservatives and Republicans generally supported LBJ's foreign policy. His escalation of the war in Southeast Asia by committing a significant number of U.S. troops met with the approval of the GOP, which favored a hard-line policy against communism. Although they accepted LBJ's overall goal, however, Republicans did not, in Ford's words, "endorse his day to day handling of the situation." Many Republicans agreed with Goldwater that Johnson should stop playing general and let the members of the military do their jobs.[45] Complaining that the president was not prosecuting the war forcefully enough to win, conservative Republicans found themselves in the unique position of defending an internationalist policy to increasingly isolationist Democrats. Believing that the United States' security and reputation required that the government take a tough stance against communism wherever it appeared, Republicans warned against getting "bogged down" in a land war and pushed Johnson to resolve the situation as quickly as possible by utilizing the full extent of U.S. air power.[46]

Republicans also disliked the way the Johnson administration handled the increasing disorder and violence of protest movements. To them, Johnson's Civil Rights Act appeared only to have stirred things up further. The nonviolent demonstrations of civil rights workers met with growing violence in the South. Thousands of black and white young people working to register southern voters in the Mississippi Summer Freedom Project faced arrests, beatings, and shootings. At least three workers were murdered during the summer of 1964. Increasingly, the Student Nonviolent Coordinating Committee questioned the wisdom of employing a nonviolent strategy and began using militant Black Power slogans. In the

North, protests exploded into urban riots that seemed to become an annual tradition.

Meanwhile, white students involved in the Mississippi project returned
to their schools radicalized by their experiences in the South and ready to
apply new insights and tactics to their growing critique of universities and
other institutions. Despite ambiguous goals and lack of organization, student demonstrations symbolized the disrespect for authority and chaos
that threatened to destroy everything conservatives believed in. Instead of
treating protesters as criminals as the Right advocated, liberals in government blamed society, exonerated the lawbreakers, and castigated the
police.[47]

The students' counterculture habits appalled conservatives as much as,
if not more than, their political activities. Right-wingers disliked but could
ignore rock and roll, men's long hair, and love beads. They found the
sexual revolution much harder to accept. "The Pill," used widely after the
early 1960s, eliminated the fear of pregnancy, thus opening the door for
freer sexual relations. The widespread use of drugs further encouraged
the shedding of inhibitions and the development of alternative life-styles.
Desiring to "tune in, turn on, and drop out," young people challenged the
basic values of most Americans, especially conservatives. Many people,
shocked by scenes from Haight Ashbury and college campuses, began to
reassess the traditionalist ideas of Goldwater that they had found old-
fashioned only a few years earlier.[48]

By 1966, middle-class and ethnic whites appeared restive and resentful
of a liberal government that taxed them to support apparently ungrateful
and dangerous people. The war in Vietnam required more and more
troops but yielded few concrete results. LBJ's ability to honor his promise to produce both guns and butter seemed questionable, especially in
light of his growing credibility gap. The 1965 state and local elections
returned a majority of Democrats, but polls indicated slight gains for the
Republicans.[49]

Republicans thus looked toward the 1966 elections with the renewed
hope of proving that they were still a viable national party. Bliss and his
staff worked overtime to ensure that dynamic young candidates challenged Democrats and had solid party structures to support them. Concentrating on the South, the Midwest, and major cities, the GOP counted
on the growing concern over Vietnam, inflation, and the burgeoning federal bureaucracy to help them regain power in Congress. LBJ and his aides
realized that they were confronted with not only serious political issues but

also an organized Republican opposition. They also attributed losses at the polls to traditional off-year slippage and the weakening of the party by southern defections.[50]

Democrats did not expect in 1966 the extent of Republican gains so soon after LBJ's landslide victory. A record 56.7 million Americans voted in the off-year contests, which secured Republicans forty-seven additional seats in the House, three more seats in the Senate, and eight new governorships. Even though the election did not give the GOP a majority in either house, it certainly put Republicans in a stronger position to dam up the flood of Great Society legislation. *U.S. News and World Report* announced that "the big bash" was over. Although Ray Bliss credited the victory to a "combination of issues and the right candidates and effective organization," he also believed that the desire for a real two-party system was one of the most important factors in the victory. Although at least a few Democrats blamed their losses on "backlash," perhaps a more realistic assessment of the election returns is that voters simply wanted to return to the political center.[51]

Conservatives, however, did not see it that way. Exulting in the victories of new conservative governors—Claude Kirk in Florida, Paul Laxalt in Nevada, John Williams in Arizona, and Ronald Reagan in California—the Right felt vindicated for 1964 and more confident of its position within the party. The ACU reported that 133 of the 153 House candidates it had recommended won, while only 31 of the 87 candidates endorsed by the liberal Ripon Society were elected. A secondary result of these victories was the increasing influence that conservatives gained in the Republican Governors' Association and Congress.[52] Although these gains certainly did not indicate that conservatives had unanimous support from all factions of the party, they did show that despite the humiliating defeat of 1964, the Right still had popular support and an effective organization.

The years from 1964 to 1966 had witnessed the maturation and transformation of the conservative movement and the deepening of its hold on the Republican Party. As the rest of the GOP reflected on the defeat of 1964, conservatives sought to ensure that it never happened again by preaching and practicing unity and by rebuilding the party. Right-wingers also attempted to work with other factions of the GOP and strengthened their base of support by establishing numerous extraparty groups. They exorcised the extremist demon from the movement without surrendering their principles. The Right looked on 1964 not as a defeat but rather as a solid beginning for its movement.

7

VICTORY?

Republicans, buoyed by their victories in 1966, looked eagerly toward the 1968 presidential campaign. Anxious to take advantage of the shifting circumstances of the late 1960s and the slow but steady increase in party registrants, they utilized their momentum to develop a strong foundation for 1968. Bliss traveled across the country presenting workshops on how to build support in urban and suburban areas. He encouraged Republican groups to coordinate their efforts, and he recruited qualified candidates on the precinct level. Devoted to making the party "a long range effective force in this country," Bliss focused particularly on preparing local officials and candidates in the hopes that the party could win from the bottom up. Congressional Republican leaders, also energized by the election, worked on presenting positive alternatives and forming a united opposition to the Democratic administration.[1]

The Republican national chair also continued to emphasize the importance of party unity, which became even more crucial as competition for the 1968 presidential nomination intensified. In addition to Bliss, party leaders such as House Campaign Committee chair Melvin Laird, House minority leader Gerald Ford, former president Dwight Eisenhower, and Eisenhower's interior secretary Fred Seaton proudly acclaimed the cohesiveness and determination of the party as 1968 approached.[2] Leading Republicans, with ever fresh memories of the factionalism that had doomed the party in 1964, announced to the media and party workers that ideological labels were a thing of the past. Even liberal Ripon Society members believed that it was time to "bridge the ideological gap" by recognizing that conservatives were focusing on areas of agreement and by encouraging activists of both factions to cooperate with each other. Republicans, the editors of the society's journal stressed, should seek "unity through creativity rather than through mere accommodation."[3]

As the various factions pursued areas of agreement, most Republicans expected a moderate candidate to be nominated in 1968. Although some conservatives took exception, others felt the nomination of a moderate was necessary for the party's survival. Michigan governor George Romney set the pace as the early front-runner. The former president of American Motors had been considered for the nomination in 1964 but had decided to run for governor instead. His "split the ticket" campaign in 1964 combined with his close relationship with Rockefeller and his performance as governor alienated many conservatives and earned him a reputation as a moderate. A blunt, sincere man, Romney benefited from the guidance and encouragement of Eisenhower.[4]

Romney was ill-prepared for the constant scrutiny he received as the first formal candidate, however, and as the primary season began, his candidacy fell apart. Although he had worked to pacify lingering conservative animosity and even Goldwater said he could support him, Romney's contradictory and vacillating statements undermined his legitimacy as a candidate. The most famous of these also indicated the impact of the media on his campaign. On a local Detroit television talk show, Romney claimed that he "had the greatest brainwashing that anybody can get when you go over to Vietnam." No one attached much significance to his statement until the *New York Times* reported it almost a week later; the furor that then developed severely weakened Romney's campaign. Moreover, rumors flew that Romney was just a stalking horse for Rockefeller, who allegedly paid for much of the Michigan governor's campaign and talked him out of quitting before the actual primary took place.[5]

The disintegration of Romney's candidacy left the field open for Richard Nixon. The former vice president realized soon after the 1964 election that he wanted the 1968 nomination but that it would be worthless unless the party was rebuilt and reunified. Working under that assumption, Nixon vigorously played the postelection role of unifier and regular party man. As the media praised him and the *Indianapolis News* commended his "needed voice of sanity," Nixon chastised those who had ignored Goldwater in 1964 and stressed that both Left and Right should have a voice in party politics to allow the party to broaden "its reservoir of intellectual talent." Goldwater, grateful for Nixon's unswerving support, publicly thanked him at the first RNC meeting following the election and promised his assistance if Nixon should ever want to utilize his gratitude "for selfish reasons." Although years later Goldwater claimed that everything Nixon had ever done was "for selfish reasons," in the mid-1960s his early statement of support was a boon to the budding Nixon campaign and a source of worry to right-wingers who favored a more avowedly conservative candidate.[6]

Nixon, knowing that he could not win the nomination without conservative support, set out to woo the Right even before he announced his candidacy. He invited right-wing intellectuals to private meetings to discuss the political situation. In addition, he gave speeches advocating a hard-line stance on Vietnam and an antistatist domestic policy, and he willingly campaigned for conservative candidates during the 1966 campaign. He hired Patrick Buchanan, a staunch conservative, as a speechwriter to give his words the proper right-wing flavor.[7] Nixon paid particular attention to courting southern conservatives, who had proven so important to Goldwater.

Right-wingers expressed ambiguous feelings about Nixon. Very few conservatives trusted him and many suspected that he had an ulterior motive behind every move, but many, especially regular party members, supported him out of loyalty for his actions in 1964 or because they believed he was the only "electable" choice. Ranging from novelist Taylor Caldwell to China Lobby member Anna Chennault to *National Review* editor Frank Meyer, Nixon's conservative supporters helped to convince others that he was the best challenger to any of the Democratic contenders. Both Nixon and the Right realized that they needed each other—Nixon, if he wanted to be elected, and the Right, if members wanted to increase their influence in the party.[8]

Nixon also needed support from more moderate elements of the party. Eisenhower's support was unstinting and, unlike that of 1960, unambiguous. Going so far as to break personal precedent, he endorsed Nixon before the convention. Even Eisenhower's friend, financier William Robinson, who had a rather "low" opinion of Nixon, expressed his "great admiration" for the way in which Nixon conducted his "pre-convention campaign." Although Nixon certainly did not evoke the enthusiasm among young people that Goldwater and Reagan did, he did have support among the Young Republicans and at least 7,000 members of the National Youth for Nixon organization. Moreover, the *National Review* noted that the Nixon for President Committee had a "galaxy of old-line Republican notables on the letterhead."[9]

Nixon's effective courting of both the right and center factions of his party put him in a good position to win the nomination at the convention in Miami Beach. In fact, Nixon had, in the disapproving words of William Rusher, "with calipers and footrule" located the "exact center" of the party and "occupied it." By staking out the middle ground and leaning slightly to the right, Nixon made his competitors seem extremist and un-reasonable. Moreover, by spending the first six months of 1967 traveling overseas visiting heads of state, Nixon reinvoked memories of his past diplomatic service.[10] His only real problem was the loser image that haunted him following his defeats in 1960 and 1962. Entering the primaries with very little competition, he won enough delegates to make him the front-runner going into the convention, which helped erase the loser image.

Ironically, despite his primary victories and front-runner status, Nixon's campaign faced its most serious challenges as the convention drew nearer. Overconfidence was one danger, but more significant were the last-minute candidacies of two men who inspired more emotion and enthusiasm than Nixon. Although they had little chance of depriving him of the nomination, they were a threat to the perception of unity and consensus he had nurtured. Their candidacies had the potential to turn the convention into a free-for-all.

Nelson Rockefeller, Nixon's perennial nemesis, charged in from the Left. Supporting Romney long after everyone else gave up, Rockefeller announced in March his decision to stay out of the race. But again his actions belied his words as he hired advisers and speechwriters and began to set up an organization. He was therefore ready when the riots following Martin Luther King, Jr.'s, assassination and the demonstrations on college campuses convinced him that he was needed. In late April 1968, he formally entered the race. He had waited too long, however, and had changed his mind too often to be able to unite the party behind him. His vacillation had already alienated many of his liberal supporters, just as his actions in 1964 had irritated conservatives. His only possible strategy in 1968, therefore, was to play up Nixon's loser image. To that end, he published polls showing that he could gain more votes than Nixon against possible Democratic candidates. In this way, Rockefeller hoped to raise enough doubt to stop Nixon on the first ballot. He could then await a call from a deadlocked convention.[11] His candidacy was based on a faint hope that depended on many variables: the polls, which contradicted one another; the public, which was never *that* enthusiastic; and the success of fellow candidate Ronald Reagan, which proved to be too little too late.

Reagan's candidacy, though not strong enough to win the nomination or to help Rockefeller, gave Nixon cause for alarm and provided ample evidence of the growing power of the conservative wing of the party. Reagan had made his debut as a conservative spokesperson in a highly acclaimed speech supporting Goldwater in 1964. Almost immediately, conservatives had encouraged him to run for the governorship of California. Espousing ideals as conservative as Goldwater's but presenting them in a more attractive form, Reagan kept the California party united as he easily won his race by a large margin.[12]

Talk of a Reagan presidency began soon after his gubernatorial victory. The *Houston Post* reported that Reagan represented "a hope for the future" for right-wingers who saw him as a "conservative with enough mass appeal to win a national election." Indeed, due in part to his movie career, a November 1966 Gallup poll showed that 75 percent of Americans recognized him and that 54 percent had a favorable impression. With support from prominent public figures like John Wayne, Reagan was a strong contender despite his lack of administrative and political experience.[13]

Reagan delayed becoming a formal candidate for the nomination, however, because he had pledged during his 1966 gubernatorial campaign that he would not enter the race in 1968. As a result, although he traveled around the country making appearances and articulating his positions on the important issues of the day, his constituents were never certain whether or not he would shed his favorite son status to become a real candidate. Following a strategy similar to Rockefeller's, Reagan strategists, principally Thomas Reed and F. Clifton White, planned on building enough support to stop Nixon on the first ballot and to take the nomination from him on subsequent tallies.[14]

Reagan thus complicated the situation for some Republican conservatives. F. Clifton White and William Rusher eagerly and consistently supported his candidacy, but others delayed giving an endorsement. Many, like Barry Goldwater and William F. Buckley, Jr., felt that Reagan needed time to mature as a politician. They felt his inexperience would hurt him in the election. Moreover, Reagan's "half-hearted effort," in Goldwater's words, threatened to accomplish for Rockefeller what he could not do for himself: deadlock the convention and allow the New York governor to run off with the nomination. Frank Meyer agreed, complaining that the "urgent necessity of stopping Rockefeller" was being forgotten in the rush of activity in both the Nixon and Reagan camps.[15] The professional political conservatives were determined not to be carried away by emotion as they had been in 1964. As a result, although many of the delegates believed in Reagan wholeheartedly, they supported Nixon because they thought he could win.

This ambiguity posed a serious problem for Nixon. Having won the primaries, he still needed to make certain that he had the support of southern conservatives at the convention. The South played a crucial role in the nomination process in 1968. The GOP's Operation Dixie had expanded party membership south of the Mason-Dixon line. By 1968, the region controlled 26.7 percent of the voting strength at the convention, or 356 votes, more than half the number necessary for nomination. Southern political leaders realized that these numbers afforded them a certain amount of leverage. They had committed to Goldwater early in 1964 and thus had lost their bargaining power; they would not make the same mistake again. As a result, they held off, allowing the candidates to woo them before they made any final decisions. Since many delegates were torn between the candidates, this strategy also gave them time to make up their minds.[16]

Southern Republicans considered themselves closer to Reagan philosophically. His narrow view of the power of the federal government and his outspoken antipathy for demonstrators of all varieties appealed to them. In early caucuses, many state delegations wanted to vote for him, but they were concerned about his continued refusal to announce his candidacy. They did not intend to waste their newfound power on someone who was not going to go all the way. This difficulty became most apparent in a series of meetings with the southern delegations that the presidential contenders held in May 1968. Reagan gave an unusually poor performance followed by a firm denial of his intention to run. Reagan's strategy had been to declare his candidacy at the last minute to delay breaking his 1966 pledge not to run in 1968 and to avoid any unfavorable polls. It was a mistake that ultimately doomed any chance of holding off Nixon.[17]

Nixon had a more positive experience during his meeting with southern delegates. Although he did not fathom the depth of southern support for Reagan, he did recognize that a problem existed. As a result, he redoubled efforts to convince southern delegates that he was the man who could win the election. He assured them that he did not support busing as a form of integration, that he had supported the open housing bill only as a political expedient, and that he was still a firm anticommunist. Most significantly, he convinced South Carolina senator Strom Thurmond that he could win.[18]

The importance of Thurmond's support cannot be overemphasized. Thurmond had led the Dixiecrats out of the Democratic Party in 1948 and had fought against integration his entire political career; he therefore had a solid reputation with southerners. He was more than a simple segregationist, however. Unlike some southerners who accepted federal money and interference in all but racial matters, Thurmond despised the increase in federal power almost as much as he hated communists. He had switched party allegiances in 1964 and worked hard for Goldwater. In 1968, although he felt closer philosophically to Reagan, he believed, as he told countless audiences across the South, that "a vote for Reagan is a vote for Rockefeller." Thurmond's support proved instrumental in winning over the South Carolina delegation and in keeping many of the other southern delegations firmly behind Nixon.[19]

By the time of the convention, Nixon had thus covered all bases. He believed that he had solid backing in the South and enough support in the West and border states to balance whatever he might lose in the Northeast. All he had to do was to quell ideological passions and prevent breakaway delegates from starting a hemorrhage.

Reagan, however, was attempting to undermine these efforts. He finally came out as a formal candidate on the Monday of the convention. He spent most of his time visiting delegations trying to secure votes by convincing people that Nixon could be stopped. Concentrating on southern delegations, Reagan found the situation frustrating because many states followed the unit rule, which meant that everyone voted the way the majority wanted on the first ballot. Reagan discovered that he was too late to change the position of most of these groups. Many of the delegates' hearts were with him, but their votes went to Nixon.[20]

For a brief period, the issue of the vice presidency nearly provided Reagan with the break he needed to change the flow of events. Southerners were very concerned that Nixon might choose a northern liberal to balance the ticket. Early in the week, Nixon had assured southern political leaders that he would not choose anyone who would "divide the party." Thurmond and others took this to mean that he would not tap someone unacceptable to the South. The situation appeared to be under control until Wednesday evening, when the *Miami Herald* ran a story that Nixon planned to nominate Oregon senator Mark Hatfield, a well-known liberal, as his running mate. Reagan's campaign staff wasted no time in telling delegates that Nixon was going to betray the South. Frantic, Nixon supporters played "put-up-or-shut-up" politics, offering to bet their fellow delegates that the story was wrong. The tactic worked. When the roll call took place, the southern delegations fell in line for Nixon, who won the nomination with almost 30 votes to spare.[21]

With victory in hand, Nixon continued to play up to the southern delegates concerning the vice presidency. Although Nixon had already decided on Maryland governor Spiro Agnew, he invited various groups to his suite to discuss the matter so that important political leaders, particularly Thurmond, would think they had a say in the decision. Nixon listened to various suggestions before introducing Agnew's name himself. Once Nixon ascertained that Agnew would be acceptable to Thurmond and the South, the decision was announced. The fact that Nixon felt it necessary to use this subterfuge was in itself an indication of the power held by southern conservatives. Nixon realized that he needed their continued support to win the election. Moreover, the choice of Agnew further revealed Nixon's recognition of the increasing number of conservative voters. Agnew, who had run for office in 1966 as a Rockefeller liberal, had transformed himself into a tough law-and-order advocate after the riots following King's assassination.[22]

Nixon's victory over Reagan did not mean that right-wingers surrendered their influence or abandoned their conviction that conservatism represented the future of the party. In fact, the Right played a crucial role in the campaigns of all of the major contenders for the nomination. Since right-wing pressure ensured that Rockefeller had no real chance of winning, the main battle ensued between conservatives supporting Nixon and those backing Reagan. Even more significantly, the two groups fought over the conservative southern delegations, which had been crucial to the nomination of Goldwater in 1964.[23]

Both Reagan and Nixon, in their own ways, were heirs to Goldwater's legacy. With his more eloquent speeches echoing Goldwater's themes in *The Conscience of a Conservative*, Reagan won the hearts and minds of many conservative Republicans. Nixon, with years of national political experience, received the votes of Republican conservatives. On the other hand, although he was a centrist rather than a conservative, Nixon "spoke conservatively" enough to win the respect of Reagan supporters such as Donald Lukens, who realized that the candidate emphasized many of the themes Goldwater had advocated during his campaign. Moreover, Nixon's search for the "center" had always been conducted from the Right. He moved left when he believed it was necessary to build coalitions or to achieve broader goals, but the shift was usually temporary and the extent of the shift was usually quite limited. Clearly, he felt most at home on the right side of the middle of the road.

In addition, Nixon recognized the utility of the organization White had created from 1960 to 1964, and he attempted to emulate it. Although Reagan won White's loyalty, Nixon employed his techniques and many of his ex-coworkers, including Draft Goldwater Committee chair Peter O'Donnell, Finance Committee member Jeremiah Milbank, Jr., and head of field operations Richard Kleindienst. White, who had delayed Reagan's campaign until 1967 because of Reagan's position as governor, was forced to watch as Nixon used his programs to get elected.[24]

In the end, then, the competition between Reagan and Nixon did not represent a contest between conservatism and liberalism; rather, it was a battle between different types of conservatives. Reagan had the support of the grass roots, but Nixon had the backing of conservative political leaders, which was enough in 1968. In fact, at the time, few Republicans recognized the extent of the Right's role in deciding the nomination of 1968. It would be years before the depth of conservative control of the GOP was realized and even longer before members of the grass roots would be able to make their preferences known and their power felt. The fact that the right wing could wield such influence without the dramatics of 1964 indicated its maturity as a movement and the party's perhaps unconscious recognition of its power.

In the meantime, the turbulent events of 1968 made Nixon's election and his conservative proposals more tenable. First, shocking developments occurred in Vietnam. In January, the North Vietnamese mounted the Tet Offensive. In a surprise move, the Vietcong and the North Vietnamese attacked cities throughout the south, including Saigon. Before they were beaten back by American and South Vietnamese troops, the enemy was photographed even within the confines of the U.S. embassy. Shocked Americans questioned what they had been told about the war. They were willing to accept deaths in a fight they thought they were winning, but they were less amenable to throwing away young people's lives when the cause seemed to be lost. Many questioned the wisdom and strategy of the war.[25]

Conservatives were especially frustrated by the offensive. For years, they had been pressuring Johnson to "fight or get out" of Vietnam. The public's reaction to the offensive seemed to validate their argument. Either the military should be allowed to use its full firepower potential, or the entire war should be abandoned. Moreover, since Americans found it difficult to believe that a developing country could outfight the United States, the conservatives' argument that Johnson was restraining military leaders gained credence.

Right-wingers were divided over which option they preferred, however. *National Review* editors argued that driving back the Tet Offensive "constitut[ed] possibly the longest step forward . . . in the entire war." This was obviously the time to continue the drive into North Vietnam. John Birch Society members disagreed; they did not see any positive results of the battle. To them, Tet further illustrated the uselessness of the "disastrous defensive strategy" Americans had been ordered to use. Since they foresaw no change in policy, they argued that abandonment was the best option. In any case, they insisted, something must be done.[26]

Death in a battle zone was one thing; murder in American cities was something else. The assassinations of Martin Luther King, Jr., in April and Robert Kennedy in June made people wonder about their own safety. The riots that followed King's murder intensified Americans' fears that they were not even secure on their own streets and in their own homes. During the week after King's death, ghettos in 125 cities exploded in frustration and anger. Federal troops protected the White House, and the army was called in to calm violence in Chicago and Baltimore.[27]

The violence on college campuses was also becoming all too commonplace. In April 1968, a student protest at Columbia University escalated when a group of white and black militants seized several university buildings and held them for over a week before the police removed them, in some cases brutally. Although the students ended up in jail, they had managed to close down the university. On other campuses across the country in the following months, similar scenarios developed as the New Left became more confrontational. Working-class police and blue-collar television viewers found the spectacle of militant college students puzzling. Blue-collar workers who could not afford to send their children to college, much less to Ivy League schools, saw these demonstrators as spoiled students wasting their opportunities. Class resentments accounted at least partly for the roughness with which the students were handled and the antipathy with which they were viewed.[28]

The inability of working-class Americans to send their children to college was just one indication that the post-1945 economic prosperity was beginning to break down. LBJ had promised that he could win the war on poverty and the war in Indochina without placing too much strain on the American economy. Although the situation seemed stable during the early part of the decade, signs of trouble had emerged by 1968, including a growing trade deficit, volatile international financial markets, and rising inflation. Politicians complained about the escalating cost of living until LBJ agreed to a 10 percent income tax increase, which economists believed would cool off the overheated economy. Many Americans concluded that they were paying more taxes so that welfare recipients could have bigger checks. In their view, the higher taxes went directly into the pockets of those who were threatening to burn down the cities and increasing the violence on the streets. This analysis, although simplistic, seemed reasonable to people eager to see the interconnections between taxes, race, and law and order.[29]

What the middle- and working-class public left out of the equation was Vietnam, which was costing a great deal more in dollars, lives, and political capital than the Johnson administration had anticipated. The administration had expected the war to be easily winnable, but it refused to follow Johnson's plan. The Tet Offensive might not have been a military victory for the North Vietnamese, but it was certainly a psychological one. For the first time, the American public took a good look at U.S. involvement in the conflict and did not like what they saw. While some wanted to cut American losses and pull out, others doubled their determination to win.

The mounting uncertainty and frustration led to a change in political perceptions and priorities. The appeals Johnson had made in 1964 for the creation of a Great Society seemed less attractive in 1968, and the simplistic answers of Goldwater appeared more appropriate. Goldwater seemed much less foolish in 1968 in pointing out that the country was rushing into a "morass of indecision, weakness and bankruptcy." Moreover, conservatives benefited from the "revolt," as one Michigan constituent put it, of the "people who are paying the taxes and bearing the brunt of inflation."[30]

Conservatives agreed that the country faced a serious danger that the "tired formulas of liberalism" could not solve. Comparing the events of the spring of 1968 to the American Civil War, conservatives braced themselves for revolution. They worried that the American people might ignore the signs and prefer to "sleep through" this second civil war. It seemed clear to the Right that the American system was in need of an overhaul, that the problems could not be solved by implementing more civil rights legislation or antipoverty programs. The "crisis," Frank Meyer explained, resulted from "the corrosion of national morale." Meyer held out the hope, however, that the necessary "national renewal" would emerge from the "crucible of crisis." To conservatives who finally saw their ideas being taken seriously by segments of the American public, that possibility seemed very real.[31]

Johnson's domestic and international problems undermined the Democratic coalition that had sustained the party since 1936. As early as 1966, liberal intellectuals had warned their colleagues that success often eroded the will and need to reform. The New Deal coalition, they predicted, was in the process of breaking apart. The American public, tired of racial problems, welfare programs, and continuous warfare, wanted a change.[32] The beleaguered Johnson, ever the politician, had come to the same conclusion. In March 1968, he stunned the nation by withdrawing from the race, leaving the Democratic nomination open.

Johnson's withdrawal did not save the Democratic Party from destroying itself. Since Johnson had been in power, he received much of the blame for the nation's problems, but he was not the only object of popular resentments. The overwhelmingly Democratic Congress that had appropriated the money and raised the taxes also suffered as the American public turned against the Great Society and questioned the war. Rather than working together to use what support they still had to build a new coalition, Democrats squabbled over the nomination and blamed one another for the problems.

This party cannibalism plagued the Democratic National Convention in Chicago. As prowar and antiwar candidates fought each other inside the convention hall, Chicago police battled protesters in the streets while Americans watched the televised turbulence in horror. Outside, even bystanders and journalists became objects of police violence. Chicago mayor Richard Daley cordoned off the convention center with barbed wire and made certain that plenty of law enforcement officers were always on hand. In fact, most of the time, police outnumbered demonstrators. Delegates inside could smell the tear gas while they watched what was later termed a "police riot" on television. Vice President Hubert Humphrey, who had impeccable liberal credentials but who favored continuing the Vietnam

War, waged a battle against the leading antiwar contender, Minnesota senator Eugene McCarthy. Humphrey won the nomination, but many wondered if his success had been worth the price.[33]

While Humphrey and the Democrats represented Nixon's major competition, the wild card in the race was Independent Party candidate George Wallace, former governor of Alabama. Wallace first entered the national spotlight in 1963 when he "stood in the schoolhouse door" to prevent the integration of the University of Alabama. He astonished and frightened Democrats and Republicans in 1964 when he entered several northern primaries and won a significant number of votes. In the wake of Tet, escalating prices, riots, and the Chicago convention, Wallace again threatened to pick up the votes of the discontented, frustrated, and angry. His simple solutions and blunt language appealed to people who were tired of the same old rhetoric and frightened by the turbulence around them.[34]

Wallace was a Democrat, but his philosophy was more akin to that of conservative Republicans, especially in regard to individualism and states' rights. However, significant differences did exist, as worried conservatives pointed out in an effort to stop Wallace from befouling the conservative image once more with the taint of extremism. John Ashbrook, in an ACU report, contended that Wallace was a racist rather than a true states' rights advocate because he gladly accepted federal interference when it was economically advantageous but rejected federal intrusions involving civil rights issues. Frank Meyer classified Wallace as a populist rather than a conservative. Explaining that not all strands of antiliberal thought were necessarily good, Meyer condemned populism for being "in its own way as alien to the American conservative conception of constitutional republican government as is liberalism." Viewing Wallace as an "impostor" and a "dangerous" man, Buckley resented his "abuse of the rhetoric and analysis of conservatism for ends that are wholly individual." Ford worried that Wallace would siphon off enough votes to prevent the election of a majority president.[35] Conservatives disagreed vehemently on Wallace's intentions and goals, but most recognized, as did Democrats, that he would cost Republicans more votes than Democrats.

Nixon, especially, was aware of Wallace's potential impact. Relying on what one southern Republican called the "Holy Trinity" of conservatism —Barry Goldwater, Strom Thurmond, and John Tower—Nixon was able to retain his southern support.[36] Not wanting to concede the entire South to Wallace, Nixon pulled out all the stops to win the border states and the Carolinas. Encouraging voters "not to waste your vote," Nixon captured all but the five states of the Deep South.

In large part, Nixon was able to accomplish this because of the support he had received during the fall campaign from conservatives. The endorsement of prominent right-wingers such as Goldwater, Buckley, and Clare Booth Luce was crucial in convincing the public that Nixon was the conservative candidate. More importantly, Nixon won the support of people who worked for Reagan before the convention. People such as William Rusher and Marvin Liebman recognized that Nixon was, according to Rusher, "the candidate of a strictly and highly conservative bloc." Even Reagan backers who did not trust Nixon's conservatism at least trusted the people who backed him. Moreover, Nixon had depended so heavily on the Right for his nomination that many conservatives assumed that he must be, "within the limits of his inherently ambiguous personality," a conservative. As a result, conservatives viewed him as preferable to all other candidates.[37]

Although Wallace was a problem, Humphrey was the real enemy. Obliged to support the administration he had been part of, Humphrey nevertheless distanced himself enough to win the endorsement of many liberal intellectuals and doves who were much more comfortable with him than with his competitors. This distancing, combined with last-minute talk before the election of negotiations to end the war, increased public support for Humphrey and exacerbated Republican fears of a repeat of 1960.

Although Nixon carried all but eighteen states, beating Humphrey by an electoral margin of 301 to 191, the popular vote indicated that it was a much closer race. The GOP realized a net gain of five senators, four congressmen, and five governors but did not secure a majority in either house. Despite this lack of a popular or congressional mandate, Nixon and Republicans in general still found victory sweet. After all, just four years after being overwhelmed in the Johnson landslide, Republicans had managed to defeat LBJ and his successor and put a moderately conservative man in the White House. The return of Goldwater to the Senate as well as the election of four new conservative congressmen further heartened the Right.

In fact, 1968 was an important year in the evolution of the Right's role in the GOP. Although some people wanted to read them out of the party after the 1964 disaster, conservatives learned from their mistakes and refused to give up their power base. Their behavior during the 1968 nomination process exemplified this determination. Refusing to be carried away by emotion, they pursued a successful strategy in a bid to back the most ideologically acceptable candidate who could win. For many, that candidate was Nixon; for others, it was Reagan. In either case, conservatives made important tactical decisions and played key roles in the campaign. No longer outsiders in their own party, conservatives now held the party machinery in their hands.

Although Nixon won the nomination, Reagan was crucial to the continued growth of the conservative movement, which, without a legitimate figure to articulate its philosophy, would have risked being saddled with the extremist label again. Reagan, who possessed all of Goldwater's good points but none of his faults, believed deeply in the principles of conservatism, communicated them in a reasonable manner, and knew when to compromise with moderates. He was a master of the soft sell. Although he did not win the nomination in 1968, the loyalty he engendered among delegates hinted of the strength he would have in future years.

Although Nixon's victory and Reagan's emergence were certainly important, they took on added significance in the context of the changing circumstances of the country. As cities burned and young people fought with the police, Americans saw their past way of life slipping away. Anger and frustration at the politically awakening minorities and at the government's seeming unwillingness to condemn protesters and troublemakers had caused many white, middle-class citizens to reexamine their faith in Johnson's liberal policies. As political scientist Kevin Phillips predicted in *The Emerging Republican Majority*, white America's response to socioeconomic changes in the black community would eventually result in permanent Republican strength. Moreover, he argued that the movement of the population south and west played a significant role by shifting the locus of power away from the East Coast.[38] Conservatives, who gained much of their support from the South and Southwest, had established a political framework ready to accept the new converts.

Conservatives, in fact, had achieved a greater victory than anyone suspected at the time. The Nixon years would further the country's move to the right and strengthen the grip of conservatives on the GOP. Nixon's pragmatism and centrist tendencies could not obscure the conservatism underlying his administration. Whether through conscious effort or not, Nixon advanced the cause of conservatism.

This did not appear to be the case at first. Nixon's choice of advisers, such as Daniel P. Moynihan and Henry Kissinger, as well as his domestic agenda appalled conservatives. Always seeking the center, Nixon's policies at home combined various aspects of modern Republicanism with elements of conservatism. Revenue sharing provides the best example. Returning federal tax money to the states proved Nixon's commitment to an activist government while simultaneously fulfilling the conservative goal of maintaining local control over programs and cutting taxes. Nixon's welfare reform program, the Family Assistance Plan, horrified conservatives because of its provision for a guaranteed income. Most significantly, Nixon pressed for wage and price controls, a measure far at odds with conservative economic goals and philosophy.[39]

Nixon's foreign policy shocked the Right even more. Conservatives had never really trusted Nixon domestically, but they felt certain they could count on his anticommunism. For that reason, his trips to the Soviet Union and the People's Republic of China took the Right by surprise.[40] The nemesis of Alger Hiss opening up relations with Red China? Inconceivable. Khrushchev's kitchen opponent negotiating arms limitation talks? Unbelievable. The evidence of Nixon's betrayal was obvious.

Appearances were rather deceiving, however, for even though Nixon seemed to have betrayed conservatives, he was in fact advancing their cause. For example, he pursued a "southern strategy" from his first moment in office. This included not only attempting to appoint a southerner to the Supreme Court but also seeking to build on the discontent southerners still felt concerning civil rights. Although in hindsight Nixon's actions seem obviously exploitative, at that time they succeeded in convincing white southerners that the president was defending their interests against a hostile liberal world. The most divisive issue of the civil rights movement in the early 1970s was the use of busing to guarantee more racially balanced schools. This issue spread north as cities became divided over whether or not to implement busing plans. The battles became bitter as middle- and working-class whites framed their rejection of busing plans in terms that liberals labeled racist. To the applause of busing opponents and to the dismay of civil rights leaders, the Nixon administration postponed the implementation of court-mandated busing.[41]

In diplomacy, too, Nixon's bold moves disguised an underlying continuation of an old policy. Détente was simply containment by other means. The China Communique did not overturn U.S. policy toward the two Chinas since the United States maintained its assistance to the Taiwanese government while moving closer to diplomatic recognition of the People's Republic of China. Nixon and Mao basically agreed to disagree, hoping that the gesture would be enough to unsettle their common enemy, the Soviet Union. The new relationship did concern the Soviets, who were experiencing their own internal troubles. With changes in the international scene, the Americans and the Soviets welcomed a chance to talk. The SALT I agreement that resulted was important if for no other reason than the fact that it kept communication lines open. The agreement in fact did little to limit the arms race, which continued to escalate throughout the 1970s.[42]

If conservatives could not see the long-term implications of Nixon's policies toward China and the Soviet Union, they did approve of his handling of Vietnam. His Vietnamization policy cut casualties, maintained pressure on the Vietcong, and undercut domestic opposition.[43] As anxious as everyone else to end the fighting, conservatives were nevertheless determined to end the war with honor. As a result, they applauded Nixon's intensification of the bombing of North Vietnam even as he withdrew troops. They also commended his efforts to quiet and intimidate the antiwar movement. In the end, mainstream conservatives like William F. Buckley, Jr., concluded that the agreements reached with the North Vietnamese in January 1973 were better than any settlement Johnson could have achieved. Such conservatives accepted that these agreements did, in fact, constitute peace with honor.[44] Members of the John Birch Society and others did not agree. They believed that Nixon had sold out to the radical forces in the United States and North Vietnam just as Johnson had.[45]

Nixon's record up to that point was mixed as far as conservatives were concerned. On the one hand, he used conservative rhetoric and cultivated a conservative image with the public. He incorporated conservative spokespersons such as Buckley and Patrick Buchanan into his administration; he vetoed and fought the creation of new regulatory agencies; he pursued a harsh policy against antiwar protesters; and he fought a tough fight in Asia. On the other hand, the overall record of the Nixon years put him far to the left of the conservatives. Nixon's proposed Family Assistance Plan, wage and price controls, and revenue-sharing program demonstrated his desire to maintain a centrist policy. If his term had ended in 1973, he might have created the potential for moderate Republicans to regain control of their party.

Unfortunately for Nixon and the left wing of the party, the president had already destroyed that possibility. By his complicity in the cover-up of the break-in at Democratic headquarters in the Watergate Building in 1972, Nixon planted the seeds of his own destruction and weakened the faith of American people in their government. He also faced a challenge from the Internal Revenue Service, which audited him and fined him for underpaying his taxes, and problems with his vice president Spiro Agnew, who resigned in August 1973 amid accusations of bribery.[46]

The Democrats profited from these scandals in the short term, but conservatives were the big long-term winners. Watergate alienated Americans from their government. By suggesting that politicians cannot and should not be trusted, the scandals confirmed to many voters that conservatives had been right about the dangers of too much government. Moreover, by eliminating Nixon, the Watergate scandal undermined the centrist position in the party, thus clearing the way for conservatives.

Nixon's 1968 election was therefore ultimately a victory for conservatives. Ever the pragmatic politician, Nixon played to conservatives because he knew that they held power in the party. The fact that he took a few "liberal" steps proved more about the tactical need for political compromise than about Nixon's ideology. Nixon's bows to liberalism reflected both his desire to please as many factions as possible and his view that pure conservatism was no better for the country than pure liberalism.

The election of 1968 marked the maturation of the conservative movement. Gaining control of the Republican Party in 1964 by building an organization of loyal and enthusiastic workers, the Right survived the 1964 defeat by viewing it simply as a learning experience rather than as a failure. They spent the next four years moderating and redefining their philosophy without conceding control of the party. Consequently, by 1968, conservatives were prepared to flex their political muscles. The fracture of the liberal coalition facilitated the conservatives' attempt to maintain power. It was only a matter of time until a much more conservative candidate became president.

* * * * * * * * * * * * * * * * * * * *

CONCLUSION

    The 1968 nomination battle between Nixon and Reagan indicated how far the Republican Party had shifted to the right. From the quarrelsome, tiny band of true believers who had attempted to nominate Goldwater in 1960, conservatives had expanded and organized a movement that drafted a presidential candidate in 1964 and played the decisive role in choosing the nominee in 1968. The untutored conservatives of the early 1960s applied the lessons learned from the bitterly fought Goldwater nomination and the election battles of 1964. Emerging scarred but invigorated, the right wing worked to consolidate its new prominence in the Republican Party and to reeducate voters by moderating its tactics without surrendering the principles of conservatism. Consequently, when the actions of the liberal Johnson administration, antiwar and other political protesters, and the Black Power movement alienated many Americans, conservatives already had a political apparatus in place to take advantage of voters' discontent. They used their growing organizational strength and public appeal to decide the nomination in 1968 after the politically astute Nixon ran on a conservative platform.

Conservatives' most important achievement during the 1960s was the organization of a grassroots constituency. For years, right-wingers across the country had remained isolated from one another and alienated from politicians with whom they disagreed. They grew increasingly angry with their government. The growth of conservative organizations in the late 1950s and early 1960s provided alienated citizens with outlets for their anger and vehicles for channeling their frustrations into political action. The number and variety of these groups illustrated the depth of public dissatisfaction in the 1960s.

By encouraging the politicization of such groups, Republican conservatives nurtured a bloc of voters thoroughly committed to right-wing philosophies and goals. Conservative volunteers were usually more loyal to principles than to particular candidates. As a result, the defeat of an individual politician did not destroy the movement itself. Building from the bottom up also ensured that significant numbers of volunteers would be available to ring doorbells, stuff envelopes, and make telephone calls— essential tasks for an infant political movement. These workers often played a decisive role in expanding and advertising the movement. They provided an ideological focus for their neighbors' discontent and thus turned disgruntled citizens into voting conservatives.

In addition to recruiting a base of trained, politically experienced volunteers, the Goldwater effort in 1964 taught right-wing leaders several valuable lessons. The first evolved naturally from their reliance on grassroots organization efforts. In order to increase their numbers, conservatives developed mailing lists of like-minded individuals. During the 1964 campaign, Goldwater's staff used these lists to solicit donations and keep supporters informed. Such direct-mail techniques proved useful in the 1970s as the Right worked to form a national coalition.[1] Since much of the national media was dominated by liberals or centrists, newsletters, right-wing journals, and conservative commentators provided an essential service by keeping conservatives across the country in contact with one another and informed about important issues. Perhaps more importantly, these communication links reinforced the political structures created during the 1960s and encouraged the growth of the conservative movement.

A second lesson also emerged from the conservatives' organizational base. As their movement expanded, right-wingers learned to overlook or minimize internal differences in order to present a united front. Aware that internal disagreements had weakened them throughout the 1950s, conservatives concentrated on the wide chasm separating them from the liberals rather than on internal factional disputes. As a result, traditionalists and libertarians set aside their disagreements to campaign for Goldwater, whom each group regarded as their best chance for success. Conservatives continued this campaign for unity, both in their attempts to rid themselves and their party of the extremist taint and in their work for candidates in 1966 and 1968. This strategy would serve conservatives well in the late 1970s as disparate groups on the right worked together for a conservative victory.

Conservative unity did not mean the accommodation of fringe groups, however. The most valuable lesson gleaned from the 1964 experience was the importance of shedding the image of extremism. Dedication to principle was one thing; fanaticism was another. Extremism undermined the movement's struggle by associating conservatism with "crackpot" ideas in the public mind. Moreover, right-wing extremism alienated moderate Republicans, thus weakening the Right's power base inside the party. Conservatives needed the Republican Party's name, apparatus, and money to win national office. Misunderstandings and misrepresentations only exacerbated factional differences in the party. The Right's early reluctance to repudiate extremism compounded the problem. Blame also rested with liberal Republicans who had labeled Goldwater an extremist without realizing that the smear would spread to the entire party. This taint of extremism proved difficult to purge.

The problem of being associated with extremism ultimately threatened conservatives' greatest achievement of the 1960s—the transformation of conservatism into a legitimate, mainstream political alternative. Through the efforts of people such as Goldwater and William F. Buckley, Jr., conservatism shed some of its stodgy, old-fashioned character and became more sophisticated, attractive, and dynamic. Right-wingers of the 1960s came across as educated, resolute individuals, not as lunatics. Countless Americans rejected Goldwater for the presidency yet saw him as the more decent and honest of the two candidates. In fact, many people voted against him precisely because they believed he would practice what he preached. More important for the movement's long-term development, conservative ideas were presented seriously to a national audience. Most Americans were not ready to accept those principles in 1964 but drew on them in subsequent years to interpret the United States' changed political landscape.

The Right's capture of the Republican Party fully legitimized conservatism. The growth of an energized constituency paved the way for right-wingers to seize control of the GOP. Intent on building from the precinct level up instead of merely imposing their ideas from the top, conservatives cultivated the support of county chairs and state workers who felt neglected by the national party. This strategy avoided direct confrontations with liberal Republicans and ensured that when victory came on the national level, it was complete.

The fact that conservatives did not reach their ultimate goal until Ronald Reagan's election in 1980 does not diminish the significance of their achievements during the 1960s or obscure the connections between the two movements. If there had been no Barry Goldwater, there could have been no Ronald Reagan. Although the movements surrounding the two men differed in style and goals, the conservatives of the 1970s and 1980s built on the structures created in the 1960s and utilized the techniques and the personnel cultivated during that time.

Conservatives also benefited from the shifting circumstances of the late 1960s and 1970s. The war in Vietnam, the Watergate scandals, and the student and civil rights demonstrations alarmed Americans and alienated many people from their representatives in Washington. As a result, the conservatives' antigovernment platform became more appealing. Simultaneously, the failure of Jimmy Carter's administration to curtail high unemployment and inflation created a wider audience for conservative economic theories. At the same time, frustrated Americans demanded that action be taken to free the hostages in Iran and to deal with the attendant growing disrespect for the Stars and Stripes around the world. The Soviet invasion of Afghanistan and the Sandista revolution in Nicaragua seemed to indicate that the United States was losing the Cold War and provided further proof of the impotence of American foreign policy. Finally, angry Christians and other social traditionalists mounted an attack against liberalism for allegedly undermining the moral fabric of American society.

Ronald Reagan skillfully united these forces. Through his amiable personality, tremendous communications skills, and talented staff of writers, he successfully linked capitalism to morality and democracy to create a broad-based movement.[2] While some right-wingers toyed with the idea of creating a national third party, most, like Reagan, favored remaining within the GOP, where they had achieved so many gains.[3] From the beginning of his Republican career, Reagan had established close ties with the right-wing network in the GOP, and he profited from that network in 1980.

Aware that conservative campaign rhetoric in the early 1960s rarely produced the desired outcome, conservatives blended new and old techniques to achieve different results.[4] New political action committees and conservative think tanks, energized by the support of grassroots groups and the use of direct-mail techniques, steadily enlarged the conservative constituency. Reagan's ability to use the Goldwater networks, combined with the final disintegration of the New Deal coalition and the ongoing economic and diplomatic crises facing Carter, ensured the conservatives' long-awaited triumph in 1980.[5]

The New Right of the 1980s would not have emerged without the "old" Right of the 1960s, but important differences remained between the two movements. While fear of the "Red Menace" existed in both movements, the New Right of the 1980s emphasized a different blend of nationalism and anticommunism. For example, William Buckley favored the Panama Canal Treaty because it accommodated Panamanian nationalism and undercut hostility toward the United States, therefore discouraging the growth of communism in Latin America. Reagan, on the other hand, exploited New Right nationalism by campaigning against the treaty in 1980 on the grounds that it denied the United States its property for no acceptable reason.[6]

The presence of social conservatives and religious evangelicals within the New Right was another distinguishing factor. Traditionalists had been an important part of the Goldwater movement; certainly, Goldwater had played to them in his attacks on the immorality of the Johnson administration. The religious Right, however, was not the most vocal or visible part of that coalition. The situation was very different in 1980, when televangelists such as Jerry Falwell and Pat Robertson helped to hold the New Right coalition together. Their power frightened libertarians and old-line conservatives like Goldwater.

These differences mark the conservative movement of the 1960s as distinctive and important in its own right. It was more than simply a stepping stone for the New Right. As right-wingers created a viable political organization, they gained control of the Republican Party in the 1960s and enhanced their public profile. They did not put a pure conservative in the White House at that time, but they created an apparatus that enabled them to do so by 1980. The Right finally followed Barry Goldwater's advice from the 1960 campaign—it grew up.

NOTES

ABBREVIATIONS

The following abbreviations are used throughout the notes.

AHF	Arizona Historical Foundation, Tempe, Arizona
CAH	Center for American History, University of Texas, Austin, Texas
COHP	Columbia Oral History Project, Oral History Collection, Columbia University, New York, New York
CUL	Division of Rare and Manuscript Collections, Cornell University Library, Ithaca, New York
DDEL	Dwight D. Eisenhower Library, Abilene, Kansas
GRFL	Gerald R. Ford Library, Ann Arbor, Michigan
HIWRP	Hoover Institution on War, Revolution and Peace, Stanford University, Stanford, California
JFKL	John Fitzgerald Kennedy Library, Columbia Point, Massachusetts
LBJL	Lyndon Baines Johnson Library, Austin, Texas
RCCN	*Republican Congressional Committee Newsletter*
RNC Papers	Republican National Committee Papers, National Archives and Records Administration, Washington, D.C.; reprinted with permission of the Republican National Committee.
RNPP Papers	Richard Nixon Pre-Presidential Papers, National Archives and Records Administration, Pacific Southwest Region, Laguna Niguel, California
RNVP Papers	Richard Nixon Vice Presidential Papers, National Archives and Records Administration, Pacific Southwest Region, Laguna Niguel, California
SDC	Social Documents Collection, University of Iowa Library, Iowa City, Iowa
YUL	Yale University Library, New Haven, Connecticut

INTRODUCTION

1 Hans Engh, "The John Birch Society," *The Nation*, 11 March 1961, pp. 209–10; Schlesinger, *A Thousand Days*, 754.

CHAPTER ONE

1 Patterson, *Congressional Conservatism*, chaps. 9, 10.
2 The term "Eastern Establishment" is used in this book as conservatives used it:

it refers to a group of Republicans who accepted New Deal–style reforms and an internationalist foreign policy. For a discussion of the composition of the liberal faction, see Griffith, "Dwight D. Eisenhower and the Corporate Commonwealth"; Theodore White, *America in Search of Itself*, 55–63; Ferguson and Rogers, *Right Turn*, 53; Rae, *Decline and Fall of the Liberal Republicans*, 10–46; and Goldwater, *Goldwater*, 115–16.

3 Goldwater, *Goldwater*, 116; Ferguson and Rogers, *Right Turn*, 63.

4 Griffith, "Dwight D. Eisenhower and the Corporate Commonwealth," 88; Paul G. Hoffman, "How Eisenhower Saved the Republican Party," *Collier's*, 26 October 1956, pp. 44–47.

5 Miles, *Odyssey of the American Right*, 47–120.

6 See Patterson, *Mr. Republican*, chaps. 26–27, 32–35. William Knowland was suggested as Taft's replacement, but his failure to win the California gubernatorial race and his lack of strength ended all such plans. See Reinhard, *Republican Right*, 142–44, and Rusher, *Rise of the Right*, 66.

7 Kirk, *Conservative Mind*, 7–8. See Nash, *Conservative Intellectual Tradition*, 36–84, for a full discussion of the traditionalist school. For examples of traditionalist writings, see Weaver, *Ideas Have Consequences*; Nisbet, *Quest for Community*; and Nock, *Memoirs of a Superfluous Man*.

8 Nash, *Conservative Intellectual Tradition*, 35. For a discussion of the libertarians, see ibid., 3–35.

9 Burnham, *Struggle for the World*, 1. Burnham called his continuing column in the *National Review* "The Third World War." See Nash, *Conservative Intellectual Tradition*, 84–131. See Miles, *Odyssey of the American Right*, 47–123, for a discussion of postwar conservative foreign policy. For Eisenhower's efforts to talk with the Soviets, see, for example, Divine, *Eisenhower and the Cold War*, and Ambrose, *Eisenhower*, 519–21, 532–37. See also information on the anti-Khrushchev rally sponsored by Crusade for America and the *National Review* in "Forum, NR (1959)," box 7, General Correspondence, Buckley Papers, YUL.

10 For a discussion of this unification, see Nash, *Conservative Intellectual Tradition*, 131–220. Buckley's most recent biographer, John Judis, rightly credits Buckley with playing the decisive role in the resurgence of conservatism. See Judis, *William F. Buckley, Jr.*, 14. For an example of the Right's frustration with liberal institutions, see Richard Whalen, " 'McCarthyism' Revisited," *Human Events*, 11 February 1959, pp. 1–2. For information on the impact of the conservative press, see Nash, *Conservative Intellectual Tradition*, 27–28, 124–25, 148–53. See also Reinhard, *Republican Right*, 171–72.

11 Judis, *William F. Buckley, Jr.*, chaps. 1–5. For an example of Buckley's views on a controversial issue of the early 1950s, see Buckley and Bozell, *McCarthy and His Enemies*, esp. chap. 13.

12 William Rusher to Rev. Richard Ginder, 28 May 1958, "Ginder, Rev. Richard (1958)," box 5, General Correspondence, Buckley Papers, YUL.

13 M. Stanton Evans, *Revolt on the Campus*, 34–35. One example of the impact of the conservative press on youth can be found in a letter to the editor of the

National Review, 16 July 1960, pp. 30–31, in which A. Louise Sperling wrote: "If I had not been introduced to *National Review* as a college sophomore, I feel certain that I would be a typical ritualistic Liberal today. . . . Without the benefit of exposure to conservative criticism, reason and principles, [the average college freshman] will perhaps never have the opportunity and satisfaction of committing himself to a guiding philosophy through the process of rational, deliberate exclusion." For a brief description and history of conservative youth groups, see Cain, *They'd Rather Be Right*, 156–77; William F. Buckley, Jr., "The Young Americans for Freedom," *National Review*, 24 September 1960, pp. 172–73; and "History of the Young Republicans," booklet, [1972?], box 7, RNC Papers.

14 The loyalty oath requirement was a provision of the National Defense Act of 1958 specifying that students must take a loyalty oath to be eligible for student loans. Many students, particularly those at Yale and Harvard universities, protested this provision strenuously. See William F. Buckley, Jr., "Please Note Our Highmindedness," *National Review*, 5 December 1959, pp. 513–14. See "The Week," *National Review*, 16 January 1960, p. 28, for sketchy details of the National Student Committee for the Loyalty Oath. For an opposing view, see Gerald W. Johnson, "An Outburst of Servility," *New Republic*, 8 February 1960, p. 11.

15 Douglas Caddy, form invitation, 16 August 1960, "Young Americans for Freedom (1960)," box 2, General Correspondence, Buckley Papers, YUL; Rusher, *Rise of the Right*, 79.

16 Whalen, "'McCarthyism' Revisited," 2. See Miles, *Odyssey of the American Right*, 222–41, for a discussion of the response of conservatives to the liberalization, in their opinion, of the culture.

17 The quickest way to grasp the breadth and number of these grassroots movements is to examine the guide of the Social Documents Collection at the University of Iowa Library. This collection, which contains almost 200 reels of microfilm, catalogs in alphabetical order by group the publications of a wide variety of conservative/radical groups. Many of these publications had a very small audience, but their existence indicates the strength of antiliberal feeling in the country.

18 Group Research, Inc., "The Finances of the Right Wing: A Study of the Size and Sources of Income of 30 Selected Operations," 1 September 1964, Special Report #16, "Finances of Right Wing," box 88, Liebman Collection, HIWRP.

19 American Survival Party, "Survival," ASP6, n.d., A99, reel 13, and Committee to Warn of the Arrival of Communist Merchandise on the Local Business Scene, "1963 Guide to Communist Imports on the Business Scene," 8 July 1963, C127, reel 36, both in SDC.

20 Congress of Freedom, Inc., "Freedom Facts," 5 July 1960, F33, reel 54, SDC.

21 Constructive Action, Inc., pamphlet, n.d., C51, reel 37, SDC. The Committee of One Million fought to keep Communist China out of the United Nations. Many prominent politicians, of varying ideological beliefs, were members, including Paul Douglas, Walter Judd, and Kenneth Keating. Many of the

papers of the committee can be found in the Liebman Collection, HIWRP. For listings of anticommunist, Christian, and/or conservative organizations, see Group Research, Inc., "Finances of the Right Wing," appendix B; SDC guide; and *National Directory of "Rightist" Groups*. For a liberal view of Schwarz, see Phil Kerby, "The Cold War Sells Razors," *The Nation*, 4 November 1961, pp. 339–41. See also Ben Gilmore to Ted Humes, 9 December 1963, "Humes Correspondence (1962–65)," Humes Papers, AHF, and *The Spirit*, March 1964, A49, reel 8, SDC.

22 Welch, *New Americanism*, 115–52. For more on the John Birch Society, see Lipset and Raab, *Politics of Unreason*, 248–50.

23 Howard Buffet, "Beware the Judas Goat Or: Where Do Conservatives Go from Here?," *Human Events*, 11 May 1957, n.p.; Richard Weaver, "The Middle of the Road: Where It Leads," *Human Events*, 24 March 1956, n.p.; Clarence Manion to William F. Buckley, Jr., 25 July 1958, "Manion, Clarence (1958)," box 6, General Correspondence, Buckley Papers, YUL.

24 Frank Meyer to William F. Buckley, Jr., et al., memo, 10 May 1960, "Interoffice Memos (1960)," box 10, and Douglas Caddy, form invitation, 16 August 1960, "Young Americans for Freedom (1960)," box 12, both in General Correspondence, Buckley Papers, YUL.

25 George E. Sokolsky, transcript of remarks on Mike Wallace's television show, station WNTA, 21 March 1960, "Sokolsky, George E. (1960)," box 12, General Correspondence, Buckley Papers, YUL; John J. Synon, "You Bet I Am a Republican," *Human Events*, 28 July 1960, pp. 315–16.

26 Barry Goldwater, interview by Ed Edwin, 15 June 1967, OH21, transcript, COHP.

27 Max Eastman to William F. Buckley, Jr., 28 November 1958, "Eastman, Max (1958)," box 5, and William F. Buckley, Jr., to Revilo Oliver, 3 September 1959, "Oliver, Revilo P. (1959)," box 9, both in General Correspondence, Buckley Papers, YUL.

28 Reinhard, *Republican Right*, 142–44; "'56 Nears, Nixon-Knowland Rivalry Grows," *U.S. News and World Report*, July 16, 1954, pp. 60–62; William L. Roper, "California: Four Feet—One Pair of Shoes," *New Republic*, 27 September 1954, pp. 11–12.

29 W. Henry McFarland, in *American Flag Committee Newsletter*, July 1960, A35, reel 6, SDC; L. Brent Bozell, "National Trends," *National Review*, 19 November 1955, p. 5.

30 Nash, *Conservative Intellectual Tradition*, 137; Rossiter, *Conservatism in America*, 230, 224–29. See also Nash, *Conservative Intellectual Tradition*, 197–98. I am indebted to Nash for much of the information in this paragraph.

31 "Yes, I Fear Washington," *New Republic*, 4 January 1960, p. 5; "TRB from Washington," *New Republic*, 28 March 1960, p. 2; Schlesinger, *Vital Center*, 11–34.

32 Daniel Bell et al., *Radical Right*, 57, 58–61. For information on McCarthy, see Oshinsky, *A Conspiracy So Immense*; Griffith, *Politics of Fear*; and Fried, *Men against McCarthy*. For the conservative perspective, see, for example, Buckley and Bozell, *McCarthy and His Enemies*.

33 Elizabeth Churchill Brown, "The Secret of Political Success: How to Convert the Unconverted," *Human Events*, 25 August 1958, pp. 2–4; William F. Buckley, Jr., to Kent Courtney, 3 November 1959, "Courtney, Kent (1959)," box 7, correspondence between William F. Buckley, Jr., and George Lincoln Rockwell, "Rockwell, Lincoln (1958)," letters, " 'American Mercury' Controversy (1960)," box 10, correspondence between William F. Buckley, Jr., and Robert Welch, "Welch, Robert (1958)," box 6, and William F. Buckley, Jr., to Revilo Oliver, 3 September 1959, "Oliver, Revilo P. (1959)," box 9, all in General Correspondence, Buckley Papers, YUL.

CHAPTER TWO

1 Hartz, *Liberal Tradition*, 3–20; Hofstadter, *American Political Tradition*. For extremely helpful and insightful discussions of this era, see Pells, *Liberal Mind*, 117–83, and Daniel Bell, *End of Ideology*, 393, 402–3.

2 For a general introduction to the 1950s, see Gilbert, *Another Chance*, 7–191; O'Neill, *Coming Apart*, 3–25; Siegel, *Troubled Journey*, 86–130; and Goldman, *Crucial Decade*. On Eisenhower's presidency, see Alexander, *Holding the Line*, and Greenstein, *Hidden-Hand Presidency*.

3 Alexander, *Holding the Line*, 160; Larson, *A Republican Looks at His Party*, 1–19; Eisenhower, quoted in Alexander, *Holding the Line*, 191.

4 Patterson, *Mr. Republican*, 588–98; Reinhard, *Republican Right*, 89, 98–99; Ambrose, *Eisenhower*, 155–227; Eisenhower, *Eisenhower Diaries*, 1 April 1953, pp. 233–34; Reichard, *Reaffirmation of Republicanism*, 237. Even the Bricker Amendment debate, which could have proven disastrous, eventually ended. Although Bricker never gave up, his support dwindled and the dispute died down. For more information, see S.J. Res. 102, 82d Cong., 1st sess., 14 September 1951; "Senator Bricker on His Chances," *Newsweek*, 16 May 1955, p. 34; Ambrose, *Eisenhower*, 66–70; Tanabaum, *Bricker Amendment Controversy*; John Bricker to Dwight Eisenhower, 4 June 1956, "C.A. July 1956," box 123, Bricker Papers, Ohio Historical Society, Columbus, Ohio; and Meade Alcorn, interview by Ed Edwin, 5 June 1967, OH163, transcript, 138, COHP.

5 For example, Nelson Rockefeller wrote to Richard Nixon: "Under you and the President the Republican Party is now emerging, at home and abroad, as the great and liberal party of the future" (Nelson Rockefeller to Richard Nixon, 7 November [1956], "Rockefeller, Nelson A. [1955–59]," box 650, series 320, RNVP Papers). Barry Goldwater, in a speech at an Eisenhower-Nixon dinner, commented that in order for Republicans to return to being Republicans they needed to become more conservative (Barry Goldwater, speech, 27 January 1960, box 3H493, Goldwater Collection, CAH).

6 Barry Goldwater, "The Preservation of Our Basic Institutions," speech on Senate floor, 8 April 1957, in *Vital Speeches*, May 15, 1957, pp. 455–59.

7 Eisenhower, *Waging Peace*, 376.

8 William Hines, "Republicans Close Ranks to Deny Rift in Party," *Washington*

Evening Star, 10 April 1957; Barry Goldwater to Richard Nixon, 16 December 1958, "Goldwater, Barry (1953–59)," box 293, series 320, RNVP Papers; Barry Goldwater, speech on Senate floor, *Congressional Record* (6 May 1960), 86th Cong., 2d sess., 106, pt. 7:9524; "GOP Rift Widened by Goldwater Speech," *Washington Evening Star*, 16 March 1960; John Bricker to Richard Nixon, 20 November 1958, "Bricker, Hon. John," box 102, series 320, RNVP Papers; "Fresh Leadership," *Human Events*, 31 March 1958, p. 1; Herbert Hoover, [20 February 1960?], quoted in "The Week," *National Review*, 27 February 1960, p. 124.

9 "Sen. Goldwater Reports: 8 Million Quit GOP since '54," *Denver Post*, 16 March 1959; Reinhard, *Republican Right*, 145. See also Paul M. Butler, Chairman's Report, 1958, 27 February 1959, "Chairman's Report (1958)," box 122, Democratic National Committee Papers, JFKL, and Arthur Schlesinger, Jr., Memorandum for the President, 27 August 1962, "PL2 Elections, Campaigns (8/21/62–8/31/62)," box 692, White House Central Files, JFKL.

10 "The Week," *National Review*, 30 January 1960, p. 60; Max Eastman, letter to the editor, *National Review*, 9 April 1960, p. 244; "Can Nixon Assume Taft's Mantle?," *Human Events*, 6 October 1958, p. 1.

11 Gilbert, *Another Chance*, 54–75, 116–19; Siegel, *Troubled Journey*, 105–15; Baritz, *Good Life*, 56–104; May, *Homeward Bound*, 11. For the intellectual perspective, see Pells, *Liberal Mind*, 183–261, and Lasch, *Culture of Narcissism*, 267–320.

12 Nixon, *Six Crises*, 215. See also Eisenhower, *Waging Peace*, chaps. 4, 11, 22, and Ambrose, *Eisenhower*, chaps. 14–16, 20–21.

13 Alexander, *Holding the Line*, 256–61.

14 Parmet, *Eisenhower and the American Crusades*, 513; Eisenhower, *Waging Peace*, 505–12; Halberstam, *The Fifties*, 702.

15 Eisenhower, *Waging Peace*, 543–59; Ambrose, *Eisenhower*, 571–80.

16 Alexander, *Holding the Line*, 242; Eisenhower, *Waging Peace*, 305–6.

17 Alexander, *Holding the Line*, 268–71.

18 Parmet, *The Democrats*, 142–44; Rutland, *The Democrats: From Jefferson to Carter*, 211–18.

19 Biographies of Nixon are numerous and vary from psychohistory to autobiography. See, for example, Ambrose, *Nixon: The Education of a Politician*; Brodie, *Richard Nixon*; Parmet, *Richard Nixon*; Wicker, *One of Us*; and Nixon, *RN* and *Six Crises*.

20 Richard Nixon, "The Economy" (first television talk), 1 November 1960, "RN's Copies (#2)," box 2, series 45, Richard Nixon to Nelson Rockefeller, 15 January 1957, "Rockefeller, Nelson A. (1955–59)," box 650, series 320, and Richard Nixon, statement in Fresno, California, 4 November 1960, "RN's Copies (#1)," box 2, series 45, all in RNVP Papers. For his civil rights views, see Parmet, *Richard Nixon*, 268–69, 383–84, and Wicker, *One of Us*, 226, 238.

21 James Hagerty, interview #1 by Ed Edwin, 2 March 1967, OH91, transcript, 38, COHP; Nixon, *RN*, 185–93, 203–14.

22 Ibid., 214, 215.

23 Reinhard, *Republican Right*, 152; Barry Goldwater to Richard Nixon, 16 December 1958, "Goldwater, Barry (1953–59)," box 293, Alfred Kohlberg to Richard Nixon, 5 December 1957, 17 February 1960, "Kohlberg, Alfred," box 423, and Ronald Reagan to Richard Nixon, 15 July 1960, "Reagan, Ronald, Mr. and Mrs.," box 621, all in series 320, RNVP Papers. The latter is the famous letter in which Reagan states that under JFK's "tousled boyish haircut is still old Karl Marx."

24 "Can Nixon Assume Taft's Mantle?," *Human Events*, 6 October 1958, p. 1; "20 Questions about Dick Nixon," *Human Events*, 22 September 1960, pp. 441–44; Robert J. Needles, letter to the editor, *National Review*, 16 January 1960, p. 53; "The Week," *National Review*, 18 June 1960, p. 380; L. Brent Bozell, "Mr. Nixon's Moment of Truth," *National Review*, 8 October 1960, p. 204; *Closer Up*, 22 July 1960, C35, reel 28, SDC.

25 Wicker, *One of Us*, 239; Parmet, *Richard Nixon*, preface.

26 Parmet, *Richard Nixon*, 176–77, 186–87.

27 Goldwater, *With No Apologies*, 62. No scholarly biography of Goldwater exists at this time. Most accounts are campaign biographies or other such propaganda. His memoirs offer his side of the story and, especially for his early life, are extremely helpful. For information on the 1958 campaign, see ibid., 62–63, 88–95.

28 "Man of the Hour," *Human Events*, 1 December 1958, p. 1; Goldwater, *With No Apologies*, 74–77, 95–100; and Barry Goldwater, Notes to Diary, 25 June 1976, box 3, Alpha File, Goldwater Papers, AHF.

29 Goldwater, *With No Apologies*, 100; "For the Record," *National Review*, 18 June 1960, p. 379; " 'Conscience of a Conservative' Senator Goldwater Has Raised an Inspiring Standard," *Human Events*, 19 May 1960, p. 4; Goldwater, *Conscience of a Conservative*, 18, 21, 97–134. Although the original printing was 10,000 copies, the book ultimately sold more than 3.5 million copies and made the *New York Times'* nonfiction best-seller list.

30 Holmes Alexander, memo, 1 July 1960, "Goldwater, Barry (1960)," box 10, Roger Milliken to William F. Buckley, Jr., 28 March 1960 (dictated 25 March), "Milliken, Roger (1960)," box 10, and Clarence Manion to Daniel Buckley, 9 July 1959, "Manion, Clarence (1959)," box 8, all in General Correspondence, Buckley Papers, YUL.

31 Frank S. Meyer, "A Man of Principle," *National Review*, 23 April 1960, pp. 269–70. For Goldwater's impact on youth, see Reinhard, *Republican Right*, 172–73.

32 Patterson, *Mr. Republican*, 315–34.

33 Ibid., 474–96.

34 Barry Goldwater, *Face the Nation* transcript, [19 April 1960], "Goldwater, Barry (1953–59)," box 293, series 320, RNVP Papers. See also "How Goldwater Won," *Human Events*, 24 November 1958, p. 1; "Man of the Hour," *Human Events*, 1 December 1958, p. 1; "For the Record," *National Review*, 23 April 1960, p. 251, 2 July 1960, p. 411; "The Week," *National Review*, 21 May 1960, p. 316; letters to the editor, *National Review*, 7 May 1960, pp. 310–11, 18

June 1960, p. 405, 16 July 1960, p. 29; Mr. and Mrs. Ronald Reagan to Nixon Headquarters, telegram, 23 July 1960, "Reagan, Ronald, Mr. and Mrs.," box 621, series 320, RNVP Papers; and "He Says 'Would Accept If Offered' Goldwater for Vice President?," *American Statesman* (Salt Lake City, Utah), 27 November 1959. None of Nixon's biographies mentions that he considered Goldwater as a possibility for the vice presidential nomination.

35 Goldwater, *With No Apologies*, 101–3; G. D. Shorey to Barry Goldwater, 11 July 1960, box 3H493, Goldwater Collection, CAH; Goldwater, *With No Apologies*, 104.

36 I found evidence of three groups besides Shorey's: Aubrey Barker's Goldwater for President Committee, Frank Cullen Brophy's Americans for Goldwater, and Kent Courtney's Goldwater for President clubs. Information on these groups can be found in box 3H497, Goldwater Collection, CAH; Aubrey Barker to Paul Talbert, 2 July 1960, "Goldwater Clubs, California," box 3H498, and Barry Goldwater to Aubrey Barker, 12 July 1960, box 3H497, both in Goldwater Collection, CAH; and Aubrey Barker to "Fellow American," 3 June 1960, "Goldwater, Barry, Clippings (1960)," box 293, series 320, RNVP Papers.

37 Clif White to Bob Finch, 8 September 1959, "White, F. Clifton," box 812, series 320, RNVP Papers.

38 For a brief comparison of the two men, see Richard Whalen, "Rockefeller: The Roosevelt Republican," *Human Events*, 16 June 1960, pp. 1–4, and Theodore White, *1960*, 65–68.

39 Milton Eisenhower, interview #2 by Ed Edwin, 21 June 1967, OH292, transcript, 48, COHP; William Robinson to Dwight Eisenhower, 10 February 1959, "Eisenhower (January–February 1959)," box 3, Robinson Papers, DDEL. For a discussion of Nixon's views on Rockefeller's defense policy, see Ambrose, *Nixon: The Education of a Politician*, 536.

40 Nelson Rockefeller, transcript of statement, 26 December 1959, "Rockefeller, Nelson A. (1955–59)," box 650, series 320, RNVP Papers; *National Review*, 2 January 1960, p. 5, 16 January 1960, pp. 30–31, 30 January 1960, pp. 63–64; Nelson Rockefeller, text of statement, 9 June 1960, *Washington Post*; Ambrose, *Nixon: The Education of a Politician*, 540. For an account of these events, see Theodore White, *1960*, 67–77. For an interesting discussion of why Rockefeller did not run in 1960, see Wicker, *One of Us*, 221–23.

41 Ambrose, *Nixon: The Education of a Politician*, 551; Nixon, *Six Crises*, 314; Rockefeller, quoted in John Dreiske, "Rockefeller Blasts Hopes of Unity," *Chicago Sun-Times*, 23 July 1960. Rockefeller, in his statement the morning after the meeting, said that "these [statements] constitute the basic positions for which I have been fighting" (Nelson Rockefeller, text of statement, 23 July 1960, "Rep. Party Platform [July 1960]," box 1, Merriam Papers, DDEL). On the other hand, Nixon's staff reported that "on no single substantive issue . . . did [Nixon] retreat from, drop, or significantly alter a prior position or program or policy recommendation" ([Chuck Lichenstein], Memorandum on the Joint Nixon-Rockefeller Statement of July 23, 1960, 15 September 1960, "1960 Election Chapter," box 1, series 258, RNVP Papers).

42 Ambrose, *Nixon: The Education of a Politician*, 552; Robert Finch, interview by Ed Edwin, 1967, OH20, transcript, 39, COHP.

43 W. H. Lawrence, "Pact Opens Way for Party Amity," *New York Times*, 24 July 1960; Russell Baker, "Goldwater Hits Platform Accord," *New York Times*, 24 July 1960; Goldwater, *With No Apologies*, 109–17; Barry Goldwater, "Goldwater Calls Nixon-Rockefeller Meeting a Republican Munich," press release, 23 July 1960, "Sen. Barry Goldwater," box 29, Liebman Collection, HIWRP; Goldwater for President Coordinating Committee, press release, 24 July 1960, box 3H493, Goldwater Collection, CAH.

44 Paul Fannin, nominating speech, 27 July 1960, box 3H493, Goldwater Collection, CAH; Goldwater, *With No Apologies*, 115; Barry Goldwater to Richard Nixon, telegram, n.d., "Goldwater, Barry, Clippings (1960)," box 293, series 320, RNVP Papers; Barry Goldwater, "Conservatives Should Support Nixon," n.d., box 3H493, Goldwater Collection, CAH.

45 Barry Goldwater, speech withdrawing name from nomination, 27 July 1960, reprinted in *New York Times*, 28 July 1960; Richard Nixon, transcript of tape 4 for *Six Crises* manuscript, n.d., "Unlabeled #1," box 1, series 258, RNPP Papers.

46 Barry Goldwater, "Conservatives Should Support Nixon," *Human Events*, 4 August 1960, pp. 33–34; Roger Milliken to William F. Buckley, Jr., 8 November 1960, "Milliken, Roger (1960)," box 10, General Correspondence, Buckley Papers, YUL; "20 Questions about Dick Nixon," *Human Events*, 22 September 1960, pp. 441–44. See also pertinent memos in "Interoffice Memos (1960)," box 10, General Correspondence, Buckley Papers, YUL. For a more detailed discussion of the debate among the members of the *National Review*'s editorial board, see Judis, *William F. Buckley, Jr.*, 178–79.

47 "Republican Old Guard Rallying to Goldwater as Its Last Hope," *New York Times*, 23 July 1960; Rusher, *Rise of the Right*, 89–91; F. Clifton White, *Suite 3505*, 25–36.

48 Mayer, *Republican Party*, 509; Ambrose, *Nixon: The Education of a Politician*, 605.

49 Ambrose, *Nixon: The Education of a Politician*, 606.

CHAPTER THREE

1 H. H. Steeven, letter to the editor, *National Review*, 2 December 1960, pp. 356–57; "Who Lost the Election?," *National Review*, 19 November 1960, pp. 298–300; Robert S. Allen and Paul Scott, "Senator Bridges Quits Nixon, Says Rockefeller Can Triumph," *Whittier (Calif.) Daily News*, 27 February 1961; Theodore White, *1960*, 352; L. Brent Bozell, "The Intimidation of Richard Nixon," *National Review*, 19 November 1960, p. 304.

2 Nixon, *Six Crises*, 419; Research Division, Partial Analysis of 1960 Campaign Expenditures, 17 March 1961, "PL3 Fund Raising (4/15/61)," box 693, White House Central Files, JFKL; Matusow, *Unraveling of America*, 27–29; Ambrose,

Nixon: The Education of a Politician, 607–8. The criticism that he ran a "me-too" campaign upset Nixon more than any other complaint. Perhaps thinking of his political future, he defended his campaign in his 1962 book, *Six Crises*: "I did not attack [JFK] or members of his family personally. But on the issues, I drew the line between us coldly and clearly and could not have hit him harder than I did, with any sense of responsibility" (419).

3 Eisenhower's role in the campaign was complicated. First, Nixon and Eisenhower had a rather ambiguous relationship—they respected one another, but each had misgivings about the other. In fact, Stephen Ambrose claims that Eisenhower's ambiguous feelings toward Nixon as well as the problems involved in the campaign might have cost Nixon the election. See Ambrose, *Nixon: The Education of a Politician*, 548, 617, 619–20, and *Eisenhower*, 593–94, 599–601. Second, as vice president, Nixon had to defend Eisenhower's record or risk alienating him, even when he did not agree with his policies. See Nixon, *RN*, 217. Third, Eisenhower did not participate in the campaign until the end, despite the fact, according to Milton Eisenhower, that "Dick Nixon was clearly the president's choice." See Milton Eisenhower, interview #2 by Ed Edwin, 1967, OH292, transcript, 49, COHP. According to both Eisenhower and Nixon, the president played a limited role in the campaign by mutual agreement. Nixon wanted Eisenhower to make a "non-political" tour, during which he would "talk in support of the policies that Dick was expounding" but not about the campaign itself. See Dwight Eisenhower to William Robinson, 21 September 1966, "Nixon, Richard M. (1966) (1)," box 8, Special Name Series, Post-Presidential Papers, DDEL. The president was scheduled for an intensive campaign tour during the last two weeks before the election. This, too, was cut short, however, after Mrs. Eisenhower telephoned Mrs. Nixon and asked her to have Nixon convince the president to decrease his campaigning due to his poor health. After Eisenhower's doctor also spoke to the vice president, Nixon insisted the president not take on a strenuous tour. The president reluctantly agreed. See Nixon, *RN*, 222; Ambrose, *Eisenhower*, 602; and "Rockefeller and the Republicans," *New York Post*, 26 November 1960.

4 Thruston Morton, Address to the RNC, 6 January 1961, "RNC Press Releases (1961)," box 34, 2d ser., and RNC Research Division, "Metropolitan Areas and Key Counties in the Presidential Election of 1960" (1965), national summary of 1960 election, p. 2, box 16, both in RNC Papers; Charles Lichenstein, memo on *The Odds against Us*, 16 September 1961, "1960 Election Chapter," box 1, series 258, RNPP Papers.

5 Thruston Morton, Address to the RNC, 6 January 1961, "RNC Press Releases (1961)," box 34, 2d ser., RNC Papers; William Miller, transcript of address, 17 October 1961, "Miller, Hon. William E.," box 519, and Stephen Shadegg to Richard Nixon, 22 December 1960, "Shadegg, Stephen C.," box 687, both in series 320, RNPP Papers; T. L. Vandervliet, letter to the editor, *National Review*, 3 December 1960, pp. 356–57; Reinhard, *Republican Right*, 164.

6 Theodore White, *1960*, 359; Sale, *Power Shift*, 109–10. The Southern Rim,

according to Sale, includes everything south of an imaginary line running west from the northern border of North Carolina to just above San Francisco.

7 V. O. Key, *Southern Politics in State and Nation,* is the standard work on early twentieth-century southern politics. See also Phillips, *Emerging Republican Majority,* 193–98; Black and Black, *Politics and Society,* 3–72; and Bartley and Graham, *Southern Politics,* 81–110. For more in-depth discussions of this transformation, see Cobb, *Industrialization and Southern Society,* 99–120; Wright, *Old South, New South,* 239–74; Daniel, "Going among Strangers"; Sale, *Power Shift,* 17–53; and Black and Black, *Politics and Society,* 23–49.

8 Black and Black, *Politics and Society,* 58–64, 215, 246.

9 Daniel, "Going among Strangers," 910; Black and Black, *Politics and Society,* 236; Phillips, *Emerging Republican Majority,* 203; Theodore White, *1960,* 359; Reinhard, *Republican Right,* 169.

10 Bartley and Graham, *Southern Politics,* 86, 87. Ironically, the GOP was aided in 1956 by substantial numbers of black votes in response to the *Brown v. Board of Education* decision. See Black and Black, *Politics and Society,* 265, 272–73; Mayer, *Republican Party,* 518; and Bartley and Graham, *Southern Politics,* 92, 96, 98–103. The editors of *The Nation* asserted that Tower won because liberal Democrats defected from his reactionary opponent, not because Texas was turning Republican *or* conservative. See "Low in the Saddle," editorial, *The Nation,* 10 June 1961, p. 491.

11 See Sale, *Power Shift,* 90–124, for a discussion of southern conservatives. A more historical analysis of the continuation of southern conservative values can be found in Cobb, *Industrialization and Southern Society,* 151, 154–56. For a discussion of southern culture, see, among others, Reed, *Southerners* and *Enduring South.*

12 "Shaping GOP Policy," *Advance* 1 (February 1961): 8; Emil Frankel, "Crisis in Republican Tradition," *Advance* 3 (July 1961): 15–18; Mrs. Arthur Larson and Thomas Kuchel, letters to the editor, *Advance* 2 (April 1961): 27; Richard Nixon, letter to the editor, *Advance* 4 (November 1961): 19.

13 Nelson Rockefeller, press conference, 8 March 1962, "Rockefeller, Nelson (Nellie's Flap, June 1960) (folder 1 of 2)," box 650, series 320, and William Miller, transcript of "Ask Ken Keating," 4 June 1961, "Miller, William E.," box 519, series 320, both in RNPP Papers.

14 "The Collapse of the GOP," *National Review,* 8 May 1962, pp. 314–15. George Sokolsky stated in an address to the New York Young Women's Republican Club: "I'm not interested in practical politics tonight; it's practical politics that are taking this country to ruin. . . . What we need are people with the faith and idealism to rise above party politics and compromises, because both the Republican and Democratic parties are meaningless today. They ignore the real problems facing America." See "The Week," *National Review,* 17 June 1961, p. 370. Bruce Chapman, publisher of the Republican magazine *Advance,* wrote to the *National Review* (7 October 1961, pp. 242–43) asking why conservatives did not back Republican candidates to prove this was a right-wing renaissance. William F. Buckley, Jr., replied, "Conservatives are concerned for Republican success only insofar as they further conservative principle."

15 There are numerous biographies of Kennedy and books dealing with his administration. Among others, see Parmet, *Jack* and *JFK*; Burner and West, *The Torch Is Passed*; Schlesinger, *A Thousand Days*; Sorenson, *Kennedy*; Matusow, *Unraveling of America*, 30–32; Ambrose, *Nixon: The Education of a Politician*, 584–87; and Gilbert, *Another Chance*, 191–211.

16 Parmet, *Jack*, 465–78.

17 Schlesinger, *A Thousand Days*, 741–49; "The Return from Niagra Falls," editorial, *The Nation*, 1 April 1961, pp. 273–74; Ted Lewis, "Kennedy: Profile of a Technician," *The Nation*, 2 February 1963, p. 93.

18 JFK, quoted in Matusow, *Unraveling of America*, 33. For a discussion of JFK's economic views, see Parmet, *JFK*, 65–66, 76–77, 90–95.

19 George T. Altman, "The Tax-Cut Mirage," *The Nation*, 16 February 1963, pp. 137–38; "He Poisoned the Well," editorial, *The Nation*, 9 June 1962, p. 505; "Tax Cuts and Military Budget," editorial, *The Nation*, 16 June 1962, p. 525. For JFK's relationship with business interests, see Heath, *John F. Kennedy and the Business Community*, 1–22, 123–29.

20 Heath, *John F. Kennedy and the Business Community*, 10–11; Ferguson, "From Normalcy to New Deal"; Ferguson and Rogers, *Right Turn*, 50.

21 Rae, *Decline and Fall of the Liberal Republicans*, 49–53.

22 Parmet, *JFK*, 249–76; Burner and West, *The Torch Is Passed*, 161–63; Matusow, *Unraveling of America*, 60; Leuchtenburg, *Troubled Feast*, 144; Garrow, *Bearing the Cross*, 307; Sorenson, *Kennedy*, 470–506. For JFK's senatorial views, see Parmet, *Jack*, 409–14.

23 Brauer, *John F. Kennedy*, 24–29, 79–88; Samuel J. Ervin to Louis F. Lawler, 24 September 1962, "FE4-1 Presidential Powers," box 100, and Hubert Humphrey to John Bailey, 16 February 1963, "PL Political Affairs (9/1/62–2/28/63)," box 680, both in White House Central Files, JFKL; Martin Luther King, Jr., "Fumbling on the New Frontier," *The Nation*, 3 March 1962, pp. 190–93, and "Bold Design for a New South," *The Nation*, 30 March 1963, pp. 259–62; Matusow, *Unraveling of America*, 60–96; Leuchtenburg, *Troubled Feast*, 142–53.

24 Reinhard, *Republican Right*, 153; "Civil Rights and the GOP," editorial, *The Nation*, 13 July 1963, pp. 21–22; "Winds of Change," editorial, *The Nation*, 18 May 1963, p. 414; Brauer, *John F. Kennedy*, 223–24; Javits, *Javits*, 343–44. The editors of *Advance*, in fact, believed that Democratic failure in the civil rights movement provided the GOP with the opportunity to reclaim its role as a leading exponent of minorities. See "Civil Rights: A Republican Imperative," *Advance* 3 (July 1961): 6–9.

25 Goldwater, *Conscience of a Conservative*, 31–37; Robert Parker, "Bobby in the Black Belt," *National Review*, 20 May 1961, p. 309; W. H. Von Dreele, "It Happens in New York," *National Review*, 25 February 1961, pp. 113–14; "Let Us Try, at Least, to Understand," *National Review*, 3 June 1961, p. 338; Robert Lewis Taylor, "On the Palm Beach Frontier," *National Review*, 10 April 1962, pp. 241–42; Jackie Robinson, "The GOP: For White Men Only," *Saturday Evening Post*, 10–17 August 1963, pp. 10–12; Brauer, *John F. Kennedy*, 298–

99; Cobb, *Industrialization and Southern Society*, 153–54; Brauer, *John F. Kennedy*, 301–3. As early as 1961, the *National Review* received a letter hinting at the development of a backlash. John Wyndham noted that "the little people who ride the buses and streetcars and subways" were ready to act; they just needed direction. See John Wyndham, letter to the editor, *National Review*, 17 June 1961, p. 375.

26 Robert L. Schulz to John F. Kennedy, telegram, received 20 July 1961, and John F. Kennedy to Dwight D. Eisenhower, 17 May 1962, both in "FG2 Eisenhower, Dwight D.," box 110, John F. Kennedy to Barry Goldwater, 25 February 1961, "Goldwater, Barry," box 1013, Name File, and John M. Bailey to William E. Miller, 4 August 1961, "PL (4/1/61–10/20/61)," box 680, all in White House Central Files, JFKL; Gerald R. Ford to Dennis C. Kolenda, 27 May 1963, "Foreign Affairs (13)," and Dean Rusk, Address to Economic Club of New York, 22 April 1963, "Foreign Affairs (12)," both in box B5, Legislative File, Congressional Papers, Ford Papers, GRFL.

27 "Cuba, RIP," *National Review*, 6 May 1961, pp. 269–70; "The Week," *National Review*, 15 July 1961, p. 5. See also Goldwater, *With No Apologies*, 135–40; Parmet, *JFK*, 177; Walton, *Cold War and Counterrevolution*, 49–54; "History Will Not Absolve Him," editorial, *The Nation*, 6 May 1961, pp. 382–83; Dean Rusk, quoted in Siegel, *Troubled Journey*, 136; and "After Quarantine," editorial, *The Nation*, 3 November 1962, pp. 277–79.

28 Parmet, *JFK*, 131–56; Schlesinger, *Thousand Days*, 745–47; "The Vietnam Booby Trap," editorial, *The Nation*, 10 March 1962, p. 205; "Vietnam: Fact and Fiction," editorial, *The Nation*, 2 March 1963, p. 169; Stormer, *None Dare Call It Treason*, 54–92. Each issue of the *National Review* during the years 1961–64 contained at least one article expressing concern over the political intentions and actions of the emerging nations of the world.

29 Goldwater, *Conscience of a Conservative*, 99, 95; Javits, *Order of Battle*, 248–66; "The Week," *National Review*, 9 September 1961, p. 145; "The Week," *National Review*, 30 December 1961, p. 436; John F. Kennedy to Joint Senate-House Leadership, 1 September 1962, and assistant secretary of state, memo for Mr. O'Brien and Mr. Bundy, 14 February 1963, both in "PL6-3 Republican Party," box 695, White House Central Files, JFKL; Javits, *Order of Battle*, 237–43. An editorial in *Advance* ("Fiasco in Foreign Aid," *Advance* 4 [November 1961]: 2) bluntly stated that JFK's foreign aid bill met with disorganized opposition from Republicans because they could not agree on how to disagree. For a critique of the program, see James Burnham, "Ideology and Foreign Aid," *National Review*, 10 April 1962, p. 243.

30 "Senator Goldwater Speaks His Mind," *National Review*, 14 January 1961, pp. 13–14; Lester H. DuPree, letter to the editor, *National Review*, 14 January 1961, p. 30; "JFK: The Shifting Image," *National Review*, 30 January 1962, p. 50.

31 William Rusher to William F. Buckley, Jr., 23 May 1963, "Interoffice Memos (Apr. 1963–Dec. 1963), n.d.," box 26, General Correspondence, Buckley Papers, YUL; Group Research, Inc., "The Finances of the Right Wing: A Study

of the Size and Sources of Income of 30 Selected Operations," 1 September 1964, Special Report #16, "Finances of Right Wing," box 88, Liebman Collection, HIWRP; Wesley McCune, Group Research, Inc., "The Right-wingers: Who They Are and What They Have Done in 1963," "Right Wing," box 3J6, Goldwater Collection, CAH; "T.R.B. from Washington," *New Republic*, 28 March 1960, p. 2; Fred J. Cook, "The Ultras: Aims, Affiliations, and Finances of the Radical Right," *The Nation*, 30 June 1962, pp. 565–602; and "American Political Extremism in the 1960s," *Journal of Social Issues* 19 (April 1963). Rusher claimed that the press realized a radical movement existed only after a Kennedy speech on the subject in Seattle in September 1961. For examples of liberal reports on the Right, see A. Barth, "Report on the Rampageous Right," *New York Times Magazine*, 29 April 1962, pp. 93–96; J. Brant, "The Anti-Communist Hoax," *New Republic*, 28 May 1962, pp. 15–19, 4 June 1962, pp. 17–20; Arthur Schlesinger, Jr., "The Threat of the Radical Right," *New York Times Magazine*, 17 June 1962, pp. 10–11; Roscoe Fleming, "Onward Christian Rightists!," *The Nation*, 31 March 1962, pp. 275–77; and "How to Be a Conservative," *The Nation*, 12 October 1963, p. 210.

32 Sanford Gottlieb, "A Program to Counter Right-Wing Influence on U.S. Foreign Policy," n.d., attached to Marcus Raskin to Lee C. White, 23 January 1962, "The Radical Right," box 12, General File, Lee C. White File, White House Staff Files, Presidential Papers, Gale W. McGee to Steve Smith, 8 September 1961, attached to Stephen E. Smith to Theodore Sorenson, memo, 12 September 1964, "Politics, Prior 1964 Campaign (9/12/61–6/30/62)," box 36, Subject Files, Sorenson Papers, Gale McGee to Mike Feldman, memo, 14 August 1963, "Right-Wing Movement, Part I," box 106, President's Office Files, Presidential Papers, and Wright Patman to the President, 24 August 1963, attached to Lawrence O'Brien to Wright Patman, 4 September 1963, "PL7 Publicity, Publications," box 695, White House Central Files, all in JFKL.

33 Gale W. McGee to Steve Smith, 8 September 1961, attached to Stephen E. Smith to Theodore Sorenson, memo, 12 September 1964, "Politics, Prior 1964 Campaign (9/12/61–6/30/62)," box 36, Subject Files, Sorenson Papers, JFKL. See, for example, Confidential Report #6, 19 February 1962, "The Radical Right," box 12, General File, Lee C. White File, White House Staff Files, Presidential Papers, JFKL.

34 Journals and newspapers were quick to note this phenomenon. See John R. Williams, letter to the editor, *National Review*, 21 October 1961, p. 279; "Congressional GOP Leaders Left in Air—Refuse to Name Over-all Chief," *Los Angeles Times*, 9 January 1961; Nelson Rockefeller, press conference, 8 March 1962, "Rockefeller, Nelson (Nellie's Flap, June 1960) (folder 1 of 2)," box 650, series 320, RNVP Papers; and Gerald Griffin, "Leadership of Republicans after January 20 Seen Diffuse," *Baltimore Sun*, 4 December 1960.

35 Ambrose, *Nixon: The Education of a Politician*, 626–42; Nixon, *RN*, 236. Nixon apparently believed that he *was* the head of the "loyal opposition."

36 John Bricker to Richard Nixon, 31 August 1961, "Bricker, Hon. John," box

102, series 320, RNPP Papers; Dwight Eisenhower to Richard Nixon, 11 September 1961, and Richard Nixon to Dwight Eisenhower, 25 July 1961, both in "Nixon, Richard M. (only)," box 2, Special Name Series, Post-Presidential Papers, DDEL; Ambrose, *Nixon: The Education of a Politician*, 645–49; Nixon, *RN*, 237–40. Bricker wrote Nixon: "I personally want you to stay in this presidential picture. It is going to be most difficult as a private citizen." Eisenhower commented: "If you run and win . . . you offset to a large extent the razor-thin margin by which you lost the Presidential race last November. . . . I see no reason why, if you are elected Governor, you cannot, if you wish, make the 1964 Presidential race—and I think you would be in a far more powerful position as Governor, controlling a large delegation, than otherwise."

37 Ambrose, *Nixon: The Education of a Politician*, 650–68, 672; Nixon, *RN*, 241–44. See also Lawrence E. Davies, "California GOP Vows Full Unity," *New York Times*, 6 August 1962. Ronald Reagan served as a moderator between Nixon and the conservatives. See Ronald Reagan, transcript of televised address, 4 November 1962, "Reagan, Ronald, Mr. and Mrs.," box 621, series 320, RNPP Papers. Nixon's staff came to the same conclusion as Nixon concerning the cause of his defeat: "Our analysis is that the Cuban developments changed the voting materially in the last two weeks. Prior to that time Dick was even or ahead in the public and private polls." See Maurice Stans to Arthur Summerfield, 26 November 1962, "Stans, Maurice H.," box 4, series III, Summerfield Papers, DDEL.

38 Nixon, *RN*, 244–59; "Mr. Nixon and the Press," editorial, *The Nation*, 17 November 1962, pp. 318–19; "Battle for State GOP Control as Nixon Leaves," and Garry McCarthy, "Nixon Loses Party Voice—Goldwater," both in *Los Angeles Herald Examiner*, 3 May 1963.

39 Underwood and Daniels, *Governor Rockefeller*, 3–12; William Rusher, quoted in Kramer and Roberts, *"I Never Wanted to Be Vice-President,"* 5; Pierre Salinger to Dennis Losness, 1 May 1962, "Rockefeller, Nelson A.," Name File, Presidential Papers, JFKL; Goldwater, *With No Apologies*, 158; Reinhard, *Republican Right*, 176.

40 Reinhard, *Republican Right*, 177; Gervasi, *The Real Rockefeller*, 243–44, 249–56; "The Block-Goldwater Movement in the GOP," *Newsweek*, 22 July 1963, pp. 19–20. For a text of the press release, see *New York Times*, 15 July 1963.

41 Reinhard, *Republican Right*, 159; "The Week," *National Review*, 17 December 1960, p. 365; General Douglas MacArthur to Barry Goldwater, 3 February 1961, "General Douglas MacArthur," Alpha File, Goldwater Papers, AHF; Eliot Bernat, letter to the editor, *National Review*, 3 December 1960, pp. 356–57. Besides appearing frequently in the *National Review* and *Human Events*, Goldwater was the subject of major stories in *U.S. News and World Report* (7 August 1961), *Time* (23 June 1961), and *Life* (1 January 1961) even before he became an official candidate. He wrote to Marvin Liebman: "The problem of the conservatives is to gain positions of control within the local, state and national Republican organizations, and unless they are willing and able to do this, nothing of a conservative nature . . . will come of the next convention." See

Barry Goldwater to Marvin Liebman, 30 January 1961, "Americans for Conservative Action," box 59, Liebman Collection, HIWRP. For some of Goldwater's criticisms of JFK, see L. Brent Bozell, "Putting Power to Use," *National Review*, 17 December 1960, p. 373; "Goldwater Sees Economic Slide," *New York Times*, 27 July 1962; and "Goldwater Hails Young Republican Conference on Minority, Ethnic Groups," 17 April 1963, RNC press release, "Republican National Committee Press Releases (1963)," box 6, RNC Papers.

42 Richard Nixon to Dwight Eisenhower, 16 August 1963, "Nixon, Richard M. (2)," box 8, Special Name Series, Post-Presidential Papers, DDEL.

43 RNC news release, 8 January 1963, "RNC News Releases (1963)," box 6, RNC Papers; "Straw in the Wind," *Washington Post*, 10 January 1963; Reinhard, *Republican Right*, 165–67; "Blurred Image," *Commonweal*, 21 April 1961, p. 93. See Mayer, *Republican Party*, 523–24, for a discussion of the "cult of personality" that gripped the parties during the 1960s and affected candidate presentation. In 1963 the RNC appointed the Leo Burnett Company, the nation's sixth largest advertising agency, to handle its account. For several transcripts of television shows, see "1961–65, Joint Senate-House Republican Leadership, Staff Director and Consultant (2)," box 12, Humphrey Papers, DDEL. For the liberal Republican view of the show, see "Ideas and Images," *Advance* 5 (March 1962): 19–20. A typical cartoon of the era depicted two clowns wearing "I'm Ev" and "I'm Charlie" buttons who entertainingly twirled hats on their canes as an old woman sitting in a rocking chair looked pained. The caption read: "Doctor, Nonsense! All you need is a few chuckles." See *Washington Post* cartoon, in Democratic National Committee, *The 1962 Democratic Fact Book*, "Democratic National Committee Fact Book 1962," box 12, Attorney General's Correspondence, Personal Correspondence, Robert F. Kennedy Papers, JFKL.

44 Dwight Eisenhower to Leonard Finder, 10 June 1963, "Finder-Eisenhower Correspondence (1955–69)," box 1, Finder Papers, DDEL.

45 "Bircher Making Gains in GOP," *Los Angeles Times*, 14 April 1962; Richard Nixon, statement concerning Robert Welch and the John Birch Society, 1 March 1962, "Nixon, Richard M. (2)," box 8, and Richard Nixon to Dwight Eisenhower, 5 March 1962, "Nixon, Richard M.," box 4, both in Special Name Series, Post-Presidential Papers, DDEL; Richard Nixon to Nelson Rockefeller, 5 March 1962, "Rockefeller, Nelson (Nellie's Flap, June 1960) (folder 1 of 2)," box 650, series 320, RNPP Papers.

46 George Romney to Dwight D. Eisenhower, 12 September 1962, "Romney, George (1962)," box 17, Special Name Series, Post-Presidential Papers; Leonard Finder to Harry Bremner, 3 June 1964, "Propaganda Correspondence," box 15, Finder Papers, DDEL. See files on Birch material in boxes 16–18, ibid.

47 Reinhard, *Republican Right*, 168; Mayer, *Republican Party*, 530. For more detailed information, see "Big Cities Project," Stull Papers, RNC Papers. See, for example, Clare B. Williams, statement, 10 March 1963, "Republican National Committee Press Releases (1963)," box 6, RNC Papers. Conservatives also recognized the significant role youth would play in the forthcoming elections.

See L. Brent Bozell, "Challenge for Conservatives, II," *National Review*, 14 January 1961, p. 12.

48 The Executive Committee decided it would cause less confusion in Washington if the organization dropped "National" from the title. For consistency, I will always refer to it as the RCC except in direct quotations. See Executive Committee of RCC, Minutes of Meeting, 14–15 December 1962, black binder, box 4, Republican Citizens' Committee Records, CUL.

49 Dwight Eisenhower to Bryce Harlow, 21 March 1962, "Political Affairs 3 (PL3) (2) NRCC," William Miller, form letter, 31 May 1962, "Political Affairs 3 (PL3) (3) NRCC, Govs. Conf. (7/1/62)," and Dwight Eisenhower to Barry Goldwater, 20 June 1962, and Barry Goldwater to Dwight Eisenhower, 9 June 1962, both in "Political Affairs 3 (PL3) (1) NRCC," all in box 19, 1962 Principal File, Post-Presidential Papers, DDEL; Ambrose, *Eisenhower*, 644–45.

50 Dwight Eisenhower to R. Douglas Stuart, 19 July 1962, "Political Affairs 3 (PL3) (1) NRCC, Govs. Conf. (7/1/62)," Don Frey to Dwight Eisenhower, 13 November 1962, "Political Affairs 3 (PL3) (1) NRCC," and Dwight Eisenhower to William Miller, 3 July 1962, "Political Affairs 3 (PL3) (1) NRCC, Govs. Conf. (7/1/62)," all in box 19, 1962 Principal File, Post-Presidential Papers, DDEL; Dwight Eisenhower to William Miller, 2 July 1962, "List, Founding and Sustaining Members," box 1, Republican Citizens' Committee Records, CUL.

51 Organizing Committee of RCC, memo, 30 June 1962, and Executive Committee of RCC, Minutes of Meeting, 6–7 October 1962, black binder, both in box 4, Republican Citizens' Committee Records, CUL.

52 Kenneth Keating to Dwight Eisenhower, 6 July 1962, "Political Affairs 3 (PL3) (2) NRCC," and Dwight Eisenhower to Harry Darby, 6 November 1962, "Political Affairs 3 (PL3) (1) NRCC," both in box 19, 1962 Principal File, Post-Presidential Papers, DDEL; Organizing Committee of RCC, Minutes of Meeting, 6–7 October 1962, black binder, box 4, Republican Citizens' Committee Records, CUL.

53 Barry Goldwater to William Miller, 2 July 1962, "26 RNC (1962)," box 19, Goldwater Papers, AHF. Not all conservatives disliked the new organization. George Humphrey, a self-proclaimed member of the "Old Guard," felt that the advantages of harmony outweighed other considerations. Of course, he was also a close friend of Eisenhower. See George Humphrey to Dwight Eisenhower, 3 July 1962, and Dwight Eisenhower to George Humphrey, 5 July 1962, both in "Political Affairs 3 (PL3) (2) NRCC," and Joseph Sheffield to Dwight Eisenhower, 29 August 1962, "Political Affairs 3 (PL3) (2) NRCC, Govs. Conf. (7/1/62)," all in box 19, 1962 Principal File, Post-Presidential Papers, DDEL. See also Organizing Committee of RCC, Minutes of Meeting, 6–7 October 1962, and Organizing Committee of RCC, Confidential Memo Re: Developments since Gettysburg, 23 July 1962, black binder, both in box 4, Republican Citizens' Committee Records, CUL.

54 Rae, *Decline and Fall of the Liberal Republicans*, 67–68; F. Clifton White to C. R. Barr et al., Confidential Memo, 9 July 1962, "National Republican Citizens'

Committee," box 19, White Papers, CUL; Charles White to Dwight Eisenhower, 5 July 1962, "Political Affairs 3 (PL3) (3) NRCC, Govs. Conf. (7/1/62)," Leonard Hall to Dwight Eisenhower, 2 July 1962, "Political Affairs 3 (PL3) (2) NRCC," Dwight Eisenhower to Alfred Gruenther, 5 July 1962, "Political Affairs 3 (PL3) (1) NRCC," and Walter Thayer to Dwight Eisenhower, 16 October 1962, "Political Affairs 3 (PL3) (2) NRCC, Govs. Conf. (7/1/62)," all in box 19, 1962 Principal File, Post-Presidential Papers, DDEL.

55 RCC news release, 31 March 1964, "March 31st Announcement Release," box 2, Republican Citizens' Committee Records, CUL; Milton Eisenhower, interview #2, 56–58, COHP.

CHAPTER FOUR

1 Jonathan Rieder, "The Rise of the Silent Majority," in Fraser and Gerstle, *Rise and Fall of the New Deal Order*, 243–68.

2 Robert D. Enoch, "A New Era Is Dawning," *ACA Newsletter*, 27 July 1964, and Alice Widenor, "Middle Class against Welfare State," *ACA Newsletter*, 24 August 1964, both in A2, reel 1, SDC; Mildred Willis Harris, letter to the editor, *National Review*, 11 March 1961, p. 160; Tom Anderson, "For Once Conservatives Have a Choice," *American Way*, 14 January 1964, A54, reel 8, SDC.

3 Gale McGee to Mike Feldman, memo, 14 August 1963, pp. 66–67, "Right-Wing Movement, Part I," box 106, President's Office Files, Presidential Papers, JFKL.

4 Rusher attributes this growing attention to a conscious decision made by liberal leaders in both parties to destroy the conservative movement. Although his discussion is at times permeated with the tone of a self-righteous martyr, his point contains a basic truth. Liberals saw all conservatives as radicals, so it was natural that they would want to eliminate them. Rusher takes this point to a paranoiac extreme, however. See Rusher, *Rise of the Right*, 117–27.

5 William F. Buckley, Jr., "The Uproar," *National Review*, 22 April 1961, pp. 241–43; Marvin Liebman to "All Concerned," 16 January 1962, "National Review," box 99, Liebman Collection, HIWRP; Clarence Manion, letter to the editor, *National Review*, 6 May 1961, p. 290; William F. Buckley, Jr., to Roger Milliken, 25 April 1961, "Milliken, Roger (1961)," box 15, General Correspondence, Buckley Papers, YUL. Not all conservatives were willing to give Welch and his group the benefit of the doubt. Arthur G. McDowell in the *Council against Aggression Newsletter* (5 June 1961, C54, reel 54, SDC) compared Welch's program to communism.

6 Rusher, *Rise of the Right*, 117–18; "Extremism Is Thicker Than Water," *National Review*, 16 December 1961, p. 404; "Liberal Screams," *America's Future*, 21 June 1963, A19, reel 3, SDC; "The Question of Robert Welch," *National Review*, 13 February 1962, pp. 83–88; William F. Buckley, Jr., to Spruille Braden, 12 February 1962, "National Review," box 99, Liebman Collection, HIWRP; Barry Goldwater and John Tower, letters to the editor, *National Re-*

view, 27 February 1962, p. 140; Ronald Reagan, letter to the editor, *National Review,* 13 March 1962, p. 177; Barry Goldwater to Glenn O. Young, 26 March 1962, reprinted in *American Advisor,* May 1962, A70, reel 12, SDC.

7 P. A. DeValle to Barry Goldwater, n.d., reprinted in *American Advisor,* May 1962, A70, reel 12, SDC. See also letters to the editor, *National Review,* 27 February 1962, p. 140, 24 April 1962, p. 303, and William F. Buckley, Jr., to Spruille Braden, 12 February 1962, "Braden, Spruille (1962)," box 18, General Correspondence, Buckley Papers, YUL.

8 William F. Buckley, Jr., to Edward Foley, 17 April 1962, "Foley, Edward T. (1962)," box 20, General Correspondence, Buckley Papers, YUL.

9 "A Letter from a Father to a Son Who Was Straying from the 'Straight and Narrow' Conservative Road," *ACA Newsletter,* 27 July 1964, A2, reel 1, "Those Terrible Ultra Extremists Who Want to Restore Our Constitution," *Closer Up,* 10 November 1961, C35, reel 28, and "Liberal Screams," *America's Future,* 21 June 1963, A19, reel 3, all in SDC; "The Week," *National Review,* 4 June 1963, p. 435.

10 Richard Nixon, "Organizing for Republican Victory in '62 and '64," 5 May 1961, "Nixon, Richard M. (only)," box 2, Special Name Series, Post-Presidential Papers, DDEL; Marvin Liebman to Robert Bauman, 9 November 1964, "Background of ACU Meetings (12/1 and 12/19/64)," box 57, Liebman Collection, HIWRP; "The Big Show," *America's Future,* 1 January 1960, A19, reel 2, and Congress of Freedom, Inc., *Freedom Facts,* July 1960, F33, reel 54, both in SDC; George Sokolsky, quoted in "The Week," *National Review,* 17 June 1961, p. 370.

11 W. Henry MacFarland, Jr., *American Flag Committee Newsletter* 47 (July 1960), A35, reel 6, SDC; F. Clifton White, interview by author, tape recording, Ashland, Ohio, 21 October 1987.

12 For a history of the Conservative Party in New York, see Rusher, *Rise of the Right,* 95–98, 131–35; Underwood and Daniels, *Governor Rockefeller,* 64–65; Conservative Party of Kansas, pamphlet, 1963, C137, reel 36, SDC; "The Week," *National Review,* 18 December 1962, p. 46; "Strength Shown by L.I. Rightists," *New York Times,* 26 July 1962; "Javits Will Run for a New Term," *New York Times,* 17 July 1962; "The Conservative Party (N.Y.) Is Here to Stay," *National Review,* 23 October 1962, pp. 301–2.

13 Frank Meyer, "Only Four Years to 1964," *National Review,* 3 December 1960, p. 344; L. Brent Bozell, "The Challenge to Conservatives, I," *National Review,* 3 December 1960, p. 343; William Rusher, "Crossroads for the GOP," *National Review,* 12 February 1963, pp. 109–12. In response to a letter to the editor from Bruce Chapman (*National Review,* 7 October 1961, p. 243), Buckley explained that "conservatives are concerned for Republican successes only insofar as they further conservative principle."

14 For background on these groups, see chapter 1. Although they were organized under a national organization, local chapters of the Young Republicans and Young Americans for Freedom were basically autonomous, which meant that the extremity of each group's political beliefs varied considerably. Internal

struggles for control also occurred, which, of course, influenced the workings of the groups. See Green, Turner, and Germino, "Responsible and Irresponsible Right-Wing Groups," 8, and William Madden to William Rusher, 14 July 1962, and William Rusher to William Madden, 17 July 1962, both in "National Review," box 99, Liebman Collection, HIWRP. In 1963 Senator Strom Thurmond resigned from the Board of Directors of Young Americans for Freedom because the group had appealed for funds for Goldwater's campaign in a mailing that also included a letter from Thurmond encouraging recipients to donate money to the group. See Harry Dent to Walter Jenkins, 27 December 1963, "PL6-3 Republican Party (11/22/63–2/29/64)," EX PL6-3, box 119, White House Central Files, LBJL, and Rorabaugh, *Berkeley at War*, 33.

15 "The Week," *National Review*, 16 January 1960, p. 28; "Revolt on the Campus," *America's Future*, 26 May 1961, A19, reel 2, SDC; "The Week," *National Review*, 4 June 1963, p. 436; *Conservative View*, 27 April 1962, C44, reel 31, SDC. For examples of such articles, see "The Week," *National Review*, 8 October 1960, p. 198, and Alan McCone, Jr., "Conservatives, Radicals, and Reactionaries," *Insight and Outlook*, 17 February 1959, I14, reel 64, SDC. For students' views on communism, see any issue of *Insight and Outlook, Conservative View* (C44, reel 31, SDC), or any other conservative college publication. It is amusing to compare the reporting by various journals of the conservative efforts within the National Student Association. The *National Review* claimed the right-wingers were successful, while *The Nation* tended to minimize their efforts. See Steven Roberts and Carey McWilliams, Jr., "Student Leaders and Campus Apathy," *The Nation*, 16 September 1961, pp. 155–57. *Conservative View* was published by the Iowa State University Young Americans for Freedom. *Insight and Outlook* claimed to be the oldest conservative university magazine in the country. The *New Liberal* was published by the University of Idaho Young Americans for Freedom. See "Idaho Youth Form New Anti-Red Movement," *American Eagle*, April 1962, N14, reel 80, SDC. The *New Guard* was produced by the national Young Americans for Freedom office, and the *New Individualist Review* by graduate students at the University of Chicago. See "The Week," *National Review*, 22 April 1961, p. 237.

16 Donald E. Lukens, interview by author, tape recording, Hamilton, Ohio, 6 February 1988; Barry Goldwater, interview by Ed Edwin, 15 June 1967, OH21, transcript, 76–77, COHP; George E. Sokolsky, "No Program for Youth," *National Review*, 8 October 1960, pp. 205–6.

17 George F. Hobart, "Inside the Goldwater 'Draft,'" *Advance* 2 (Spring 1963): 20–21; *America's Future*, 21 October 1960, A19, reel 2, and Constructive Action, Inc., pamphlet, n.d., C151, reel 137, both in SDC. Among others, William Rusher, Clifton White, and John Ashbrook had been very active members of the Young Republicans and used the files they maintained during that time to form the early Draft Goldwater group.

18 "GOP Woman Leader Challenges Young Republicans to 'Get-Out-the-Young-Vote in '64,'" RNC news release, 26 June 1963, "Republican National Committee Press Releases (1963)," box 6, RNC Papers; National Draft Goldwater

Committee, Minutes of Executive Committee Meeting, 9 May 1963, "Steering Committee Reports," box 9, White Papers, CUL; Rusher, *Rise of the Right*, 148; White, interview by author. Many young people sold "Goldwater in '64" buttons at the 1960 convention.

19 For further information, see the material in "Goldwater Presidential Campaign, 1964 Draft Goldwater Endeavor (1962–63)," box 4, Kitchel Papers, HIWRP; documents by Denison Kitchel in the Kitchel Papers and Free Society Association Collection copyright Stanford University.

20 For a detailed chronology of the actions of this group, see F. Clifton White, *Suite 3505*. See also White Papers, CUL.

21 Biography of F. Clifton White, 27 June 1963, "Staff Biographies," box 4, White Papers, CUL; White, interview by author; F. Clifton White to A. C. Rabel, 16 November 1962, "Chicago (December 1962)," box 20, White Papers, CUL. See also F. Clifton White, *Suite 3505*, 28–29, 34, and Rusher, *Rise of the Right*, 99–101. Not everyone believed that White was valuable to the movement. Some people closely connected with Goldwater and the draft effort, such as Stephen Shadegg, Albert Fay, and Peter O'Donnell, felt he was poorly organized and should have been replaced. See Shadegg's interviews of these men in box 3J24, Goldwater Collection, CAH.

22 F. Clifton White, "1962 Report," "Chicago (December 1962)," box 20, and [F. Clifton White to Chicago group], Confidential Memo, 24 August 1962, "Group Mailings," box 18, both in White Papers, CUL; Hobart, "Inside the Goldwater 'Draft,' " 18; F. Clifton White to Barry Goldwater, 31 January 1963, "Goldwater Correspondence," box 18, White Papers, CUL; F. Clifton White, *Suite 3505*, 48–50; Robert Chapman to F. Clifton White, 27 December 1961, "South Carolina," box 20, "Budget Figures," 27 November 1962, "Chapter X, 'Secret Meeting,' " box 9, and [White to Chicago group], Confidential Memo, 24 August 1962, "Group Mailings," box 18, all in White Papers, CUL. See F. Clifton White, *Suite 3505*, 61–76, for a description of his financial troubles in 1962. On several occasions, the group would have folded if White had not used his family savings to keep it afloat.

23 White, interview by author.

24 Goldwater, *Goldwater*, 121–22; Goldwater interview, 28–29, COHP; Goldwater, *Why Not Victory?*; Rosalie Gordon, book review of *Why Not Victory?*, *America's Future*, 1 June 1962, A19, reel 2, SDC; reviews reprinted in Shadegg, *What Happened to Goldwater?*, 48–49. Books concerning Goldwater included three biographies and a "history" depicting him as the hero: Jack Bell, *Mr. Conservative: Barry Goldwater*; Shadegg, *Barry Goldwater: Freedom Is His Flight Plan*; McDowell, *Barry Goldwater: Portrait of an Arizonan*; and Schlafly, *A Choice, Not an Echo*.

25 William Rusher to Barry Goldwater, 9 November 1961, "Steering Committee Reports," box 9, White Papers, CUL; F. Clifton White, interview by Stephen Shadegg, December 1964, envelope "Clif White (12/64)," box 3J24, Goldwater Collection, CAH; Barry Goldwater to F. Clifton White, 12 June 1963, "Goldwater Correspondence," box 18, and "Agenda, Executive Officers," 2

December 1962, "Chicago (December 1962)," box 20, both in White Papers, CUL; Albert Fay and Stephen Shadegg, transcript of telephone conversation, 29 March 1963, envelope "Albert Fay (3/29/63)," "Conversations," box 3J4, Goldwater Collection, CAH. In his latest memoir, Goldwater denies any knowledge of what transpired with White's group. Since White sent him periodic letters keeping him updated, this hardly seems possible. See Goldwater, *Goldwater*, 134.

26 William Rusher to Barry Goldwater, 23, 18 January 1963, "Goldwater Correspondence," box 18, White Papers, CUL; F. Clifton White to Barry Goldwater, 7 June 1963, "Goldwater Presidential Campaign Correspondence, General (1963)," box 4, Kitchel Papers, HIWRP; William Rusher to Barry Goldwater, 18 January 1963, Frank Meyer to Barry Goldwater, 11 February 1963, and F. Clifton White to Barry Goldwater, 31 January 1963, all in "Goldwater Correspondence," box 18, White Papers, CUL. Members of White's committee were particularly frantic in January 1963 because, at a meeting early in the month, Goldwater told White that he did not want the nomination and would stop any draft effort. See F. Clifton White, *Suite 3505*, 115–26.

27 Barry Goldwater to Kenneth Kellar, 4 December 1962, and Kenneth Kellar to Denison Kitchel, 11 December 1962, both in "Kellar, Kenneth C. (1962–79)," box 2, Kitchel Papers, HIWRP; Barry Goldwater to Dean Burch, 14 January 1963, "Burch, Dean, Correspondence," box 20, Goldwater Papers, AHF; Barry Goldwater to F. Clifton White, 12 June 1963, "Goldwater Presidential Campaign Correspondence, General (1963)," box 4, Kitchel Papers, HIWRP; Barry Goldwater to William Rusher, 22 January 1963, "Goldwater Correspondence," box 18, White Papers, CUL; White, interview by Shadegg, 20; Barry Goldwater to Frank Meyer, n.d., "Goldwater, Barry, Correspondence," box 25, General Correspondence, Buckley Papers, YUL; Barry Goldwater to Frank Meyer, 20 February 1963, "Goldwater Presidential Campaign Correspondence, General (1963)," box 4, Kitchel Papers, HIWRP; Barry Goldwater to Dean Burch, 21 January 1963, "Burch, Dean, Correspondence," box 20, Goldwater Papers, AHF; Goldwater, *With No Apologies*, 157–58; Barry Goldwater, Notes to Diary, 25 June 1976, box 3, Alpha File, Goldwater Papers, AHF; Denison Kitchel to Kenneth Kellar, 8 April 1963, "Goldwater Presidential Campaign Correspondence, General (1963)," box 4, Kitchel Papers, HIWRP; Goldwater, *With No Apologies*, 161.

28 F. Clifton White, *Suite 3505*, 115–26; Shadegg, *What Happened to Goldwater?*, 57–62.

29 National Draft Goldwater Committee, press release, 8 April 1963, "Goldwater Presidential Campaign, 1964 Draft Endeavor (1962–63)," box 4, Kitchel Papers, HIWRP; "States Which Need a NDGC Chairman," box 4, Frank J. Kovac to O. E. Towery, 13 September 1963, "Finance," box 5, Ione F. Harrington and Judy G. Fernald to "Conference Chairman," 18 April 1963, "Women (National Committee, Women's Federation)," box 20, and "Republican Governors' Meeting, Denver," [13 September 1963], "Governors' Conference Biographies," box 5, all in White Papers, CUL; Report on Goldwater

Hospitality Room at Missouri Republican Lincoln Day, 8–9 February [1963], "Goldwater Presidential Campaign, 1964 Draft Endeavor (1962–63)," box 4, Kitchel Papers, HIWRP; "Conventions," box 5, White Papers, CUL. For the complete story, see F. Clifton White, *Suite 3505*, 127–44. See also National Draft Goldwater Committee, Constitution, 8 April 1963, "Constitution," box 5, White Papers, CUL.

30 F. Clifton White, *Suite 3505*, 199–213, 264.

31 Ibid., 233–44; *Time*, 4 October 1963; Goldwater, *With No Apologies*, 156–57; Barry Goldwater, Notes to Stephen Shadegg, 18 March 1977, Goldwater Book Materials and Columns, Goldwater Papers, AHF.

32 Schlesinger, *A Thousand Days*, 18; Robert F. Kennedy to Barry Goldwater, 13 November 1963, "VIP, 1963–64, Goldberg–Gruenther," box 9, Attorney General's Correspondence, Personal Correspondence, Robert F. Kennedy Papers, JFKL; Goldwater, *Goldwater*, 29. See also the friendly correspondence between Kennedy and Goldwater, for example, Barry Goldwater to John F. Kennedy, 7 January 1963, "Goldwater, Barry (Sen.)," Name File, White House Central Files, JFKL.

33 Goldwater, *Goldwater*, 136–38; Kennedy, *Robert Kennedy in His Own Words*, 392; Subcommittee on Party Organization, Democratic National Committee, Recommendations, 25 June 1963, "Democratic National Committee, 1964 Campaign (4/1963–6/1963)," box 12, Attorney General's Correspondence, Personal Correspondence, Robert F. Kennedy Papers, JFKL; Sorenson, *Kennedy*, 754; Kennedy, *Robert Kennedy in His Own Words*, 373, 392; Schlesinger, *A Thousand Days*, 1018, 981.

34 Goldwater, *With No Apologies*, 160–61; Goldwater, *Goldwater*, 149, 154; [Stephen Shadegg], "Notes Dictated on B Side of Record #20," envelope "Dean Burch (12/64)," Goldwater Collection, CAH; F. Clifton White to "JH and DK," 18 December 1963, memo/status report, "JH," and National Draft Goldwater Committee, Minutes of Steering Committee Meeting, 11 December 1963, "Steering Committee Reports," both in box 9, White Papers, CUL; Goldwater interview, 72–73, COHP.

35 For a more detailed account of these problems following his nomination, see chapter 5. For information on the primary period, see F. Clifton White, *Suite 3505*, 263–79; Rusher, *Rise of the Right*, 157–58; "Preliminary Campaign Plan," box 8, White Papers, CUL; Burch, interview by Shadegg; L. Brent Bozell and Stephen Shadegg, transcript of telephone conversation, 19 or 20 September 1963, "Conversations," box 3J4, Goldwater Collection, CAH; and National Draft Goldwater Committee, Minutes of Steering Committee Meeting, 11 December 1963, "Steering Committee Reports," box 9, White Papers, CUL.

36 "National Goldwater Rally," box 88, Liebman Collection, HIWRP; William King, "Round Up Scheduled to Help Goldwater," *Chicago Tribune*, 28 June 1964; "Can a Conservative Republican Win?," unlabeled folder, box 8, and Memo on the Western States Republican Conference, [October 1963], "Western States Conference," box 4, both in White Papers, CUL; "Potential Gold-

water Strength at Convention Time," 16 April 1964, "PL6 Republican Party (11/22/63–7/19/64)," EX PL6-1, box 116, and Ben Gilmore, Mailing, Goldwater Clubs of Connecticut, January 1964, "PL6-3 Republican Party (11/22/63–2/29/64)," EX PL6-3, box 119, both in White House Central Files, LBJL; James Helbert, " 'Massive' Drive for Goldwater on in State," *Pittsburgh Press*, 26 June 1964; "Goldwater Victory in Young Republican Group, Rockefeller Supporters Defeated," Goldwater for President press release, 11 March 1964, "Goldwater for Pres.," box 90, Liebman Collection, HIWRP. For a complete description of the committee's activities, see the appropriate chapters in F. Clifton White, *Suite 3505*; Rusher, *Rise of the Right*; and Shadegg, *What Happened to Goldwater?*

37 "Money Comes Easy," *Business Week*, 1 August 1964, pp. 19–20; "Delegates, Not Dollars," *Commonweal*, 7 August 1964; letter to the editor, *National Review*, 22 October 1963, p. 369; National Draft Goldwater Committee, Minutes of Executive Committee Meeting, 9 May 1963, "Steering Committee Reports," box 9, White Papers, CUL; Goldwater Supporter to Goldwater Supporter, 21 February 1964, "EX PL2 (2/11/64–3/15/64)," PL2, box 82, White House Central Files, LBJL; A. A. Lausmann to Edwin Durno and Steve Shadegg, 9 April 1964, "Misc. Literature and Correspondence," box 3J9, Goldwater Collection, CAH.

38 Tom Anderson, "For Once Conservatives Have a Choice," *American Way*, 14 January 1964, A54, reel 8, and "A 'Free' Publisher Speaks Out," *ACA Newsletter*, 21 September 1964, A2, reel 1, both in SDC; Alexander Hudgins to F. Clifton White, 22 June 1964, "Other Corres., Virginia," box 10, White Papers, CUL; Stuart Long, "Austin Report," 19 July 1964, "EX PL2 (6/15/64–7/23/64)," EX PL2, box 83, and Tom Martin, transcript of editorial for KFDA-TV, 6 January 1964, "PL6-3 Republican Party (11/22/63–2/29/64)," EX PL6-3, box 119, both in White House Central Files, LBJL; *Shasta County Chronicle*, 12 March, 2, 9 April 1964, N11, reel 79, "Political Civil War Decreed?," *Closer Up*, 17 July 1964, C35, reel 28, and "Sees Socialist Taint to Barry," *Des Moines Register*, 17 April 1961, C140, reel 36, all in SDC.

39 Republican Party of Oklahoma, resolution, 20 April 1963, and State Executive Committee of the South Carolina Republican Party, resolution, 25 May 1963, both in "Goldwater Presidential Campaign Correspondence, General (1963)," box 4, Kitchel Papers, HIWRP; "Statement of Certain Republican Members of Congress," 17 June 1964, "Misc. Literature and Correspondence," box 3J8, Goldwater Collection, CAH; "List of Members of House of Representatives Actively Supporting the Candidacy of Senator Barry Goldwater," "Goldwater Rally, List for Knowland Invites," box 90, Liebman Collection, HIWRP; Dwight Eisenhower, 4 June 1964, Calls and Appointments 1964 (3), and 8 July 1964, Calls and Appointments 1964 (4), Appointment Book Series, and Dwight Eisenhower to Clarence Hill, 3 September 1963, "DDE's Views on Participating in 1964 Election," box 1, Convenience File, both in Post-Presidential Papers, DDEL; Goldwater interview, 84, COHP;

"Nixon Cites Goldwater's Shift to Eisenhower Views," *Chicago Sun-Times*, 9
June 1964.

40 "Wallace Drops Presidency Bid, Denies Any Deals," *New York Times*, 20 July
1964, pp. 1, 12; Lesher, *George Wallace*, 308–9; Matusow, *Unraveling of America*, 139; William Robinson to Ellis Slater, 2 February 1964, "Eisenhower
(1964)," box 4, Robinson Papers, DDEL.

41 Dwight D. Eisenhower to George Romney, 2 March 1962, "Romney, George
(1962)," and George Romney to Dwight D. Eisenhower, 12 December 1963,
"Romney, George (1963–66)," both in box 17, Special Name Series, and Calls
and Appointments, 1963 and 1964, Appointment Book Series, all in Post-
Presidential Papers, DDEL; Barry Goldwater to William F. Buckley, Jr., dic-
tated 28 December 1962, transcribed 2 January 1963, "Goldwater, Barry,
Correspondence," box 25, General Correspondence, Buckley Papers, YUL;
Parmet, *JFK*, 130, 272; Sorenson, *Kennedy*, 754; Kennedy, *Robert Kennedy in
His Own Words*, 76.

42 Theodore White, *1964*, 143–53; Parmet, *Richard Nixon*, 479–81; Jack Steele,
"Nixon Drive Stalls as Romney Rambles," *Washington Daily News*, 10 June
1964; J. F. Ter Horst, "Nixon Proposes Rival for Barry," *Detroit News*, 9 June
1964. For information on the Romney-Nixon talk, see William Chapman,
"Nixon Tells His Role in Romney Bid," *Washington Post*, 10 June 1964.

43 For detailed accounts of these events, see Kramer and Roberts, *"I Never
Wanted to Be Vice-President,"* 242–47, 266–86, and Theodore White, *1964*, 64–
136. According to Richard Kleindienst, head of field operations, the Goldwater for President Committee discouraged specific references to Rockefeller's
marital situation since it was receiving continual treatment in the press. Instead, Goldwater increased his emphasis on the "need for morality at all levels
of government and at all levels of our personal lives." See Richard Kleindienst
to Stephen Shadegg, 7 March 1964, envelope "Richard Kleindienst: Notes
and Conversation," Goldwater Collection, CAH.

44 Richard Nixon, "Recent Statements . . . in Response to Questions Concerning
the 1964 Campaign, Jan. 1964," "1964 Statements," box 1, series 127, and
"1964 Letters Urging Nixon to Run for Presidency," box 1, series 129, all in
RNPP Papers; Ronald Sullivan, "Nixon Will Expand His Political Staff," *New
York Times*, 13 March 1964; correspondence between Fred Seaton and Rose
Mary Woods, "Nixon 1964 Campaign, Memos of Conversations," box 8,
Seaton Papers, and Dwight Eisenhower, 19 May 1964, Calls and Appointments 1964 (2), and 18 June 1964, Calls and Appointments 1964 (3), both in
box 2, Appointment Book Series, Post-Presidential Papers, all in DDEL; The-
odore White, *1964*, 140–41; Parmet, *Richard Nixon*, 480. Eisenhower believed
Nixon was waiting in the wings for a draft. See Dwight Eisenhower to Elinor
Peabody, 16 September 1963, "Politics (PL) Nixon, Richard M. (1964)," box
2, Files of the Secretary to General D. D. Eisenhower, and Dwight Eisenhower,
12, 18 June 1964, Calls and Appointments 1964 (3), box 2, Appointment Book
Series, both in Post-Presidential Papers, DDEL.

45 Leonard Hall, interview, 19 May 1975, OH478, transcript, 45–46, Eisenhower Library Collection, DDEL; Meade Alcorn, interview by Ed Edwin, 5 June 1967, OH163, transcript, 139–40, COHP; Dwight Eisenhower, 4 June 1964, Calls and Appointments 1964 (3), box 2, Appointment Book Series, Post-Presidential Papers, William Robinson to Dwight Eisenhower, 5 July 1964, "Eisenhower (1964)," box 4, Robinson Papers, and Dwight Eisenhower, 15 May 1964, Calls and Appointments 1964 (2), Appointment Book Series, Post-Presidential Papers, all in DDEL; transcript of Eisenhower-Cronkite interview on *CBS Evening News*, 15 May 1964, "Misc. Literature and Correspondence," box 3J8, Goldwater Collection, CAH; Ambrose, *Eisenhower*, 651–53.

46 See Dwight Eisenhower, 23 May, 5, 6, 11, 12, 16, 17, 29 June 1964, Calls and Appointments 1964 (3), Appointment Book Series, Post-Presidential Papers, DDEL. This also meshes with Eisenhower's public image. He always made certain that someone else served as front man and disliked being connected to controversy. See Greenstein, *Hidden-Hand Presidency*, 80–92, and Ambrose, *Eisenhower*, 653.

47 Travis Cross, typed manuscript of Notes for Shadegg, envelope "Travis Cross (1/6/65)," "Conversations," box 3J4, Goldwater Collection, CAH; Reinhard, *Republican Right*, 190; Theodore White, *1964*, 154–61.

48 Dwight Eisenhower, 24 June 1964, Calls and Appointments 1964 (3), 6, 7 July 1964, Calls and Appointments 1964 (4), box 2, Appointment Book Series, Post-Presidential Papers, DDEL; Ambrose, *Nixon: The Triumph of a Politician*, 52–53.

49 Draft Scranton National Campaign Committee, news release, 5 June 1964, "A15–38," box A15, General Correspondence and Constituent Case File, Ford Papers, GRFL; George McDowell to Lee Edwards, n.d., "L. E.," box 9, White Papers, CUL; Nelson Rockefeller to Gerald R. Ford, 16 June 1964, "A15–38," box A15, General Correspondence and Constituent Case File, Ford Papers, GRFL.

50 Theodore White, *1964*, 197–98; "Goldwater Heads Captive GOP," 27 July 1964, "Political Memo from COPE," no. 15-64, "Goldwater," box 48 (475), Files of Frederick Panzer, LBJL; "If Goldwater Were Elected President," cartoon, "1964 Campaign Anti-Goldwater Hate Literature," box 2, series 127, RNPP Papers; Shadegg, *What Happened to Goldwater?*, 152–54; Ted Lewis, "Capitol Stuff," *New York Daily News*, 15 July 1964; Reinhard, *Republican Right*, 192; Goldwater, *With No Apologies*, 185–86.

51 Confidential Memo to Goldwater Chairmen, 1 July 1964, "Convention Memos," box 7, White Papers, CUL; Joe Hatcher, "Goldwater Money Flowing at Convention," *Nashville Tennessean*, 14 July 1964; Burch and White, interviews by Shadegg.

52 John S. D. Eisenhower, "Notes," 12 July 1964, Calls and Appointments 1964 (4), box 2, Appointment Book Series, Post-Presidential Papers, DDEL; Theodore White, *1964*, 200–202; Reinhard, *Republican Right*, 193–94; "Remarks by Nelson Rockefeller in Support of the Scott Amendment," in *Official Report of the Proceedings of the Twenty-Eighth Republican National Convention Held in*

San Francisco, California, July 13, 14, 15, 16, 1964 (Washington, D.C.: Republican National Committee, 1964), box 10, Goldwater Papers, AHF. Shadegg believed that Rockefeller enjoyed his martyrdom. See Shadegg, *What Happened to Goldwater?*, 161. Rockefeller's nominators certainly used the incident to his advantage in their speeches for him. See "Speeches Nominating and Seconding Nelson Rockefeller for President," in ibid., 313–22. William Rusher claimed that the boos came not from the Goldwater delegates but from the gallery. See Rusher, *Rise of the Right*, 166.

53 See Reinhard, *Republican Right*, 195; William H. McKeon, memo, n.d., "Office Files of F. P. (Material Dealing with Rep. William Miller)," box 542 (1087), Files of Frederick Panzer, LBJL.

54 "Speeches Nominating and Seconding Barry Goldwater for President," in *Proceedings*, 301–13; Richard Nixon, "Speech Introducing Goldwater to Convention," in ibid., 408–12.

55 Barry Goldwater, Final Notes on Final Draft of Speech Accepting the Nomination, unlabeled folder, box 20, 1964 Presidential Campaign Papers, Goldwater Papers, AHF; Barry Goldwater, "Speech Accepting the Nomination," in *Proceedings*, 413–19.

56 "Convention Notes," *ACA Newsletter*, 19 August 1964, A2, reel 1, SDC; Burch, interview by Shadegg; Chuck Lichenstein, interview by Stephen Shadegg, n.d., envelope "Chuck Lichenstein (12/64)," box 3J24, Goldwater Collection, CAH; Theodore White, *1964*, 217; Nixon, *RN*, 260; F. Clifton White, *Suite 3505*, 14–15; White, interview by Shadegg; Goldwater interview, 82, COHP; Ambrose, *Nixon: The Triumph of a Politician*, 54.

57 "Goldwater Ideas Held Peril to Basic GOP Philosophy," *Charleston (W.V.) Gazette-Mail*, 16 August 1964; Statement to Be Released by Jim Farley on Behalf of the President, [20 July 1964], "PL6-3 7/20/64–9/19/64," EX PL6-3, box 117, White House Central Files, LBJL.

58 Transcript of the Proceedings of the RNC Organizational Meeting, 17 July 1964, box 8, Good Files, RNC Papers.

59 F. Clifton White, *Suite 3505*, 406; White, interview by author.

60 "Text of Nixon, Goldwater Notes," *Los Angeles Times*, 10 August 1964; Nixon, *RN*, 261–62; Dwight Eisenhower, 27 July 1964, Calls and Appointments 1964 (4), 4 August 1964, Calls and Appointments 1964 (5), box 2, Appointment Book Series, Post-Presidential Papers, DDEL.

61 Dwight Eisenhower, 29 July 1964, Calls and Appointments 1964 (4), 10 August 1964, Calls and Appointments 1964 (5), box 2, Appointment Book Series, Post-Presidential Papers, DDEL; "Confidential Proceedings of Closed Session Meeting of Republican Unity Conference," 12 August 1964, "PL6-3 Republican Party (7/20/64–9/19/64)," EX PL6-3, box 117, White House Central Files, LBJL.

62 "Confidential Proceedings," 77–87.

63 Dwight Eisenhower to Milton Eisenhower, 14 August 1964, "Correspondence (1964)," box 15, Milton Eisenhower Papers, DDEL.

CHAPTER FIVE

1 For accounts of the riots, see *New York Times*, 19–26 July 1964, and *Time*, 17, 24, 29, 31 July 1964. Theodore White devotes an entire chapter to the riots and their effect on the presidential campaign. See Theodore White, *1964*, chap. 8. See also *Time*, 31 July 1964, pp. 11–18; Muse, *American Negro Revolution*, 148–59; Brooks, *Walls Come Tumbling Down*, 236–59; and Goldman, *Tragedy of Lyndon Johnson*, 174–75.

2 Goldman, *Tragedy of Lyndon Johnson*, 173–74; "The Real Problem," editorial, *The Nation*, 10 August 1964, p. 41.

3 Goldwater, in his memoirs, claims that he and LBJ agreed to keep civil rights out of the campaign. See Goldwater, *With No Apologies*, 192–93. Meanwhile, *Time* reported that their meeting was "icily formal" and that both agreed, rather innocuously, that "racial tension should be avoided." See *Time*, 31 July 1964, p. 9, and Matusow, *Unraveling of America*, 139.

4 Evans and Novak, *Lyndon B. Johnson*, 360–82, 407–34.

5 Bernard R. Gifford, "War on Poverty: Assumptions, History, and Results—A Flawed but Important Effort," in Kaplan and Cuciti, *The Great Society*, 62. For an in-depth discussion of the limitations of the war on poverty, see Matusow, *Unraveling of America*, 217–71; Conkin, *Big Daddy from the Pedernales*, 235–42; and Moynihan, *Maximum Feasible Misunderstanding*.

6 "Deeper and Deeper," editorial, *The Nation*, 7 September 1964, p. 81; Gerald Ford to Mrs. J. D. Eppinaga, 11 August 1964, "Foreign Affairs (913)," box B12, Legislative File, Congressional Papers, Ford Papers, GRFL; "Shortening the Fuse," editorial, *The Nation*, 24 August 1964, p. 61. For a history of the war, see Herring, *America's Longest War*. For Johnson's reactions to the Tonkin Gulf incident, see Evans and Novak, *Lyndon B. Johnson*, 531–34, and Goldman, *Tragedy of Lyndon Johnson*, 175–83. LBJ telephoned Goldwater prior to his press conference, and Goldwater issued a supportive statement.

7 Barry Goldwater, "What Are the Issues on Which Voters Should Decide the 1964 Election?," "On Business and the Economy," statements for publication, "Mag., Newspapers, and Other Articles by BG," box 20, 1964 Presidential Campaign Papers, Goldwater Papers, AHF; Goldwater, *Conscience of a Conservative*, chap. 7; Barry Goldwater, "A Free and Prosperous American Agriculture," "To Promote the General Welfare," and "How Do You Feel about Federal Aid to Depressed Areas?," statements for publication, box 20, 1964 Presidential Campaign Papers, Goldwater Papers, AHF.

8 Barry Goldwater, "What Are the Issues?," "Captive Nations Form Statement," and "Defense Policy," statements for publication, "Mag., Newspaper, and Other Articles by BG," box 20, 1964 Presidential Campaign Papers, Goldwater Papers, AHF.

9 Shadegg expressed similar ideas in *What Happened to Goldwater?*, 186. F. Clifton White insisted that the "illusion of radicalism" surrounded Goldwater in *Suite 3505*, 409.

10 Reagan enacted much of the Goldwater platform but under very different economic and political circumstances.

11 Goldwater, *With No Apologies*, 167, 188. See also Goldwater, "To Promote the General Welfare."

12 Matusow, *Unraveling of America*, 147.

13 Ibid., 137; Norman Mailer, "In the Red Light: A History of the Republican Convention in 1964," *Esquire*, November 1964, p. 87; "Citizens for Goldwater-Miller," n.d., "Formation," box 5, White Papers, CUL; "Why 'Independent' Goldwater Groups?," *ACA Newsletter*, 21 September 1964, A2, reel 1, SDC. Lieutenant General James H. Doolittle and Clare Booth Luce were honorary cochairs of Citizens for Goldwater-Miller. See Shadegg, *What Happened to Goldwater?*, 186–88, for a more detailed discussion of the workings of the committee. Pennsylvania and New York were two states in which the citizens' organizations worked harder than the party regulars. See [state chair of Pennsylvania] to Bill Gill, 1 August 1965, "Humes Correspondence (1962–65)," Humes Papers, AHF; Rita Bree to Marvin Liebman, 9 November 1964, "Goldwater Campaign," box 92, Liebman Collection, HIWRP; Oliver Pilat, "Barry Seizing GOP Reins Here," *New York Post*, 15 September 1964; and Rus Walton to Stephen Shadegg, n.d., envelope "Rus Walton (1/65)," box 3J24, Goldwater Collection, CAH.

14 "Goldwater Wins! Now *We* Go to Work!," *ACA Newsletter*, 27 July 1964, "The Keys to Victory," *ACA Newsletter*, 8 September 1964, "Negro Newspaper Endorses Barry for President," *ACA Newsletter*, 5 October 1964, and "Union Men for Barry," *ACA Newsletter*, 26 October 1964, all in A2, reel 1, SDC; Goldwater for President Committee, press release, 20 October 1964, "Fighting Aces for Goldwater," box 90, Liebman Collection, HIWRP; Admiral Ben Moreel, "A Republic—If You Can Keep It," 26 September 1964, pamphlet published by Americans for Constitutional Action, A104, reel 13, SDC; Jack Valenti to Lyndon Johnson, 13 September 1964, "EX PL2 9/6/64–9/14/64," EX PL2, box 84, White House Central Files, LBJL.

15 Barry Goldwater, interview by Ed Edwin, 15 June 1967, OH21, transcript, 13–14, COHP; F. Clifton White, *Suite 3505*, 415.

16 F. Clifton White, interview by author, tape recording, Ashland, Ohio, 21 October 1987; Alexander, *Financing the 1964 Election*, 11, 73–75; William T. Evjue, "Oil Millionaires Support Barry Goldwater," transcript of radio show "Hello Wisconsin," 3 August 1964, printed in *Capitol Times* (Madison, Wis.); Raymond P. Brandt, "GOP Contributors to Come from Western Oil, Defense Interests Rather than East," *St. Louis Post-Dispatch*, 19 July 1964; Saul Friedman, "Texas Ranchers Have Key Role in Goldwater's Campaign," *Houston Chronicle*, 26 July 1964; "Texas Ranchers Back Goldwater," *Providence (R.I.) Journal*, 27 July 1964; Warren Berry, "Goldwater Meets Money Men First," *Denver Post*, 17 July 1964; Republican National Committee, transcript of proceedings of executive session of meeting, 22 January 1965, box 8, Good Files, RNC Papers.

17 Goldman, *Tragedy of Lyndon Johnson*, 169–72, 213–56; Evans and Novak, *Lyndon B. Johnson*, 464–83; Kearns, *Lyndon Johnson*, 214–19; Conkin, *Big Daddy from the Pedernales*, 189–90; Theodore White, *1964*, chaps. 9, 12.

18 Merle Miller, *Lyndon*, 386–401; Goldman, *Tragedy of Lyndon Johnson*, 190–256; Evans and Novak, *Lyndon B. Johnson*, 465–83. For an example of staff suggestions, see Walter Heller to Lyndon Johnson, 9, 18 September 1964, "PL6-3 Republican Party (7/20/64–9/19/64)," EX PL6-3, box 117, White House Central Files, LBJL.

19 James F. Fitzpatrick to Liz Carpenter et al., 3 June 1964, "EX PL2 5/1/64–6/14/64," EX PL2, and Ken Lester to Lyndon Johnson, 7 April 1964, "EX PL2 3/17/64–4/30/64," EX PL2, both in box 83, White House Central Files, LBJL; Theodore White, *1964*, 352–53; National Independent Committee for President Johnson and Senator Humphrey, press release, 3 September 1964, "1964 Campaign, Business Idiots," box 2, series 127, RNPP Papers; Henry F. Fowler to James Rowe and Clifford Carter, 24 July 1964, "EX PL2 8/26/64–9/5/64," EX PL2, box 83, White House Central Files, LBJL.

20 Letters from Republican supporters to Johnson in Gen PL/Reps for Johnson, boxes 22 and 23, Thomas J. Deegan to Lyndon Johnson, 21 September 1964, "EX PL2 9/21/64–9/24/64," EX PL2, box 84, Drew Pearson to Bill Moyers, 2 March 1964, "EX PL2 Elections, Campaigns (2/11/63–3/15/64)," EX PL2, box 82, and Lawrence C. Merthan to Walter Jenkins, 2 October 1964, "EX PL2 10/2/64–10/4/64," EX PL2, box 84, all in White House Central Files, LBJL; Goldman, *Tragedy of Lyndon Johnson*, 228.

21 Barry Goldwater to Stephen Shadegg, 10 May 1978, Goldwater Book Materials and Columns, Goldwater Papers, AHF. For a discussion of the development of Johnson's credibility problems, see, among others, Turner, *Lyndon Johnson's Dual War*, 140–41.

22 Goldman, *Tragedy of Lyndon Johnson*, 249–52. Theodore White makes much of the fact that Goldwater refused to exploit Jenkins's arrest. See Theodore White, *1964*, 367–69. See also Dwight Eisenhower, 12 September 1964, Calls and Appointments 1964 (6), box 2, Appointment Book Series, Post-Presidential Papers, DDEL.

23 Henry H. Wilson, Jr., to Lawrence O'Brien, 8 July 1964, "EX PL2 6/15/64–7/23/64," EX PL2, box 83, and John Kenneth Galbraith to Lyndon Johnson, 3 August 1964, "PL2 Elections, Campaigns (1964–66)," C.F. PL/ST#15–32, box 77, both in White House Central Files, LBJL; "The Shoo-In Fallacy," editorial, *The Nation*, 10 February 1964, p. 130; "The Silent Vote," editorial, *The Nation*, 26 October 1964, p. 261; Goldman, *Tragedy of Lyndon Johnson*, 232–38.

24 Peter O'Donnell to Barry Goldwater, 12 January 1964, "Letter to BG from POD," box 9, White Papers, CUL; Rusher, *Rise of the Right*, 157–59; Shadegg, *What Happened to Goldwater?*, 171–84; Richard Kleindienst to Stephen Shadegg, 18 November 1964, envelope "Richard Kleindienst: Notes and Conversation," box 3J23, Jim Day, telephone interview by Stephen Shadegg, n.d., envelope "Jim Day (12/64)," box 3J24, and F. Clifton White, interview by Stephen Shadegg, December 1964, envelope "Clif White (12/64)," box 3J24, all in Goldwater Collection, CAH. Rusher claims that Goldwater felt that White and his crew had forced him into a candidacy he did not want and that

therefore Goldwater did not want to appoint White as chair. See Rusher, *Rise of the Right*, 169–70. Shadegg asserts that White did not want to be appointed chair of the citizens' committee because citizens' committees usually work at odds with the regular party and he was closely connected to the party. See Shadegg, *What Happened to Goldwater?*, 185–86. In his memoirs, Goldwater admitted that at that time loyalty and friendship had been much more important to him than any other concerns. See Goldwater, *With No Apologies*, 166.

25 John Gardiner and Ann Bowler to F. Clifton White, 14 August 1964, "California," box 1, Charles Eden to F. Clifton White, 25 September 1964, "St. Org.– Rhode Island," box 4, D. Lorraine Yerkes to F. Clifton White, 12 August 1964, "Florida–St. Org.," box 1, and Robert Goldwater to Denison Kitchel, 20 July 1964, "Arizona," box 1, all in White Papers, CUL. Karl Hess's memoir is filled with insinuations about the professional politicians of the Draft Goldwater Committee who tried to force Goldwater to compromise his principles to become more marketable. See Hess, *In a Cause That Will Triumph*, chaps. 1, 2. Kitchel told Nixon that Richard Kleindienst deserved more credit than White for winning the nomination. See Denison Kitchel to Richard Nixon, 29 March 1968, "Nixon, Richard (1960–68)," box 3, Kitchel Papers, HIWRP. For the other side of the story, see the pertinent chapters in F. Clifton White, *Suite 3505*; Rusher, *Rise of the Right*; and Shadegg, *What Happened to Goldwater?*

26 Peter O'Donnell and Stephen Shadegg, transcript of conversation, July 1964, envelope "Peter O'Donnell (12/64)," and Doug Whitlock, interview by Stephen Shadegg, n.d., envelope "Doug Whitlock (12/64)," both in box 3J24, Goldwater Collection, CAH. See also Shadegg, *What Happened to Goldwater?*, 177–78, 271–72; Reinhard, *Republican Right*, 200; and Barry Goldwater to Stephen Shadegg, 30 July 1964, "Correspondence between Shadegg and Goldwater," box 3H513, Goldwater Collection, CAH.

27 Rowland Evans and Robert Novak, "Inside Report: The Scapegoats," *New York Herald Tribune*, 4 October 1964; Denison Kitchel to Jean Hawkins, 5 July 1977, "Hawkins, Jean (Mrs. Paul M.), Undated (1965–80)," box 2, Kitchel Papers, HIWRP; Rus Walton and Stephen Shadegg, transcript of conversations, 11 February, 27 January 1965, n.d., envelope "Rus Walton (1/65)," box 3J24, Goldwater Collection, CAH; Denison Kitchel to Karl Lamb, 30 March 1965, "Lamb, Karl (1965)," box 2, Kitchel Papers, HIWRP.

28 Karl A. Lamb, "Under One Roof: Barry Goldwater's Campaign Staff," in Cosman and Huckshorn, *Republican Politics*, 17–21.

29 [Stephen Shadegg], "Notes Dictated on B Side of Record #20," envelope "Dean Burch (12/64)," Goldwater Collection, CAH; Whitlock, interview by Shadegg; John Grenier, interview by Stephen Shadegg, n.d., envelope "John Grenier (12/64)," box 3J24, Goldwater Collection, CAH; Kleindienst, conversation with Shadegg; F. Clifton White, *Suite 3505*, 415–16; Denison Kitchel to John Grenier, 11 March 1965, "Grenier, John (1965)," box 2, Kitchel Papers, HIWRP; Wayne Hood, telephone interview by Stephen Shadegg, December 1964, envelope "Wayne Hood (12/64)," box 3J24, and Travis Cross, interview by Stephen Shadegg, 6 January 1965, envelope "Travis Cross (1/6/65)," "Conversations," box 3J4, both in Goldwater Collection, CAH.

30 David S. Broder, "GOP Chiefs Meet to Map Reorganization," *Washington Evening Star*, 17 July 1964; Joseph A. Loftus, "GOP Committee Gets a New Look," *New York Times*, 3 September 1964; Laurence Stern, "Barry's Aides to Start Vast GOP Reshuffle," *Washington Post*, 26 July 1964; Carleton Kent, "GOP Committee Gets a Key Role," *Chicago Sun-Times*, 18 July 1964; Charles Bartlett, "Republican Committee Upheaval," *Washington Star*, 3 September 1964; Dwight Eisenhower, 9 September 1964, Calls and Appointments 1964 (6), box 2, Appointment Book Series, Post-Presidential Papers, DDEL; Theodore White, *1964*, 333-34.

31 John O. Beatty to William F. Knowland, 23 September 1964, "California," box 1, White Papers, CUL; [state chair of Pennsylvania] to Bill Gill, 1 August 1965, "Humes Correspondence (1962-65)," Humes Papers, AHF. For examples, see Shadegg, *What Happened to Goldwater?*, 174-75, 208, 265; F. Clifton White, *Suite 3505*, 16; Rusher, *Rise of the Right*, 157; White, interview by Shadegg; O'Donnell, conversation with Shadegg; and White, interview by author.

32 Shadegg, *What Happened to Goldwater?*, 213-15, 217-18, 231-37, 239-40.

33 Arthur J. Brandt to Dean Burch, 15 September 1964, "Politics, A/B, Misc.," box 64, Summerfield Papers, DDEL; Clyde B. Pinson to James M. Day, 30 August 1964, "West Virginia," box 4, and Barbara S. Lucy to F. Clifton White, 23 October 1964, "New Hampshire," box 3, both in White Papers, CUL.

34 Advertisement, *National Chronicle*, 4 November 1965, N11, reel 79, and Douglas Eby, "Operation Cover Up," *American Capsule News*, 8 August 1964, A21, reel 4, both in SDC; Welch, *New Americanism*; "Golden Steamroller," *American Capsule News*, 16 August 1963, A21, reel 4, SDC. For opposition, see Dagmar Reedy to William Miller, 13 August 1964, "John Birch Society," box 55, Miller Papers, CUL; Jean Powell, "Ex-Resident of Arizona Urges All to Heed Barry Goldwater's Civil Rights Deeds," *ACA Newsletter*, 24 August 1964, A2, reel 1, SDC; and George Lincoln Rockwell to William F. Buckley, Jr., 9 September 1963, "Rockwell, Lincoln (1963)," box 27, General Correspondence, Buckley Papers, YUL.

35 Raymond C. Swain to Lyndon Johnson, 18 July 1964, Gen PL/Reps for Johnson, box 22, Jack Valenti to Lyndon Johnson, 7 September 1964, "EX PL2 9/6/64-9/14/64," EX PL2, box 84, and Jack Valenti to Bill Moyers et al., 14 September 1964, "EX PL2 9/6/64-9/14/64," EX PL2, box 84, all in White House Central Files, LBJL; "Record of Senator Barry Goldwater," 1 August 1963, "Office Files of Bill Moyers: Goldwater (2 of 2)," box 32 (1350), Files of Bill Moyers, LBJL; "Study of Goldwater's Right-Wing Activity Shows Early Extremist Links and Continuing Help from Far Right," Group Research Report, 15 October 1964, and "Barry Goldwater and the Organized Right," 12 October 1964, Special Report #17, both in "Wilson: Right Wing," box 5, Files of Henry Wilson, LBJL; Bill Moyers to Lloyd Wright (DNC), 14 September 1964, "EX PL2 9/6/64-9/14/64," EX PL2, box 84, White House Central Files, LBJL; memo, 28 July 1964, "Office Files of Moyers: Campaign (2 of 2)," box 53 (1359), Files of Bill Moyers, LBJL.

36 Theodore White, *1964*, 322.

37 Ibid., 323; Goldwater, *With No Apologies*, 197; Burnett Anderson to George Reedy, 15 August 1964, "PL6-3 Republican Party (7/20/64–9/19/64)," EX PL6-3, box 117, and Fred Dutton (Research Division, DNC), "The Goldwater Candidacy and the Christian Conscience: The Response of Protestant Theologians," n.d., "PL6-3 10/27/64–4/22/67," Gen PL6-3, box 120, both in White House Central Files, LBJL; *Fact: 1,189 Psychiatrists Say Goldwater Is Psychologically Unfit to Be President*, n.d., "Office Files of George Reedy (1964 Campaign Material)," box 25 (1405/1497), Files of George Reedy, LBJL.

38 *The Goldwater Cartoon Book*, n.d., "Office Files of Moyers: The Goldwater Cartoon Book," box 37 (1352–53), Files of Bill Moyers, LBJL; Jack Valenti to Bill Moyers et al., 14 September 1964, "EX PL2 9/6/64–9/14/64," EX PL2, box 84, White House Central Files, LBJL; Page Huidekoper Wilson, "Through a Looking Glass Darkly: A Political Fantasy," n.d., "Office Files of Moyers: Goldwater (2 of 2)," box 32 (1350), Files of Bill Moyers, LBJL.

39 "The California Primary," editorial, *The Nation*, 15 June 1964, p. 593; "Plight of the Moderates," editorial, *The Nation*, 29 June 1964, p. 641; Carey McWilliams, "High Noon in the Cow Palace," *The Nation*, 27 July 1964, pp. 23–27; Carey McWilliams, "Goldwaterism: The New Ideology," *The Nation*, 24 August 1964, pp. 68–71; Arthur M. Schlesinger, Jr., Notes on RFK, n.d., "Kennedy, Robert, 1964 Campaign, Notes by AMS," box P-6, Private Files, Schlesinger Papers, Robert Kennedy, Address at Liberal Party Dinner, 24 September 1964, "9/24/64 Liberal Party Dinner, NYC," box 20, 1964 Campaign File, Senate Papers, Robert F. Kennedy Papers, and Eugene A. Theroux (associate director of Young Citizens for Johnson-Humphrey) to J. K. Galbraith, 29 September 1964, "Presidential Campaign 1964, General (8/18/64–11/7/64), Undated Notes," box 51, General Correspondence, Galbraith Papers, all in JFKL.

40 Chuck Lichenstein, interview by Stephen Shadegg, box 3J24, Goldwater Collection, CAH; Dwight Eisenhower, 21 August 1964, Calls and Appointments 1964 (5), box 2, Appointment Book Series, Post-Presidential Papers, DDEL; White, interview by Shadegg; "Goldwater 'Unpopular' with the Voters?: Not So—Says Stan Evans," *ACA Newsletter*, 10 August 1964, A2, reel 1, SDC; Shadegg, interview by reporter for *FACT* magazine, n.d., envelope "Fact Magazine," "Conversations," box 3J4, Goldwater Collection, CAH; John Grenier to Barry Goldwater, 8 February 1965, "Grenier, John (1965)," box 2, Kitchel Papers, HIWRP.

41 Norris J. Nelson to Arthur Summerfield, 28 August 1964, "Politics, N/O/P, Misc.," box 65, Summerfield Papers, DDEL; "On Guard," *The Spirit*, July–August 1964, A49, reel 8, SDC; Grenier, interview by Shadegg; David Laurence, "What Goldwater Said on the A-Bomb," *New York Herald Tribune*, 28 May 1964.

42 Shadegg devotes an entire chapter to this phenomenon. See Shadegg, *What Happened to Goldwater?*, chap. 35. The *National Review* constantly pointed out the unbalanced treatment Goldwater received from the press. See, for exam-

ple, William F. Buckley, Jr., "The Vile Campaign," *National Review*, 6 October 1964, pp. 853–58.

43 See, for example, Saul Kohler, "Goldwater Stirs Fund Problem for State GOP," *Philadelphia Inquirer*, 26 July 1964; Peter Byrnes to Rita Bree, 23 September 1964, "Peter Byrnes, Correspondence," box 11, White Papers, CUL; and Political Background, Wisconsin, 6 October 1964, "Wisconsin (Oct. 6, 1964)," box 5, and Campaign Notes, Michigan, "Michigan (Oct. 16, 1964)," box 4, both in series 127, RNPP Papers.

44 Charles P. Taft to Richard Nixon, 2 October 1964, "1964 Campaign Committee to Support Moderate Republicans," box 2, series 127, RNPP Papers; Robert G. Spivak, "Watch on the Potomac: The Republican Refugees," 27 July 1964, Publishers' Newspaper Syndicate Release, "PL6-3 7/22/64–7/31/64," EX PL6-3, box 119, White House Central Files, LBJL; Alexander, *Financing the 1964 Election*, 12.

45 James Hagerty, interview #1 by Ed Edwin, 2 March 1967, OH91, transcript, 46, COHP; " 'Moderately Yours' Becoming Extremely Popular," *RCCN*, 28 August 1964, p. 5.

46 Keith Russell and Patty Russell to Lyndon Johnson, 25 October 1964, "PL/Reps for Johnson (11/2/64–12/4/64)," Gen PL/Reps for Johnson, box 23, Francis S. Levien to Lyndon Johnson, 29 July 1964, "PL/Reps for Johnson (11/22/63–8/20/64)," EX PL/Humphrey, H./Pro, box 26, Jack Brooks to Ivan Sinclair, 28 May 1964, "PL/Reps for Johnson (11/22/63–8/3/64)," Gen PL/Reps for Johnson, box 22, J. Kenneth Galbraith to Lyndon Johnson, 3 August 1964, "PL2 Elections, Campaigns (1964–66)," C.F. PL/St#15–32, box 77, Hubert Humphrey to Jack Valenti, 5 August 1964, "EX PL2 7/24/64–8/5/64," EX PL2, box 83, and Tom Corcoran to Bill Moyers, 30 October 1964, "PL/Reps for Johnson (10/11/64–11/10/64)," EX PL/Humphrey, H./Pro, box 26, all in White House Central Files, LBJL.

47 Gwen Barnett to Ione Harrington, 8 October 1964, "Idaho," box 2, White Papers, CUL; Burch, interview by Shadegg; David Halberstam, "Keating Stumps with Rockefeller," *New York Times*, 9 October 1964; George Romney, statement, 12 August 1964, "Michigan (Oct. 16, 1964)," box 4, series 127, RNPP Papers; Arthur Summerfield to Richard Nixon, 7 February 1968, Album IX, "Richard Nixon (1)," box 2, Summerfield Papers, DDEL. Not only did Rockefeller refuse to publicly support Goldwater, but also LBJ's staff somehow got Rockefeller's files on Goldwater and the extremists. How they acquired the files is not known, but they did think the information they gained from them would save them time and effort during the campaign. See Myer Feldman to Bill Moyers, 10 September 1964, "EX PL2 9/6/64–9/14/64," EX PL2, box 84, White House Central Files, LBJL.

48 "National Ticket Will Help House Candidates," *RCCN*, 24 July 1964; William Scranton to Barry Goldwater, 15 October 1964, "Wm Scranton," Alpha File, and William Scranton, "Introduction of Barry Goldwater," 29 October 1964, "October," box 19, 1964 Presidential Campaign Papers, both in Goldwater

Papers, AHF; "Connecticut GOP Solves Dilemma," *New York Times*, 16 August 1964.

49 Dwight Eisenhower, 31 July 1964, Calls and Appointments 1964 (4), 21 October 1964, Calls and Appointments 1964 (7), both in box 2, Appointment Book Series, Post-Presidential Papers, Dwight Eisenhower to Milton Eisenhower, 14 August 1964, "Correspondence (1964)," box 15, Milton Eisenhower Papers, Dwight Eisenhower, 8, 22 September 1964, Calls and Appointments 1964 (9), box 2, Appointment Book Series, Post-Presidential Papers, and Dwight Eisenhower to "Mr. and Mrs. Citizens of Christian County, Illinois," form letter, 19 October 1964, "Rep. Party, Service to," box 1, Convenience File, Post-Presidential Papers, all in DDEL; Nixon, *RN*, 262; Dwight Eisenhower, Address at Percy Dinner, 24 September 1964, "Illinois (Oct. 7, 29)," box 4, series 127, RNPP Papers; Dwight Eisenhower, 1 December 1964, Calls and Appointments 1964 (9), box 2, Appointment Book Series, Post-Presidential Papers, DDEL; Hagerty interview, 566–67, COHP; Dwight Eisenhower to Private James H. Lovelle, 9 September 1964, "DDE's Views on Participating in 1964 Election," box 1, Convenience File, Post-Presidential Papers, DDEL.

50 Nixon, *RN*, 263; Office of Richard Nixon, news release, 29 September 1964, and Loie Grace Gaunt to Vera Ash, 19 December 1964, both in "1964 Campaign, Schedules," box 1, Richard Nixon, form letter, and replies, "1964 Campaign, RN Fund-raising Letter and Replies," boxes 3–5, Richard Nixon to Alfred W. Wallace, 4 September 1964, "1964 Campaign, RN Fund-raising Letter and Replies," box 3, C. M. Lichenstein to Richard Nixon, 7 October 1964, "1964 Campaign, Misc. Goldwater/RNC Communications," box 2, and Richard Nixon, memo and statement, 7 October 1964, "1964 Campaign, RN Nuclear Stas [*sic*]," box 3, all in series 127, RNPP Papers; Peter B. Taub, "Victory in Store for Keating-Nixon," *Rochester Times-Union*, 5 October 1964; "Nixon Urges Stamford Meeting of Area GOP to Back Goldwater," *Stamford Advocate*, 20 October 1964; John A. Grimes, "Nixon Stumps Hard for Barry Goldwater—Motives Stir Debate," *Wall Street Journal*, 6 October 1964; Arthur Knock, "The Essential Pilgrimage of Richard Nixon," *New York Times*, 2 October 1964.

51 Donald Zerial to F. Clifton White, n.d., "Michigan," Edwin Neuger to William G. McFadzen, 7 August 1964, "St. Chrm. and Co-Chrm., Minnesota," Harold B. Estes to F. Clifton White, 5 August 1964, "St. Org., Hawaii," and Jack E. Molesworth to Eugene Clapp, 17 September 1964, "St. Org., Mass.," all in box 2, White Papers, CUL; Bob Seigrist to Richard Nixon, telephone message, 14 October 1964, "Wisconsin (October 6, 1964)," box 5, series 127, RNPP Papers; Loretta Fox and Stephen Shadegg, transcript of conversation, 17 October 1964, envelope "Loretta Fox (10/17/64)," "Conversations," box 3J4, Goldwater Collection, CAH; Shadegg, *What Happened to Goldwater?*, 271–72.

52 "Choice," draft of movie script, 1 October 1964, "Choice," box 6, White Papers, CUL; White, interview by Shadegg; Shadegg, *What Happened to Goldwater?*, 244–45; F. Clifton White, *Suite 3505*, 414–15.

53 E. Keith Hartzell to F. Clifton White, 22 October 1964, "Colorado, St. Chrm. and Co-Chrm.," box 1, White Papers, CUL.

54 Goldwater, *With No Apologies*, 166; Rowland Evans and Robert Novak, "Inside Report: Goldwater's Future," *New York Herald Tribune*, 15 October 1964; Shadegg, *What Happened to Goldwater?*, 231–37; [state chair of Pennsylvania] to Bill Gill, 1 August 1965, Humes Correspondence (1962–65)," Humes Papers, AHF; Fox, conversation with Shadegg.

55 Shadegg, "Notes after Having Breakfast with O'Donnell," envelope "Peter O'Donnell (12/64)," box 3J24, Goldwater Collection, CAH; Burch, interview by Shadegg; Dean Burch, Address before the National Press Club, 8 January 1965, "1965 Releases," box 6, RNC Papers; Barry Goldwater to Stephen Shadegg, 10 May 1978, Goldwater Book Materials and Columns, Goldwater Papers, AHF; William F. Buckley, Jr., "No Death Knell for Conservatism," *Arizona Republic*, 8 November 1964.

56 John S. Knight, "Old Conservatism Thing of the Past," *Arizona Republic*, 8 November 1964; M. Stanton Evans, "The Prospects for Conservatism," ACU Special Report, 1966, "ACU Mailings," box 58, Liebman Collection, HIWRP; "Whither the GOP?," *Arizona Republic*, 8 November 1964; Barry Goldwater, Statement on the 1964 Election, *Congressional Quarterly*, 4 November 1964, pp. 2667–68; William F. Rickenbacker et al. to Marvin Liebman, 18 January 1965, "Conservative Party," box 85, Liebman Collection, HIWRP; Kenneth Kellar to Denison Kitchel, 20 November 1964, "Kellar, Kenneth C. (1962–79)," box 2, Kitchel Papers, HIWRP.

57 White, interview by Shadegg; Sam Hay and Stephen Shadegg, transcript of conversation, envelope "Sam Hay (12/64)," and Willis Johnson, "A Personal Report on the Republican National Committee and on the National Campaign of 1964," both in box 3J24, Goldwater Collection, CAH; Richard Neville to Marvin Liebman, 24 November 1964, "Goldwater Campaign," box 92, Liebman Collection, HIWRP; Burch, interview by Shadegg; Dean Burch, Remarks before the Associated Students of the University of Utah, 15 February 1965, "1965 Releases," box 6, RNC Papers; Knight, "Old Conservatism Thing of the Past"; Burch, interview by Shadegg; Barry Goldwater to Stephen Shadegg, 23 June 1965, box 3J24, Goldwater Collection, CAH; Barry Goldwater, Address before the RNC, 22 January 1965, "1965 Releases," box 6, RNC Papers.

58 Barry Goldwater to "Bob and Harry," [1978?], unlabeled folder and box, Goldwater Papers, AHF. See also Goldwater, Statement on the 1964 Election; Dean Burch to Karl Hess, 10 August 1965, "Burch, Dean," box 1, Kitchel Papers, HIWRP; Wallace Turner, "Republican Leaders in the West Doubt That Goldwater Can Retain His Party Leadership," *New York Times*, 8 November 1964; "The Week," *National Review*, 29 June 1965, p. 534; Goldwater, *With No Apologies*, 207; and Barry Goldwater, Notes to Diary, 28 August 1972, 25 June 1976, box 3, Alpha File, Goldwater Papers, AHF.

59 Earl Mazo, "Goldwater Sees Need to Realign Two Major Parties," *New York Times*, 15 November 1964. Most Republicans disagreed with his plan. See

Feliz Belair, Jr., "GOP Skeptical of a Party Shift," *New York Times*, 17 November 1964; Roger Milliken to F. Clifton White, 16 November 1964, "Letters," box 20, White Papers, CUL; Nelson Rockefeller to Leonard Finder, 25 November 1964, "R," box 15, Finder Papers, DDEL; and Statement by Governor Rockefeller, 5 November 1964, "Post-Election Newsclipping," box 2, series 128, RNPP Papers.

60 Meade Alcorn, interview by Ed Edwin, 5 June 1967, OH163, transcript, 89–93, 118–19, COHP; Leonard Hall, interview, 19 May 1975, OH478, transcript, 17, Eisenhower Library Collection, DDEL; David Lawrence, "Voters Rejected Idea of Change," *Arizona Republic*, 8 November 1964; John Grenier to Barry Goldwater, 8 February 1965, "Grenier, John (1965)," box 2, Kitchel Papers, HIWRP; Dean Burch, Address to the GOP District Convention, 13 March 1965, "1965 Releases," box 6, RNC Papers. Mayer states that Republicans actually made little gain except on the national level in the Deep South. See Mayer, *Republican Party*, 552–55.

61 Lawrence, "Voters Rejected Idea of Change"; Jim Hooker to F. Clifton White, 9 November 1964, "Letters," box 20, White Papers, CUL; "Conservatives, Tend to Your Knitting," *American Spirit*, January 1965, A49, reel 8, SDC; M. Stanton Evans, "The Prospects for Conservatism," ACU Special Report, 1966, "ACU Mailings," box 58, Liebman Collection, HIWRP; "Some Observations on the November Election," *ACA Newsletter*, January 1965, A2, reel 1, and " 'Greatly Exaggerated,' " *America's Future*, 20 November 1964, A19, reel 3, both in SDC; Denison Kitchel to Ronald Reagan, 8 June 1966, "Reagan, Ronald (1966–80)," box 3, Kitchel Papers, HIWRP. Those at least temporarily discouraged included journalist Morrie Ryskind, who felt the country had made a fatal turn to the left ("Election Marked Beginning of End," *Arizona Republic*, 8 November 1964); Clifton White, who felt it was a "real tragedy" that millions of sacrificing conservatives had been let down (White, interview by Shadegg); and Donald E. Lukens, who kicked in his television screen and bought a plane ticket to Australia (Donald E. Lukens, interview by author, tape recording, Hamilton, Ohio, 6 February 1988).

62 Bob Hunter to Douglas Cater, 12 November 1964, "EX PL2 11/1/64–11/15/64," EX PL2, box 86, White House Central Files, LBJL; Art Buchwald, "President Who?," *Evolve*, April 1965, E8, reel 44, SDC.

63 *Washington Evening Star*, 10 November 1964; National Economic Council, Inc., "Economic Council Letter," 15 November 1964, E3, reel 44, SDC; Margaret Braden, Keynote Speech to the Arizona Federation of Republican Women, 16 January 1965, "Republican National Committee (1959–72)," box 3, Kitchel Papers, HIWRP; Dwight Eisenhower, 30 October 1964, Calls and Appointments 1964 (7), box 2, Appointment Book Series, Post-Presidential Papers, DDEL; C. L. Cooper to McGeorge Bundy, 29 October 1964, "Republican Press Releases, etc.," box 491 (478), Files of Frederick Panzer, LBJL; Bruce W. Frazer to Marvin Liebman, 15 March 1965, "American Conservative Union," box 7, Liebman Collection, HIWRP; Nixon, *RN*, 263.

64 Rusher, *New Majority Party*, 47–48.

CHAPTER SIX

1 Charles P. Taft to Richard Nixon, 2 October 1964, "1964 Campaign Committee to Support Moderate Republicans," box 2, series 127, RNPP Papers; Nelson Rockefeller to Leonard Finder, 28 August 1964, and Leonard Finder to Nelson Rockefeller, 29 September 1964, both in "R," box 15, and Dwight Eisenhower to Leonard Finder, 6 November, 1 December 1964, "Finder-Eisenhower Correspondence (1955–69)," box 1, all in Finder Papers, Dwight Eisenhower, 30 October 1964, Calls and Appointments 1964 (7), 30 November 1964, Calls and Appointments 1964 (8), box 2, Appointment Book Series, Post-Presidential Papers, all in DDEL; John D. Morris, "Eisenhower Backs GOP Unity Move," *New York Times*, 22 November 1964; Wallace Turner, "Romney Ties His Political Plans to a Parley of Full Leadership," *New York Times*, 21 November 1964.

2 Dwight Eisenhower, statement, 5 November 1964, "Finder-Eisenhower Correspondence (1955–69)," Finder Papers, DDEL; Barry Goldwater, Address before the RNC, 22 January 1965, "1965 Releases," box 6, RNC Papers; "Steer Party Back to High Center: Nixon," *Chicago Tribune*, 11 November 1964; McCandlish Phillips, "Nixon Recommends Move to the Center—Rejects Rightist Extremists," *New York Times*, 11 November 1964. Eisenhower even sent his friends a letter explaining his views on the party, which he intended as the possible basis for a statement of purpose. For example, see Dwight Eisenhower to William Robinson, 4 December 1964, "Eisenhower (1964)," box 4, Robinson Papers, DDEL.

3 Joseph Hearst, "Fight Begins for GOP Lead," *Chicago Tribune*, 6 November 1964.

4 William Scranton to Barry Goldwater, 8 January 1965, "William Scranton," Alpha File, Goldwater Papers, AHF; Dwight Eisenhower and Mark Hatfield, 8 December 1964, and Dwight Eisenhower and George Romney, 7 December 1964, both in Calls and Appointments 1964 (9), box 2, Appointment Book Series, George Romney to Dwight Eisenhower, 28 December 1964, "Romney, George (1963–66)," box 17, Special Name Series, and Dwight Eisenhower, 25 November 1964, box 2, Calls and Appointments 1964 (8), Appointment Book Series, all in Post-Presidential Papers, DDEL.

5 Kitchel's associate Kenneth Kellar and Goldwater aide Travis Cross were among those who believed Burch had not been effective. See Kenneth Kellar to Denison Kitchel, 4 January 1965, "Kellar, Kenneth C. (1962–79)," box 2, Kitchel Papers, HIWRP, and Travis Cross, interview by Stephen Shadegg, 6 January 1965, envelope "Travis Cross (1/6/65)," "Conversations," box 3J4, Goldwater Collection, CAH. For those supporting Burch, see "GOP Senatorial Leader Praises Chairman Burch . . . ," RNC press release, 8 December 1964, "National Committee Meeting, Chicago, Ill., January 22–23, 1965, Business," box 1, Good Files, RNC Papers; and Denison Kitchel to Warren Nutter, 6 January 1965, and Warren Nutter to Virginius Dabney, 15 December 1964, both in "Correspondence, General (1/16–4/30/65)," box 4, Kitchel Papers, HIWRP.

6 "GOP Shuffle," *National Review*, 26 January 1965, p. 49; Dean Burch, "The Republican Challenge for 1965," 4 January 1965, Address before the National Press Club, 8 January 1965, and statement, 12 January 1965, and Barry Goldwater, statement, 12 January 1965, all in "1965 Releases," box 6, RNC Papers; Peter O'Donnell and Stephen Shadegg, transcript of conversation, 10 February 1965, envelope "Peter O'Donnell (12/64)," box 3J24, Goldwater Collection, CAH; "GOP Shuffle," *National Review*, 26 January 1965, p. 49. Goldwater wrote Romney: "I am convinced that I am the one your group would like to see out of the Party, not Dean Burch." See Barry Goldwater to George Romney, 8 December 1964, "Nixon, Political (1965)," box 8, Seaton Papers, DDEL.

7 Transcript of the Minutes of the Executive Session of the Executive Committee of the RNC, 21 January 1965, pp. 8–15, box 8, Good Files, RNC Papers. I have not been able to discover who was at the meeting in Phoenix besides Goldwater, Burch, and Bliss. All three refused to discuss specifically what took place at that meeting. Bliss was especially cryptic in his press conference following the meeting. Instead of naming the other participants, he constantly referred to a "they" whom he would not identify. See Ray Bliss, press conference, 13 January 1965, "Press Conferences, 1965, RCB," box 8, Stull Papers, RNC Papers. Dean Burch, in an interview with the author, stated that he did not remember such a meeting ever taking place. He said that he had never met Bliss and that only Goldwater supporters were at the meeting. See Dean Burch, interview by author, tape recording, Washington, D.C., 30 June 1989. Theodore White, in his book on the election, claims the decision was made in December, but all the evidence I have examined suggests that the meeting occurred later. See Theodore White, *1968*, 37.

8 Transcript of the Minutes of the Executive Session of the Executive Committee of the RNC, 21 January 1965, p. 4, box 8, Good Files, RNC Papers.

9 Ibid., 11.

10 Ray Bliss, statement, 12 January 1965, and Barry Goldwater, statement, 12 January 1965, both in "1965 Releases," box 6, and Dean Burch to Ray Bliss, February 1965, and "Report by the Chairman to the RNC," 1 July–31 January 1966, both in "Reports, RCB," box 9, Stull Papers, all in RNC Papers.

11 F. Clifton White, interview by author, tape recording, Ashland, Ohio, 21 October 1987; Reinhard, *Republican Right*, 210–11; Ray Bliss, press conferences, 21 June, 23 July 1966, 7 April 1967, "Press Conferences (1966)," box 7, Stull Papers, RNC Papers; Max Freedman, "Goldwater's Fund-Raising Success," *Washington Evening Star*, 19 May 1965; Ray Bliss, article for *Rhode Island Republican*, April 1965, "Correspondence Received (1965–66)," box 4, and Ray Bliss, interview by *U.S. News and World Report*, 10 September 1965, "Interviews, RCB (1965)," box 1, both in Stull Papers, and "Republican Beliefs: A Handy Guide Compiled by Senator Carlson," Republican Research Memo, no. 6, 22 April 1966, *Republican Research Memos, 1–35, 1966–67* (Washington, D.C.: Research Division, RNC, n.d.), box 37, 2d ser., all in RNC Papers; Dorothy A. Elston, "What Republicans Believe In," *RCCN*, 5 July 1965, p. 4.

12 Robert E. Smylie, Address at Eisenhower Birthday Dinner, 15 October 1965,

and Barry Goldwater, Address before the RNC, 22 January 1965, both in "1965 Releases," box 6, RNC Papers; Dwight Eisenhower to Edward A. Mc-Cabe, 16 November 1966, "Romney, George (1963–66)," box 17, Special Name Series, Post-Presidential Papers, DDEL; Gerald Ford to Ralph B. Sterner, 11 April 1967, A39, box A68, and George Romney, *Meet the Press* transcript, 5 September 1965, A47, box A49, both in General Correspondence and Constituent Case File, Ford Papers, GRFL.

13 "Declaration for the Republican Coordinating Committee," 10 March 1965, in *Choice for America—Republican Answers to the Challenge of Now: Reports of the Republican Coordinating Committee, 1965–1968* (Washington, D.C.: Research Division, RNC, 1968), box 29, RNC Papers; Dwight Eisenhower to George Romney, 16 December 1965, "Romney, George (1963–66)," box 17, Special Name Series, Post-Presidential Papers, DDEL; Alf M. Landon to Dean Burch, 27 January 1965, A15, box A30, General Correspondence and Constituent Case File, Ford Papers, GRFL.

14 For a history of the association, see Robert Smylie, Notes on Speech at RNC Meeting, 23 January 1965, "National Committee Meeting, Chicago, Ill., January 22–23, 1965, Business," box 1, Good Files, RNC Papers. See also Denison Kitchel to George Humphrey, 11 December 1964, "Humphrey, George M. (1964)," box 2, Kitchel Papers, HIWRP.

15 Paul Findley to "Colleague," 9 December 1964, A17, box A68, General Correspondence and Constituent Case File, Ford Papers, GRFL.

16 For a discussion of the Ford-Halleck battle, see Reinhard, *Republican Right*, 211, and Mayer, *Republican Party*, 555. See also Gerald Ford, statement, 20 December 1964, and Charles A. Halleck, statement, 21 December 1964, both in A22, box A68, and Gerald Ford to [attached list], telegram, 18 December 1964, A22, box A16, all in General Correspondence and Constituent Case File, Ford Papers, GRFL. For Halleck's detractors, see letters in folders A25–26, box A16, General Correspondence and Constituent Case File, Ford Papers, GRFL. For criticism of Ford, see Rowland Evans and Robert Novak, "A Dinner for Barry," *Washington Post*, 4 April 1965; Cato, "Focus on Washington," *National Review*, 20 April 1965, p. 311; and "Loyal Opposition," cartoon, *National Review*, 13 July 1965, p. 581.

17 Edgar W. Hiestand to Gerald Ford, 6 January 1965, A14, box A29, Gerald Ford to "Colleague," 28 January 1965, A43, box A30, Gerald Ford to James R. Hopkins, 28 March 1967, A12, box A68, and Gerald Ford to Lloyd H. McMarran, 16 February 1967, A32, box A68, all in General Correspondence and Constituent Case File, Ford Papers, GRFL; Barry Goldwater to William F. Buckley, Jr., 5 July 1967, "Goldwater, Barry," box 43, General Correspondence, Buckley Papers, YUL; Bruce C. Ladd, Jr., "Operation Enlightenment: A Proposal for the Development of Effective Press Relations for the Republican Party," in "Uses of the Media," accordion file, box 4, RNC Papers.

18 Bryce Harlow to Mrs. George W. Reynolds, 25 October 1965, "John Birch Society Correspondence and Information," box 1, Convenience File, and Richard Nixon to Ezra Taft Benson, 22 December 1965, "Nixon, Richard M.

(1966) (1)," and Richard Nixon, Remarks, 25 September 1965, "Nixon, Richard M. (2)," both in box 8, Special Name Series, all in Post-Presidential Papers, DDEL; Melvin Laird and Ray Bliss, press conference, 22 January 1968, "1968 Press Conference," box 4, Stull Papers, RNC Papers.

19 "Extremism," 13 December 1965, in *Choice for America*; Republican Coordinating Committee, Minutes of Meeting, 13 December 1965, "Minutes of Meetings," box 1, Republican Coordinating Committee Papers, RNC Papers; Gerald Ford to C. M. Campbell, 9 January 1968, "Extremism (20)," box B111, and Gerald Ford to Paul Bulow, 12 April 1966, "Extremism (18)," box 37, both in Legislative File, Congressional Papers, Ford Papers, GRFL. For letters concerning the RCC statement on extremism, see folders in box A28, General Correspondence and Constituent Case File, Ford Papers, GRFL.

20 Denison Kitchel to George Humphrey, 11 December 1964, "Humphrey, George M. (1964)," box 2, Kitchel Papers, HIWRP; Reinhard, *Republican Right*, 216; William F. Buckley, Jr., to Frank Brophy, 18 February 1966, "Brokenshaw, Brock, etc.," box 38, General Correspondence, Buckley Papers, YUL; "The John Birch Society and the Conservative Movement," *National Review*, 19 October 1965, pp. 914–18; Arlene Croce, "Is Robert Welch's Doctrine 'Christian'?," *National Review*, 9 August 1966, p. 762.

21 Robert W. Glasgow, "Responsible Conservatism Needs to Be Redefined," *Arizona Republic*, 8 November 1964; Raymond Moley to Barry Goldwater, 6 November 1964, "Moley, Raymond (1964–75)," box 3, Kitchel Papers, HIWRP; William F. Buckley, Jr., "Senator Goldwater and the Backbiters," *National Review*, 12 January 1965, p. 16; William F. Buckley, Jr., "No Death Knell for Conservatism," *Arizona Republic*, 8 November 1964; Barry Goldwater to Denison Kitchel, 5 July 1967, "Goldwater, Barry (1964–70)," box 2, Kitchel Papers, HIWRP.

22 Richard Dougherty, "The Committee of '68: GOP Moderates Regroup," *New York Herald Tribune*, 22 November 1964; "And in This Corner . . . ," *National Review*, 23 February 1965, pp. 137–38; Charles P. Taft to "Friend," form letter, December 1965, "General Correspondence, T," box 2, Seaton Papers, DDEL; "Statements of Cash Receipts and Disbursements, NRCC," 1 June–10 September 1962, black binder, box 4, Republican Citizens' Committee Records, CUL. See also John Von Stade to Mr. Sheffield and Mr. Thayer, 22 August 1963, "Finance and Membership Report (August 23/63)," box 1, C. Wrede Petersmeyer to Leon Shimkin, 3 August 1964, "CIC Book," box 6, and Elmer Anderson to Joan Nelson, 20 September 1965, "Anderson, Elmer A.," box 6, all in Republican Citizens' Committee Records, CUL.

23 Donald E. Lukens, interview by author, tape recording, Hamilton, Ohio, 6 February 1988.

24 Denison Kitchel to Moreau Yeomans, 11 December 1964, "Goldwater Presidential Campaign, Correspondence, General (November 21–December 28, 1964)," box 4, Kitchel Papers, HIWRP; Dean Burch, Remarks before the Associated Students of the University of Utah, 15 February 1965, box 6, RNC Papers; Philip A. Ray to Barry Goldwater, 6 November 1964, "Goldwater,

Barry (1964–70)," box 2, Kitchel Papers, HIWRP; Barry Goldwater, Statement on 1964 Election, 4 November 1964, *Congressional Quarterly*, 6 November 1964, p. 2667, "November," box 19, 1964 Presidential Campaign Papers, Goldwater Papers, AHF; White, interview by author.

25 Barry Goldwater, Address before the RNC, 22 January 1965, and William Miller, statement, 12 January 1965, both in "1965 Releases," box 6, RNC Papers; Ronald Reagan to William F. Buckley, Jr., 5 November 1964, "Reagan, Ronald," box 32, General Correspondence, Buckley Papers, YUL.

26 Ronald Reagan to William F. Buckley, Jr., 5 November 1964, "Reagan, Ronald," box 32, General Correspondence, Buckley Papers, YUL; William Rusher, "The Plot to Steal the GOP," *National Review*, 12 July 1966, pp. 669–71; John Ashbrook to William F. Buckley, Jr., 10 December 1967, "Ashbrook, John," box 47, General Correspondence, Buckley Papers, YUL; John Kwapisz to Republican National Fund Committee, 9 March 1966, A4, box A47, and folders A29–A34, box A31, all in General Correspondence and Constituent Case File, Ford Papers, GRFL.

27 Rusher, "Plot to Steal the GOP"; Lukens, interview by author; Cato, "Focus on Washington," *National Review*, 1 June 1965, p. 449; Cato, "Focus on Washington," *National Review*, 13 July 1965, p. 580; William F. Buckley, Jr., "Mr. Bliss' Dilemma," *National Review*, 27 July 1965, p. 630.

28 Frank Meyer, "The Horizons of Conservatism," *National Review*, 9 March 1965, p. 197. See also Frank Meyer, "Accent the Negative," *National Review*, 7 February 1967, p. 135; Conservative Party, Inc., "New York Conservative Party Launches Organizing Drive," press release, 16 February 1962, "Conservative Party (158)," box 85, Liebman Collection, HIWRP; and David J. Jaquith et al. to "Fellow Conservative," 25 January 1967, C139, reel 36, SDC.

29 Peter W. Hoguet to "Fellow Republican," n.d., "Buckley for Mayor, Letters," box 8, and William F. Buckley, Jr., statement, 24 June 1965, "Statement by Buckley (6/24/65)," box 63, both in Liebman Collection, HIWRP. Buckley's statement is also reprinted in *National Review*, 13 July 1965, pp. 586–88. See also "The Week," *National Review*, 11 January 1966, p. 9.

30 In 1967 Opinion Research reported that among college students, support for Democrats was decreasing while support for Republicans was increasing. See Thomas Benham to Ray Bliss, 2 June 1967, "Correspondence under RCB Signature," box 1, Stull Papers, RNC Papers. Ray Bliss reported a 3 percent increase in college support for Republicans and a 6 percent decrease for Democrats. See Ray Bliss, press conference, 2 June 1967, "Press Conferences, Republican Meetings (May, June, July 1967)," box 5, Stull Papers, RNC Papers. By the convention in August 1968, the RNC reported that there were "150,000 College Young Republicans on over 900 campuses across the country." See *Official Program of the Republican National Convention*, 100.

31 "The Week," *National Review*, 15 June 1965, p. 490; "The Week," *National Review*, 29 June 1965, p. 533; M. Stanton Evans, "Liberals Strike Back at Goldwater Win," *National Review*, 12 July 1965, p. 584; "The Week," *National Review*, 21 February 1967, p. 177; "Omaha," *National Review*, 11 July 1967,

pp. 726–28; Ray Bliss, press conference, 22 November 1966, "Press Conferences (1966)," box 7, Stull Papers, RNC Papers; Minutes of the Meeting of the Republican Coordinating Committee, 28 March 1966, "Minutes of Meetings," box 1, Republican Coordinating Committee Papers, RNC Papers.

32 Ray Bliss, Speech at "Big City" Meeting, 22 October 1968, "October 22, 1968, Detroit, Michigan," box 6, Stull Papers, RNC Papers. For the Young Republicans, see "YRs' President Jack MacDonald: 'Our Only Aim Is Victory,' " *RCCN*, 7 August 1967, p. 5; Cato, "Focus on Washington," *National Review*, 9 March 1965, p. 179; Tom R. Van Sickle, "Building the Republican Future," 24 July 1965, bound volume, box 7, RNC Papers. For the College Republicans, see "The New Student Politics," College Republican National Committee Report, [1968?], box 7, RNC Papers. For the Teenage Republicans, see "TARS Program and Progress," red binder, and "TARS," looseleaf binder, both in box 4, RNC Papers; and "Lukens Cultivates Youth in Ohio's 24th District," *RCCN*, 20 February 1967, p. 7.

33 Donald Janson, "Rightists Buoyed by the Election; Open New Drives," *New York Times*, 23 November 1964; Denison Kitchel to Gordon J. Baird, 11 December 1964, "Goldwater Presidential Campaign, Correspondence, General (November 21–December 28, 1964)," box 4, Kitchel Papers, HIWRP; Peter J. Byrnes to Marvin Liebman, 23 November 1964, "Goldwater Campaign," box 92, Liebman Collection, HIWRP.

34 Richard A. Viguerie to Users of Conservative Mailing List, 10 February 1966, "Richard A. Viguerie and Co.," box 35, and John Wayne to "My Fellow American," n.d., "American Economic Foundation," box 7, both in Liebman Collection, HIWRP; E. v. Kuehnelt-Leddihn, "The Philadelphia Society," *National Review*, 2 November 1965, p. 986; Guy Davenport, "The Need to Maintain a Civilization," *National Review*, 6 April 1965, pp. 283–84; James J. Kilpatrick, "Our Man at the Golliwog Lounge," *National Review*, 22 March 1966, p. 258; Richard Viguerie to Marvin Liebman, 16 December 1965, "Richard A. Viguerie and Co.," box 35, and Marvin Liebman to Admiral Ben Moreel, 15 February 1965, "Americans for Constitutional Action," box 7, both in Liebman Collection, HIWRP. By February 1966, the list had 300,000 names on it.

35 Free Society Association, Articles of Incorporation, 10 May 1965, "By-Laws and Articles of Incorporation," box 1, Free Society Association Collection, HIWRP; "The Week," *National Review*, 29 June 1965, p. 534; Ray Bliss, interview by *U.S. News and World Report*, 10 September 1965, "Interviews, RCB (1965)," box 1, and Ray Bliss, press conference, 18 June 1965, "Press Conferences, 1965, RCB," box 8, both in Stull Papers, RNC Papers; Denison Kitchel to Herbert Klein, 27 September 1968, "Klein, Herbert G. (1968)," box 2, Kitchel Papers, HIWRP; Rusher, *Rise of the Right*, 182.

36 Confidential Preliminary Report on the American Conservative Union, n.d., "Brochure for ACU, from 1st Draft to Final Form," box 58, American Conservative Union, Constitution and By-Laws, n.d. (approved 18 December 1964), "Background of ACU Meetings (12/1 and 12/19/64)," box 57, John Ashbrook to "Fellow Conservative," 10 August 1965, and Donald Bruce and John

Ashbrook to [?], 1 February 1965, both in "American Conservative Union," box 7, and John Ashbrook to Marvin Liebman, n.d., "American Conservative Union," box 58, all in Liebman Collection, HIWRP.

37 American Conservative Union, Minutes of the Meeting of the Board of Directors, 18–19 December 1964, "Background of ACU Meetings (12/1 and 12/19/64)," box 57, and American Conservative Union, Minutes of the Meeting of the Board of Directors, 17 September 1965, "Board Meetings of ACU," box 58, both in Liebman Collection, HIWRP.

38 From the beginning, members of the ACU's rival organization, the FSA, were not happy with the ACU's existence and predicted that it would die quickly. See Denison Kitchel to Jean Hawkins, 29 March 1965, "Hawkins, Jean (Mrs. Paul M.), Undated (1965–80)," box 2, Kitchel Papers, HIWRP. By 1966, even the *National Review* reported that the group was experiencing some difficulties ("The Week," *National Review*, 14 June 1966, p. 561), and Marvin Liebman offered to reorganize it more efficiently (Marvin Liebman to John Ashbrook, 2 February 1966, "Memorandums Sent to ACU," box 59, Liebman Collection, HIWRP). For a more positive view, see Rusher, *Rise of the Right*, 182–83.

39 "Countering the 'Peaceniks,'" *America's Future*, 5 November 1965, A19, reel 3, SDC; "Young Republican President Jack MacDonald," *RCCN*, 3 June 1968, p. 7; "Real Young America," *America's Future*, 8 December 1967, A19, reel 3, SDC; John F. Lulves, Jr., "Is There a Student Conservatism?," *National Review*, 31 May 1966, pp. 530–31; Marvin Liebman, "The Young Heroes," *Insight and Outlook*, Fall 1967, I14, reel 64, SDC; Russell Kirk, "Some Hope for the Rising Generation," *National Review*, 7 March 1967, p. 255; Ted Loeffler to Social Documents Collection, 12 August 1966, C151, reel 37, SDC; David Keene to YAF Chapter Chairmen and College Conservative Council Members, November 1966, "K," box 37, Liebman Collection, HIWRP.

40 "Talk about Demonstrations!," *National Review*, 11 January 1966, p. 12; letters from YAF members to Lyndon Johnson, "Young, Alfreda," box 26, Name File, White House Central Files, LBJL; Ron Docksai, "New York State Y. A. F. Liberates SDS Office for Election Day," 6 November 1968, "Young Americans for Freedom, Misc.," box 37, Philip Wayne Cramer to College Chapter Chairmen, 10 November 1966, "L," box 37, "World Youth Crusade for Freedom, Inc.: A Report and Prospectus," box 107, and pertinent folders in box 36, all in Liebman Collection, HIWRP.

41 Russell Kirk, "Beginning in Doubt," *National Review*, 21 March 1967, p. 306; "Introducing Insight and Outlook: The Challenge of Constructive Thought," *Insight and Outlook*, Fall 1968, and J. M. O'Connell, "Thoughts for the Morning After," *Insight and Outlook*, Winter 1969, both in I14, reel 64, SDC; Rusher, *Rise of the Right*, 183–84.

42 William Rusher to William F. Buckley, Jr., 3 March 1965, "Interoffice Memos (Jan. 1965–June 1965)," box 35, General Correspondence, Buckley Papers, YUL; Robert F. Ellsworth to Bob Wilson, 18 May 1965, A4, box A29, General Correspondence and Constituent Case File, Ford Papers, GRFL; Frank Meyer to "All Concerned," 23 May 1966, "Interoffice Memos (May–Decem-

ber 1966)," box 39, and William F. Buckley, Jr., to Barry Goldwater, 18 June 1965, "Goldwater, Barry," box 35, both in General Correspondence, Buckley Papers, YUL.

43 Neil McCaffrey to William F. Buckley, Jr., William Rusher, and James McFadden, 19 April 1966, "Interoffice Memos (Jan.–April)," and Frank Meyer to "All Concerned," 23 May 1966, "Interoffice Memos (May–December 1966)," both in box 39, General Correspondence, Buckley Papers, YUL.

44 Matusow, *Unraveling of America*, chaps. 6, 8, 9; Goldman, *Tragedy of Lyndon Johnson*, 332–34. For conservative reaction, see, among others, "Those Medical Plans," *National Review*, 26 January 1965, pp. 52–54; Frank Meyer, "Is Social Security a Sacred Cow?," *National Review*, 1 June 1965, p. 463; and Milton Friedman, "Social Responsibility: A Subversive Doctrine," *National Review*, 24 August 1965, pp. 721–23.

45 Gerald Ford to Jim White, 21 April 1966, A49, box A46, General Correspondence and Constituent Case File, Ford Papers, GRFL; Barry Goldwater, *Meet the Press* transcript, 13 June 1965, "Goldwater, Barry," box 35, General Correspondence, Buckley Papers, YUL.

46 For a discussion of the war, see Herring, *America's Longest War*. For conservative views, see "Should We Bomb Red China's Bomb?," *National Review*, 12 January 1965, pp. 8–10; James Burnham, "The New Isolationism," *National Review*, 26 January 1965, p. 60; James Burnham, "Which Isolationism Is Your Isolationism?," *National Review*, 16 January 1968, p. 22; Gerald Ford to Sara Harris, 22 March 1966, A2, box A47, and Robert Ellsworth et al. to Gerald Ford, 12 May 1965, A39, box A30, both in General Correspondence and Constituent Case File, Ford Papers, GRFL; Dwight Eisenhower to George Romney, 25 July 1966, "Romney, George (1963–66)," box 17, Special Name Series, Post-Presidential Papers, DDEL; Neil McCaffrey to William F. Buckley, Jr., William Rusher, and James McFadden, 19 April 1966, "Interoffice Memos (Jan.–April)," box 39, General Correspondence, Buckley Papers, YUL; and ACU Task Force Study, "Background to the Current Situation," [1965?], "Vietnam (3)," box B31, Legislative File, Congressional Papers, Ford Papers, GRFL.

47 Matusow, *Unraveling of America*, chaps. 7, 11, 12. For conservative views, see "Why They Riot," *National Review*, 9 March 1965, pp. 178–80; Charles W. Wiley, "Who Was Malcolm X?," *National Review*, 23 March 1965, pp. 239–41; "Civil Rights '66," *National Review*, 25 January 1966, pp. 57–58; William F. Buckley, Jr., "The Protest," *National Review*, 2 May 1967, p. 470; "Students, Teachers, Bureaucrats," *National Review*, 23 March 1965, pp. 228–30; Russell Kirk, "Politically Ignorant College Students," *National Review*, 18 May 1965, p. 423; "The Week," *National Review*, 17 May 1966, p. 448; Frank Meyer, "The LSD Syndrome," *National Review*, 21 March 1967, p. 301; "Interview with a Policeman Assigned to the Watts Area," *National Review*, 7 September 1965, pp. 773–74; and Barbara Vaccariello, "L.A. Police: As Seen from Olympus," *National Review*, 24 January 1967, p. 77.

48 For discussions of the counterculture, see Matusow, *Unraveling of America*,

chap. 10; Gitlin, *The Sixties*, chap. 8; and Wolfe, *The Electric Kool-Aid Acid Test*. For a sampling of early conservative reaction to the counterculture, see "The Week," *National Review*, 18 May 1965, pp. 402–3; "The Week," *National Review*, 19 October 1965, p. 905; William S. Schlamm, "Beauty and the Beatniks," *National Review*, 11 January 1966, pp. 23–24; and "The Week," *National Review*, 5 April 1966, p. 302.

49 "Election Victories Point to GOP Resurgence," *RCCN*, 8 November 1965, pp. 1, 3; Jim Jones to Marvin Watson, 11 November 1965, "EX PL2 5/11/65–1/17/66," EX PL2, box 86, White House Central Files, LBJL. For discussions of Johnson's credibility gap, see Goldman, *Tragedy of Lyndon Johnson*, 409–10; William F. Buckley, Jr., "The State of LBJ," *National Review*, 26 January 1965, p. 56; Pyrrho, "LBJ: Political Gamester," *National Review*, 25 January 1966, pp. 67–69; and Ferdinand Nount, "Nobody Loves the Poor Prez," *National Review*, 16 January 1968, pp. 24–27.

50 Mayer, *Republican Party*, 556; Reinhard, *Republican Right*, 216; Richard Nixon, "The GOP and the South," *RCCN*, 9 May 1966, p. 2; Ray Bliss, press conference, 21 June 1966, "Press Conferences (1966)," box 7, Stull Papers, RNC Papers; "Bliss Says Midwest Looms as Major Target for GOP in '66," *RCCN*, 27 September 1965, p. 5; "Bliss Target: The Big City Vote," *RCCN*, 31 January 1966, p. 3; "Decade of Opportunity," *RCCN*, 18 July 1966, p. 5; "The Issues of '66," *RCCN*, 10 October 1966, p. 1; "Republican Women Tag War, Cost of Living as Major '66 Issues," *RCCN*, 9 May 1966, p. 5; "This Is the Time for Leadership," *RCCN*, 22 August 1966, pp. 1, 4; Charles D. Roche to Marvin Watson, 27 January 1966, "EX PL2 1/18/66–5/23/66," EX PL2, box 86, White House Central Files, LBJL.

51 Research Division of the RNC, "The 1966 Elections: A Summary Report with Supporting Tables," [1967?], box 8, RNC Papers; *U.S. News and World Report*, "A Closer Look at the Results over the Country," 21 November 1966, p. 41; Ray Bliss, interview by WEAT, 7 April 1967, "Interviews, 1967, Republican Meetings," box 1, and Ray Bliss, press conference, 13 October 1967, "Press Conferences (September–December 1967)," box 5, both in Stull Papers, RNC Papers; Marvin Watson to Lyndon Johnson, 11 November 1966, "EX PL2 11/2/66–12/3/66," EX PL2, box 87, White House Central Files, LBJL.

52 Reinhard, *Republican Right*, 217; Cato, "Focus on Washington," *National Review*, 29 November 1966, p. 1201; Cato, "Focus on Washington," *National Review*, 7 February 1967, p. 121; Cato, "Focus on Washington," *National Review*, 24 January 1967, p. 73.

CHAPTER SEVEN

1 Ray Bliss, *The Chairman's Report, 1968: To Members of the Republican National Committee*, 16–17 January 1969, "Chairman's Report (1967–68)," and Ray Bliss, interview by WBBM, 22 May 1967, and Ray Bliss, interview by *Teuschen News* (Salt Lake City, Utah), 15 April 1967, both in "Interviews, 1967, Re-

publican Meetings," all in box 1, Stull Papers, RNC Papers; A. B. Hermann to Meade Alcorn, 12 May 1967, "Re Chairman Bliss Work to Rebuild the Republican Party," box 10, Hermann Papers, CUL; Ray Bliss, press conference, 13 October 1967, "Press Conferences (September–December 1967)," box 5, and Ray Bliss to Richard Carstensen, 6 February 1967, "Correspondence under RCB Signature (1967)," box 1, both in Stull Papers, RNC Papers; Cato, "Focus on Washington," *National Review*, 13 December 1966, p. 1253.

2 Ray Bliss, interview with ABC Radio, New York City, 22 January 1968, "1968 Interviews," box 1, Melvin Laird, press conference with Ray Bliss and Howard Baker, 22 January 1968, "1968 Press Conferences," box 4, and Gerald Ford, press conference with Ray Bliss, 12 July 1967, "Press Conferences, Republican Meetings (May, June, July 1967)," box 5, all in Stull Papers, RNC Papers; Dwight Eisenhower to Fred Seaton, 23 February 1967, and Fred Seaton to Dwight Eisenhower, 18 February 1967, both in "Nixon (1967–68)," box 7, Papers of General Dwight D. Eisenhower of Augusta, Georgia, Post-Presidential Papers, DDEL.

3 "Marianne Means' Washington," 27 November 1966, "EX PL2 11/2/66–12/3/66," EX PL2, box 87, White House Central Files, LBJL; Roy E. James to A. B. Hermann, 7 December 1966, "A. B. Hermann, 1966 Files," box 10, Hermann Papers, CUL; John R. Topping et al., "Can We Bridge the Ideological Gap?," in Huebner and Petri, *Ripon Papers*, 25–45.

4 Dwight Eisenhower to George Romney, 19 May 1965, 31 December 1966, "Romney, George (1963–66)," Dwight Eisenhower to Gabriel Hauge, 16 February 1967, and Dwight Eisenhower to Barry Leithead, 24 May 1967, both in "Romney, George (1967) (4)," and Dwight Eisenhower to George Romney, 27 November 1967, and Dwight Eisenhower, "To Correct Any Misunderstanding Concerning My Opinion about Governor George Romney," 27 December 1967, both in "Romney, George (1967) (1)," all in box 17, Special Name Series, Post-Presidential Papers, DDEL.

5 Theodore White, *1968*, 36–61; "Barry Goldwater Speaks Out," *National Review*, 16 January 1968, pp. 27–28; Theodore White, *1968*, 66–70.

6 Nixon, *RN*, 264–65; "Nixon on Target," *Indianapolis News*, 9 November 1964; Richard Nixon, statement, November 1964, "Statement by RN (Nov. 1964)," box 2, series 127, RNPP Papers; Murray Kempton, "Nixon to the Rescue," *New York World Telegram*, 6 November 1964; "Who Speaks for the GOP?," *Charleston (S.C.) Evening Post*, 9 November 1964; Barry Goldwater, Address before the RNC, 22 January 1965, "1965 Releases," box 6, RNC Papers; Barry Goldwater to Stephen Shadegg, 10 May 1978, Goldwater Book Materials and Columns, Goldwater Papers, AHF.

7 "The Week," *National Review*, 2 November 1965, p. 961; "The Week," *National Review*, 6 September 1966, p. 867; Cato, "Focus on Washington," *National Review*, 6 September 1966, p. 871; "Plowing on with Richard Nixon," *National Review*, 20 September 1966, pp. 916–18; Doug Nobles to Marvin Watson, 22 September 1966, "EX PL2 8/31/66–11/1/66," EX PL2, box 86, White House Central Files, LBJL; Chester et al., *American Melodrama*, 256; Judis, *William F. Buckley, Jr.*, 279.

8 Neal B. Freeman, "The Men around Nixon," *National Review*, 17 October 1967, pp. 1118–19; "Slick Dick and the Gorgeous Grik," *American Capsule News*, October 1968, A21, reel 4, SDC; James Jackson Kilpatrick, "Crisis Seven," *National Review*, 14 November 1967, pp. 1263–74; Clare Booth Luce to Denison Kitchel, 15 August 1966, "Luce, Clare Booth (1964–74)," box 2, Kitchel Papers, HIWRP; Taylor Caldwell to Gerald Ford, 25 January 1967, A9, box A68, and Anna Chennault to Herbert M. Kalmbach, 4 October 1968, "Republican Party, National (5)," box A91, both in General Correspondence and Constituent Case File, Ford Papers, GRFL; Frank Meyer to William F. Buckley, Jr., 9 March 1968, "Interoffice Memos (Jan.–Mar.)," box 50, General Correspondence, Buckley Papers, YUL; Frank Meyer, "Thinking Aloud about 1968," *National Review*, 13 June 1967, p. 640; William Rusher, "Operation 1968," *National Review*, 17 October 1967, pp. 1115–17; "The Conservatives Crash the Gates," *National Review*, 28 November 1967, p. 1312.

9 Dwight Eisenhower, statement, n.d., "Nixon, Richard M. (1)," box 34, 1968 Principal File, Dwight Eisenhower, statement, 5 November 1966, "Nixon, Richard M.," box 8, Special Name Series, and Dwight Eisenhower to Richard Nixon, 24 October 1968, "Nixon, Richard M. (1)," box 34, 1968 Principal File, all in Post-Presidential Papers, and William Robinson to Dwight Eisenhower, 24 July 1968, "Eisenhower (1968)," box 4, Robinson Papers, all in DDEL; "TARS," looseleaf binder, box 4, RNC Papers; Fred Seaton to Gaylord Parkinson, 14 July 1967, "Nixon, Political (1967)," box 8, and Constitution of the Nixon for President Committee, 3 June 1967, "Nixon for President Committee (1967)," box 9, both in Seaton Papers, DDEL; "Next, Please?," *National Review*, 4 April 1967, p. 338.

10 William Rusher to editors, 20 October 1967, "Interoffice Memos (July–Dec.)," box 43, General Correspondence, Buckley Papers, YUL. In fact, in 1965 LBJ received numerous letters from people encouraging him to appoint Nixon as secretary of state or U.N. ambassador, for example. See "Richard Nixon," Name File, White House Central Files, LBJL.

11 Nelson Rockefeller to Gerald Ford, telegram, received 30 April 1968, "Republican Party, National (61)," box A90, General Correspondence and Constituent Case File, Ford Papers, GRFL; Theodore White, *1968*, 224–56; Walter Cronkite to Dwight Eisenhower, 8 July 1968, "PL3 (July) (Pro-Nixon)," box 14, 1968 Principal File, Post-Presidential Papers, DDEL; Theodore White, *1968*, 271–75, 277–79; Chester et al., *American Melodrama*, 379–82.

12 William F. Buckley, Jr., to Ronald Reagan, 11 November 1964, "Reagan, Ronald," box 32, General Correspondence, Buckley Papers, YUL; Wills, *Reagan's America*, 287–88, 290–91; Cannon, *President Reagan*, 11; Alistair Cooke, "Alistair Cooke Calls on Ronald Reagan," *Chicago Sun-Times*, 14 January 1968; William F. Buckley, Jr., "How Is Ronald Reagan Doing?," *National Review*, 11 January 1966, p. 17; Drew Pearson, "An Actor Is Groomed to Be President," *Washington Post*, 19 September 1966; Ronald Reagan to Leonard Finder, 7 July 1966, "Reagan, Ronald," box 24, Finder Papers, DDEL; Farley Clinton, "Ronald Reagan: A Light in the West," *National Review*, 28 June 1966, pp. 613–15.

13 Bill Boyarsky, "Reagan—The Favorite Son," *Houston Post,* 1 October 1967; George Gallup, "Reagan's Appeal Not Limited to State," Gallup Poll, 16 November 1966, copy in "Office Files of Moyers: Reagan, Ronald," box 74 (1390), Files of Bill Moyers, LBJL; John Wayne to "My Fellow American," n.d., "American Economic Foundation," box 7, Liebman Collection, HIWRP; Morton Kondracke, "Reagan Unqualified: Ripon Society," *Chicago Sun-Times,* 1 June 1968. According to Theodore White, Reagan met with friends just ten days after he won the election to discuss the presidency. See Theodore White, *1968,* 35.

14 F. Clifton White and Gill, *Why Reagan Won,* 93–94.

15 Ibid.; William Rusher to editors, 12 August 1968, "Editors' Quarterly Conference," box 49, General Correspondence, Buckley Papers, YUL; Barry Goldwater to Thomas C. Reed, 19 May 1968, "RN," Alpha File, Goldwater Papers, AHF; Frank Meyer to William F. Buckley, Jr., 9 March 1968, "Interoffice Memos (Jan.–Mar.)," box 50, General Correspondence, Buckley Papers, YUL; Hubert Humphrey, memo for files, 23 August 1967, "PL/Name Political Affairs/Name," C.F. PE2 (1966), box 76, White House Central Files, LBJL; Barry Goldwater, Notes to Diary, 8 June 1966, Alpha File, Goldwater Papers, AHF; Judis, *William F. Buckley, Jr.,* 281.

16 Chester et al., *American Melodrama,* 187, 439–40.

17 Ibid., 445; F. Clifton White and Gill, *Why Reagan Won,* 109.

18 F. Clifton White and Gill, *Why Reagan Won,* 108–9; Chester et al., *American Melodrama,* 434, 446, 476–81.

19 Cohodas, *Strom Thurmond,* 397–98; Chester et al., *American Melodrama,* 434, 459–62; F. Clifton White and Gill, *Why Reagan Won,* 108–9.

20 F. Clifton White and Gill, *Why Reagan Won,* 117–29.

21 Chester et al., *American Melodrama,* 473–75. The final count was Nixon, 692; Nelson Rockefeller, 277; Reagan, 182; Rhodes, 55; Romney, 50; Case, 22; Carlson, 20; Winthrop Rockefeller, 18; Hiram Fong, 14; Stassen, 2; and Lindsay, 1. See ibid., 475.

22 Chester et al., *American Melodrama,* 484–89.

23 Fred Seaton to Walter Williams, 8 November 1967, "Nixon for President Committee (1967)," box 9, Seaton Papers, DDEL; Wicker, *One of Us,* 342–44.

24 Donald E. Lukens, interview by author, tape recording, Hamilton, Ohio, 6 February 1988; Wills, *Nixon Agonistes,* 246–57; F. Clifton White and Gill, *Why Reagan Won,* 124.

25 Herring, *America's Longest War,* 184–94; Matusow, *Unraveling of America,* 391.

26 James W. Graham, "The Score for Tet," *National Review,* 12 March 1968, p. 226; "Tactical War in Vietnam," *American Opinion,* June 1968, pp. 63–64.

27 Matusow, *Unraveling of America,* 396.

28 Ibid., 331–35; Gitlin, *The Sixties,* 306–9; Kunen, *Strawberry Statement,* 39, 43; McQuaid, *Anxious Years,* 160; Carroll, *It Seemed Like Nothing Happened,* 56–61.

29 Edsall and Edsall, *Chain Reaction,* 71–72.

30 Barry Goldwater, statement, 7 March 1968, "Republican Party, National

(60)," box A90, and Oscar DeJong to Gerald Ford, 23 March 1968, A10, box A89, both in General Correspondence and Constituent Case File, Ford Papers, GRFL.

31 Frank Meyer, "Ten Days in April," *National Review*, 7 May 1968, p. 453; Susan L. M. Huck, "Insurrection: Is America Sleeping through Civil War?," *American Opinion*, June 1968, pp. 1–25.

32 Richard K. Goodwin, Speech at National Board Meeting of Americans for Democratic Action, 17 September 1966, "Goodwin, Richard (1965–66)," box 4, J. K. Galbraith, Speech at Americans for Democratic Action Roosevelt Day Dinner, 11 March 1966, "Galbraith, J. K. (2/1/65–3/11/66)," box 4, Arthur M. Schlesinger, Jr., Speech at Americans for Democratic Action Roosevelt Day Dinner, 31 January 1967, "Schlesinger, Arthur (12/1966–3/1967)," box 11, and Fred Dutton to Robert F. Kennedy, 3 November 1967, "Dutton, Frederick (1967–68)," box 3, all in Personal File, Senate Correspondence, Robert F. Kennedy Papers, JFKL.

33 Matusow, *Unraveling of America*, 411–22; Chester et al., *American Melodrama*, 503–604; Gitlin, *The Sixties*, 319–40.

34 For background on Wallace, see Frady, *Wallace*; Lesher, *George Wallace*; and Carlson, *George C. Wallace*.

35 John M. Ashbrook, "The Wallace Candidacy," ACU Report, February–March 1968, A4, reel 1, SDC; Frank Meyer, "The Populism of George Wallace," *National Review*, 16 May 1967, p. 527; William F. Buckley, Jr., to Neil McCaffrey, [February 1968], "McCaffrey, Neil," box 52, and William F. Buckley, Jr., to Nancy Reagan, 12 February 1968, "Reagan, Ronald and Nancy," box 53, both in General Correspondence, Buckley Papers, YUL; Gerald Ford to Donald Phillips, 7 November 1967, A26, box A68, General Correspondence and Constituent Case File, Ford Papers, GRFL.

36 Lukens, interview by author.

37 Clare Booth Luce to [attached list], telegram, 10 September 1968, "James L. Buckley, Senatorial Campaign," box 103, Liebman Collection, HIWRP; Craig Chawkins to [editors?], memo, 18 December 1968, "Interoffice Memos (Oct.–Dec. 1968), n.d.," box 50, and Bill Rusher to "My Valued Colleagues, the editors of NR," memo, 12 August 1968, box 49, both in General Correspondence, Buckley Papers, YUL; Marvin Liebman to Jeremiah Milbank, 13 August 1968, "Young Americans for Freedom, Misc.," box 37, Liebman Collection, HIWRP.

38 Phillips, *Emerging Republican Majority*, 25–42. For a somewhat milder version of the same theory, see Scammon and Wattenberg, *Real Majority*, 35–44.

39 Parmet, *Richard Nixon*, 529–61; Wicker, *One of Us*, 484–542.

40 Parmet, *Richard Nixon*, 620–24; Wicker, *One of Us*, 588–605.

41 Parmet, *Richard Nixon*, 594–605; Wicker, *One of Us*, 504–7.

42 Szulc, *Illusion of Peace*, 513–30, 559–87.

43 Parmet, *Richard Nixon*, 562–93; McQuaid, *Anxious Years*, 53–127.

44 *National Review*, 2 February 1973, p. 128; 16 February 1973, pp. 188–93; 2 March 1973, p. 247; 16 March 1973, p. 292; 27 April 1973, pp. 449–50.

45 *American Opinion,* June 1973, pp. 1–16.
46 Lukas, *Nightmare*; Theodore White, *Breach of Faith*; McQuaid, *Anxious Years,* 167–306.

CONCLUSION

1 F. Clifton White and Gill, *Why Reagan Won,* 53–54, 75.
2 Dionne, *Why Americans Hate Politics,* 252–55.
3 Rusher suggested forming a new party system along ideological lines. See Rusher, *New Majority Party.* Conservatives seriously considered his plan before deciding to stick with the GOP. See Rusher, *Rise of the Right,* 267–69, for a discussion of the debate.
4 Buchanan, *Conservative Votes, Liberal Victories,* 165–77.
5 F. Clifton White and Gill, *Why Reagan Won*; Dionne, *Why Americans Hate Politics,* 281–99; Wills, *Reagan's America,* 291–93, 308, 339–42.
6 Dionne, *Why Americans Hate Politics,* 231.

BIBLIOGRAPHY

MANUSCRIPT COLLECTIONS

Abilene, Kansas
Dwight D. Eisenhower Library
  Eisenhower Library Collection
  Dwight D. Eisenhower Papers
  Milton Eisenhower Papers
  Leonard Finder Papers
  George Humphrey Papers
  Robert Merriam Papers
  Post-Presidential Papers
  William Robinson Papers
  Fred Seaton Papers
  Arthur Summerfield Papers
Ann Arbor, Michigan
Gerald R. Ford Library
  Gerald R. Ford Papers
Austin, Texas
Center for American History, University of Texas
  Goldwater Collection
Lyndon Baines Johnson Library
  Democratic National Committee Papers
  Files of Bill Moyers
  Files of Frederick Panzer
  Files of George Reedy
  White House Central Files
  Files of Henry Wilson
Columbia Point, Massachusetts
John Fitzgerald Kennedy Library
  Democratic National Committee Papers
  John Kenneth Galbraith Papers
  John F. Kennedy Papers
  Robert F. Kennedy Papers
  Presidential Papers
  Arthur M. Schlesinger, Jr., Papers
  Theodore Sorenson Papers
  White House Central Files
Columbus, Ohio
Ohio Historical Society
  John Bricker Papers
Iowa City, Iowa
University of Iowa Library
  Social Documents Collection

Ithaca, New York
Division of Rare and Manuscript Collections, Cornell University Library
  A. B. Hermann Papers
  William E. Miller Papers
  Republican Citizens' Committee Records
  F. Clifton White Papers
Laguna Niguel, California
National Archives and Records Administration, Pacific Southwest Region
  Richard Nixon Pre-Presidential Papers
  Richard Nixon Vice Presidential Papers
New Haven, Connecticut
Yale University Library
  William F. Buckley, Jr., Papers
New York, New York
Columbia Oral History Project, Oral History Collection, Columbia University
  Reminiscences of Meade Alcorn
  Reminiscences of Milton Eisenhower
  Reminiscences of Robert Finch
  Reminiscences of Barry Goldwater
  Reminiscences of James Hagerty
Stanford, California
Hoover Institution on War, Revolution and Peace, Stanford University
  Free Society Association Collection
  Denison Kitchel Papers
  Marvin Liebman Collection
  Ralph de Toledano Papers
Tempe, Arizona
Arizona Historical Foundation
  Barry Goldwater Papers
  Theodore Humes Papers
Washington, D.C.
National Archives and Records Administration
  Republican National Committee Papers
    Jo Good Files
    Republican Coordinating Committee Papers
    Ray E. Stull Papers

MAGAZINES

American Opinion
Human Events
The Nation
National Review
New Republic

INTERVIEWS

Burch, Dean. Interview by author. Tape recording. Washington, D.C., 30 June 1989.
Lukens, Donald E. Interview by author. Tape recording. Hamilton, Ohio, 6 February 1988.
White, F. Clifton. Interview by author. Tape recording. Ashland, Ohio, 21 October 1987.

BOOKS AND JOURNAL ARTICLES

Alexander, Charles C. *Holding the Line: The Eisenhower Era, 1952–1961.* Bloomington: Indiana University Press, 1975.
Alexander, Herbert E. *Financing the 1964 Election.* Princeton, N.J.: Citizens' Research Foundation, 1966.
Ambrose, Stephen. *Eisenhower: The President.* New York: Simon and Schuster, 1984.
——. *Nixon: The Education of a Politician, 1913–1962.* New York: Simon and Schuster, 1987.
——. *Nixon: The Triumph of a Politician, 1962–1972.* New York: Simon and Schuster, 1989.
Baritz, Loren. *The Good Life: The Meaning of Success for the American Middle Class.* New York: Alfred A. Knopf, 1982.
Bartley, Numan V., and Hugh D. Graham. *Southern Politics and the Second Reconstruction.* Baltimore: Johns Hopkins University Press, 1975.
Bell, Daniel. *The End of Ideology: On the Exhaustion of Political Ideas in the Fifties.* New York: Free Press, 1960.
Bell, Daniel, et al. *The Radical Right.* New York: Criterion Books, 1955.
Bell, Jack. *Mr. Conservative: Barry Goldwater.* Garden City, N.Y.: Doubleday, 1962.
Bennett, David H. *The Party of Fear: From Nativist Movements to the New Right in American History.* Chapel Hill: University of North Carolina Press, 1988.
Black, Earl, and Merle Black. *Politics and Society in the South.* Cambridge: Harvard University Press, 1987.
Brauer, Carl B. *John F. Kennedy and the Second Reconstruction.* New York: Columbia University Press, 1977.
Brodie, Fawn. *Richard Nixon: The Shaping of His Character.* New York: W. W. Norton, 1981.
Brooks, Thomas R. *Walls Come Tumbling Down: A History of the Civil Rights Movement, 1940–1970.* Englewood Cliffs, N.J.: Prentice-Hall, 1974.
Buchanan, Patrick. *Conservative Votes, Liberal Victories: Why the Right Has Failed.* New York: Quadrangle/New York Times Book Company, 1972.
Buckley, William F., Jr., and L. Brent Bozell. *McCarthy and His Enemies: The Record and Its Meaning.* Chicago: Henry Regnery, 1954.

Burner, David, and Thomas R. West. *The Torch Is Passed: The Kennedy Brothers and American Liberalism*. New York: Atheneum, 1984.

Burnham, James. *The Struggle for the World*. New York: John Day, 1947.

Cain, Edward. *They'd Rather Be Right*. New York: Macmillan, 1963.

Cannon, Lou. *President Reagan: The Role of a Lifetime*. New York: Touchstone, 1991.

Carlson, Jody. *George C. Wallace and the Politics of Powerlessness*. New Brunswick, N.J.: Transaction Books, 1981.

Carroll, Peter N. *It Seemed Like Nothing Happened: The Tragedy and Promise of America in the 1970s*. New Brunswick, N.J.: Rutgers University Press, 1982.

Chester, Lewis, et al. *An American Melodrama: The Presidential Campaign of 1968*. New York: Viking, 1969.

Cobb, James C. *Industrialization and Southern Society, 1877–1984*. Lexington: University Press of Kentucky, 1984.

Cohodas, Nadine. *Strom Thurmond and the Politics of Southern Change*. New York: Simon and Schuster, 1993.

Conkin, Paul. *Big Daddy from the Pedernales*. Boston: Twayne, 1986.

Cosman, Bernard, and Robert J. Huckshorn, eds. *Republican Politics: The 1964 Campaign and Its Aftermath for the Party*. New York: Frederick A. Praeger, 1968.

Dallek, Robert. *Lone Star Rising: Lyndon Johnson and His Times, 1908–1960*. New York: Oxford University Press, 1991.

———. *Ronald Reagan: The Politics of Symbolism*. Cambridge: Harvard University Press, 1984.

Daniel, Pete. "Going among Strangers: Southern Reactions to World War II." *Journal of American History* 77 (December 1990): 886–911.

Dionne, E. J. *Why Americans Hate Politics*. New York: Simon and Schuster, 1991.

Divine, Robert. *Eisenhower and the Cold War*. New York: Oxford University Press, 1981.

Edsall, Thomas Byrne, and Mary D. Edsall. *Chain Reaction: The Impact of Race, Rights, and Taxes on American Politics*. New York: W. W. Norton, 1991.

Eisenhower, Dwight D. *The Eisenhower Diaries*. Edited by Robert Ferrell. New York: W. W. Norton, 1981.

———. *Waging Peace, 1956–1961*. New York: Doubleday, 1965.

Evans, M. Stanton. *Revolt on the Campus*. Chicago: Henry Regnery, 1961.

Evans, Rowland, and Robert Novak. *Lyndon B. Johnson: The Exercise of Power*. New York: New American Library, 1966.

Ferguson, Thomas. "From Normalcy to New Deal: Industrial Structure, Party Competition, and American Public Policy in the Great Depression." *International Organization* 38 (Winter 1984): 41–94.

Ferguson, Thomas, and Joel Rogers. *Right Turn: The Decline of the Democrats and the Future of American Politics*. New York: Hill and Wang, 1986.

Frady, Marshall. *Wallace*. New York: World, 1968.

Fraser, Steve, and Gary Gerstle, eds. *The Rise and Fall of the New Deal Order*. Princeton, N.J.: Princeton University Press, 1989.

Fried, Richard. *Men against McCarthy*. New York: Columbia University Press, 1976.

Garrow, David J. *Bearing the Cross: Martin Luther King, Jr., and the Southern Christian Leadership Conference*. New York: Vintage, 1986.

Gervasi, Frank. *The Real Rockefeller: The Story of the Rise, Decline, and Resurgence of the Presidential Aspirations of Nelson Rockefeller*. New York: Atheneum, 1964.

Gilbert, James. *Another Chance: Postwar America, 1945–1968*. New York: Alfred A. Knopf, 1981.

Gitlin, Todd. *The Sixties: Years of Hope, Days of Rage*. New York: Bantam, 1987.

Goldman, Eric F. *The Crucial Decade and After: America, 1945–1960*. Rev. ed. New York: Vintage, 1960.

——. *The Tragedy of Lyndon Johnson*. New York: Alfred A. Knopf, 1969.

Goldwater, Barry M. *The Conscience of a Conservative*. Shepherdsville, Ky.: Victory, 1960.

——. *Goldwater*. New York: Doubleday, 1988.

——. *Why Not Victory?* New York: McGraw-Hill, 1962.

——. *With No Apologies: The Personal and Political Memoirs of United States Senator Barry M. Goldwater*. New York: William Morrow, 1979.

Green, Barbara B., Kathryn Turner, and Dante Germino. "Responsible and Irresponsible Right-Wing Groups: A Problem in Analysis." *Journal of Social Issues* 19 (April 1963): 3–17.

Greenstein, Fred I. *The Hidden-Hand Presidency: Eisenhower as Leader*. New York: Basic Books, 1982.

Griffith, Robert. "Dwight D. Eisenhower and the Corporate Commonwealth." *American Historical Review* 87 (February 1982): 87–122.

——. *The Politics of Fear: Joseph R. McCarthy and the Senate*. Lexington: University Press of Kentucky, 1970. Reprint, Rochelle Park, N.J.: Hayden, 1970.

Halberstam, David. *The Fifties*. New York: Villard Books, 1993.

Hartz, Louis. *The Liberal Tradition in America: An Interpretation of American Political Thought since the Revolution*. New York: Harcourt, Brace, 1955.

Hayden, Tom. *Reunion: A Memoir*. New York: Random House, 1988.

Heath, Jim F. *John F. Kennedy and the Business Community*. Chicago: University of Chicago Press, 1969.

Herring, George C. *America's Longest War: The United States and Vietnam, 1950–1975*. 2d ed. New York: Alfred A. Knopf, 1979.

Hess, Karl. *In a Cause That Will Triumph*. Garden City, N.Y.: Doubleday, 1967.

Hodgson, Godfrey. *America in Our Time: From World War II to Nixon, What Happened and Why?* New York: Random House, 1976.

Hofstadter, Richard. *The American Political Tradition and the Men Who Made It*. New York: Vintage, 1954.

Huebner, Lee W., and Thomas E. Petri, eds. *The Ripon Papers, 1963–1968*. Washington, D.C.: National Press, 1968.

Javits, Jacob K. *Order of Battle: A Republican's Call to Reason*. New York: Atheneum, 1964.

Javits, Jacob K., with Rafael Steinberg. *Javits: The Autobiography of a Public Man.* Boston: Houghton Mifflin, 1981.

Judis, John. *William F. Buckley, Jr.: Patron Saint of the Conservatives.* New York: Simon and Schuster, 1988.

Kaplan, Marshall, and Peggy L. Cuciti, eds. *The Great Society and Its Legacy.* Durham, N.C.: Duke University Press, 1986.

Kearns, Doris. *Lyndon Johnson and the American Dream.* New York: Harper and Row, 1976.

Kennedy, Robert F. *Robert Kennedy in His Own Words.* Edited by Edwin Guthman and Jeffrey Shulman. New York: Bantam, 1988.

Key, V. O. *Southern Politics in State and Nation.* New York: Alfred A. Knopf, 1949.

Kirby, Jack Temple. *Rural Worlds Lost: The American South, 1920–1960.* Baton Rouge: Louisiana State University Press, 1987.

Kirk, Russell. *The Conservative Mind, from Burke to Santayana.* Chicago: University of Chicago Press, 1953.

Kolkey, Jonathan Martin. *The New Right, 1960–1968.* Washington, D.C.: University Press of America, 1982.

Kramer, Michael, and Sam Roberts. *"I Never Wanted to Be Vice-President of Anything!": An Investigative Biography of Nelson Rockefeller.* New York: Basic Books, 1976.

Kunen, James Simon. *The Strawberry Statement: Notes of a College Revolutionary.* New York: Avon, 1968.

Lasch, Christopher. *The Culture of Narcissism: American Life in an Age of Diminishing Expectations.* New York: Warner Books, 1979.

Larson, Arthur. *A Republican Looks at His Party.* New York: Harper and Row, 1956.

Lesher, Stephan. *George Wallace: American Populist.* New York: Addison-Wesley, 1994.

Leuchtenburg, William E. *A Troubled Feast: American Society since 1945.* Rev. ed. Boston: Little, Brown, 1979.

Lipset, Seymour, and Earl Raab. *The Politics of Unreason: Right Wing Extremism in America, 1790–1970.* New York: Harper and Row, 1970.

Lukas, J. Anthony. *Nightmare: The Underside of the Nixon Years.* New York: Viking, 1976.

McDowell, Edwin. *Barry Goldwater: Portrait of an Arizonan.* Chicago: Henry Regnery, 1964.

McQuaid, Kim. *The Anxious Years: America in the Vietnam-Watergate Era.* New York: Basic Books, 1989.

Matusow, Allen J. *The Unraveling of America: A History of Liberalism in the 1960s.* New York: Harper and Row, 1984.

May, Elaine Tyler. *Homeward Bound: American Families in the Cold War Era.* New York: Basic Books, 1988.

Mayer, George H. *The Republican Party, 1854–1966.* 2d ed. New York: Oxford University Press, 1967.

Miles, Michael W. *The Odyssey of the American Right*. New York: Oxford University Press, 1980.

Miller, James. *"Democracy Is in the Streets": From Port Huron to the Siege of Chicago*. New York: Simon and Schuster, 1987.

Miller, Merle. *Lyndon: An Oral Biography*. New York: G. P. Putnam's Sons, 1980.

Moynihan, Daniel Patrick. *Maximum Feasible Misunderstanding*. New York: Free Press, 1969.

Muse, Benjamin. *The American Negro Revolution: From Non-Violence to Black Power, 1963–1968*. Bloomington: Indiana University Press, 1968.

Nash, George H. *The Conservative Intellectual Tradition in America since 1945*. New York: Basic Books, 1976.

National Directory of "Rightist" Groups, Publications, and Some Individuals in the United States and Some Foreign Countries. San Francisco: Liberty and Property, 1960–64.

Nisbet, Robert. *The Quest for Community: A Study in the Ethics of Order and Freedom*. New York: Oxford University Press, 1953.

Nixon, Richard M. *RN: The Memoirs of Richard Nixon*. New York: Grosset and Dunlap, 1978.

——. *Six Crises*. Garden City, N.Y.: Doubleday, 1962.

Nock, Albert Jay. *Memoirs of a Superfluous Man*. New York: Harper and Brothers, 1943.

Official Program of the Republican National Convention. New York: Bozell and Jacobs, 1968.

Official Report of the Proceedings of the Twenty-Eighth Republican National Convention Held in San Francisco, California, July 12, 14, 15, 16, 1964. Washington, D.C.: Republican National Committee, 1964.

O'Neill, William. *Coming Apart: An Informal History of America in the 1960s*. New York: Quadrangle Books, 1971.

Oshinsky, David. *A Conspiracy So Immense: The World of Joe McCarthy*. New York: Free Press, 1983.

Parmet, Herbert. *The Democrats: The Years after FDR*. New York: Macmillan, 1976.

——. *Eisenhower and the American Crusades*. New York: Macmillan, 1972.

——. *Jack: The Struggles of John F. Kennedy*. New York: Dial Press, 1983.

——. *JFK: The Presidency of John F. Kennedy*. New York: Dial Press, 1983.

——. *Richard Nixon and His America*. Boston: Little, Brown, 1990.

Patterson, James T. *Congressional Conservatism and the New Deal: The Growth of the Conservative Coalition in Congress, 1933–1939*. Lexington: University of Kentucky Press, 1967.

——. *Mr. Republican: A Biography of Robert Taft*. Boston: Houghton Mifflin, 1972.

Pells, Richard H. *The Liberal Mind in a Conservative Age*. New York: Harper and Row, 1985.

Phillips, Kevin. *The Emerging Republican Majority*. New Rochelle, N.Y.: Arlington House, 1969.

Rae, Nicol C. *The Decline and Fall of the Liberal Republicans from 1952 to the Present*. New York: Oxford University Press, 1989.

Reed, John Shelton. *The Enduring South*. Lexington, Mass.: D. C. Heath, 1972.

——. *Southerners*. Chapel Hill: University of North Carolina Press, 1983.

Reichard, Gary W. *The Reaffirmation of Republicanism: Eisenhower and the Eighty-third Congress*. Knoxville: University of Tennessee Press, 1975.

Reinhard, David W. *The Republican Right since 1945*. Lexington: University of Kentucky Press, 1983.

Rorabaugh, W. J. *Berkeley at War: The 1960s*. New York: Oxford University Press, 1989.

Rossiter, Clinton. *Conservatism in America*. New York: Alfred A. Knopf, 1955.

Rusher, William. *The Making of the New Majority Party*. New York: Sheed and Ward, 1975.

——. *The Rise of the Right*. New York: William Morrow, 1984.

Rutland, Robert A. *The Democrats: From Jefferson to Carter*. Baton Rouge: Louisiana State University Press, 1979.

Sale, Kirkpatrick. *Power Shift: The Rise of the Southern Rim and Its Challenges to the Eastern Establishment*. New York: Vintage, 1976.

Scammon, Richard, and Ben J. Wattenberg. *The Real Majority*. New York: Coward, McCann, and Geoghehan, 1970.

Schlafly, Phyllis. *A Choice, Not an Echo*. Alton, Ill.: Pere Marquette Press, 1964.

Schlesinger, Arthur M., Jr. *A Thousand Days: John F. Kennedy in the White House*. Boston: Houghton Mifflin, 1965.

——. *The Vital Center: The Politics of Freedom*. Boston: Houghton Mifflin, 1949.

Shadegg, Stephen. *Barry Goldwater: Freedom Is His Flight Plan*. New York: Fleet, 1962.

——. *What Happened to Goldwater?: The Inside Story of the 1964 Republican Campaign*. New York: Holt, Rinehart and Winston, 1965.

Siegel, Frederick. *Troubled Journey: From Pearl Harbor to Ronald Reagan*. New York: Hill and Wang, 1984.

Sigler, Jay, ed. *The Conservative Tradition in American Thought*. New York: G. P. Putnam's Sons, 1969.

Sorenson, Theodore. *Kennedy*. New York: Harper and Row, 1965.

Steinfels, Peter. *The Neoconservatives: The Men Who Are Changing America's Politics*. New York: Simon and Schuster, 1979.

Stormer, John A. *None Dare Call It Treason*. Florissant, Mo.: Liberty Bell Press, 1964.

Szulc, Tad. *The Illusion of Peace: Foreign Policy in the Nixon Years*. New York: Viking, 1978.

Tanabaum, Duane. *The Bricker Amendment Controversy: A Test of Eisenhower's Political Leadership*. Ithaca, N.Y.: Cornell University Press, 1988.

Turner, Kathleen J. *Lyndon Johnson's Dual War: Vietnam and the Press*. Chicago: University of Chicago Press, 1985.

Underwood, James E., and William J. Daniels. *Governor Rockefeller in New York: The Apex of Pragmatic Liberalism in the United States*. Westport, Conn.: Greenwood Press, 1982.

Walton, Richard J. *Cold War and Counterrevolution: The Foreign Policy of John F. Kennedy*. New York: Viking, 1972.

Weaver, Richard. *Ideas Have Consequences*. Chicago: University of Chicago Press, 1948.

Welch, Robert. *The New Americanism*. Boston: Western Islands, 1966.

White, F. Clifton. *Suite 3505: The Story of the Draft Goldwater Movement*. New Rochelle, N.Y.: Arlington House, 1967.

White, F. Clifton, and William J. Gill. *Why Reagan Won: A Narrative History of the Conservative Movement, 1964–1981*. Chicago: Regnery Gateway, 1981.

White, Theodore. *America in Search of Itself: The Making of the President, 1956–1980*. New York: Harper and Row, 1982.

——. *Breach of Faith: The Fall of Richard Nixon*. New York: Atheneum, 1975.

——. *The Making of the President, 1960*. New York: Atheneum, 1961.

——. *The Making of the President, 1964*. New York: Atheneum, 1965.

——. *The Making of the President, 1968*. New York: Atheneum, 1969.

Wicker, Tom. *One of Us: Richard Nixon and the American Dream*. New York: Random House, 1991.

Wills, Garry. *Nixon Agonistes: The Crisis of the Self-Made Man*. Boston: Houghton Mifflin, 1970.

——. *Reagan's America: Innocents at Home*. Garden City, N.Y.: Doubleday, 1987.

Wolfe, Tom. *The Electric Kool-Aid Acid Test*. New York: Bantam, 1969.

Wright, Gavin. *Old South, New South: Revolutions in the Southern Economy since the Civil War*. New York: Basic Books, 1986.

INDEX

Agnew, Spiro, 127
Alcorn, Meade, 22
All Republican Conference, 55, 56, 57
American Conservative Union, 114–15, 119, 186 (n. 38)
Americans for Constitutional Action, 61, 87
Anticommunism, 10–11, 48–49
"Arizona Mafia," 69, 92, 99
Ashbrook, John, 2, 37, 162 (n. 17); and White's committee, 66; and conservatives' future, 112; and Wallace, 132
Asia-Firsters, 9

Baker, Bobby, 89–90, 99
Baroody, William, 69, 91–92
Bell, Daniel, 16, 20
Black Power movement, 83, 117–18, 138
Bliss, Ray, 55; as RNC chair, 106–7, 120, 181 (n. 7); and extremism, 109–10; and conservatives, 112, 113; and Free Society Association, 114; and 1966 elections, 119
Bozell, L. Brent, 16, 29, 30, 39
Bricker, John, 23, 24, 51, 147 (n. 4), 157 (n. 35)
Bridges, Styles, 24, 39
Buchanan, Patrick, 122, 136
Buckley, William F., Jr., 15; background, 11–12; on extremism, 17; and John Birch Society, 55, 62–63, 100; and 1965 New York City mayoral race, 113; and Reagan, 124–25; and Wallace, 132; support for Nixon, 133, 136; and evolution of conservative movement, 140, 142, 144 (n. 10); and GOP, 153 (n. 14)

Burch, Dean, 68, 69, 71; as RNC chair, 79, 91–92, 100–101; resignation, 105–6, 108, 111, 181 (n. 7)
Burnham, James, 10, 18, 49, 144 (n. 9)

Castro, Fidel, 26, 48
Chambers, Whittaker, 11
China Lobby, 122
Citizens for Goldwater-Miller, 87
Civil Rights Act of 1964, 70, 75, 79, 83, 86, 88, 117
Civil rights movement: during the 1950s, 25, 38; Nixon's views on, 28; effect on Democratic Party, 42; Kennedy's views on, 46–47, 50; Republicans' views on, 47–48, 154 (n. 24); during 1964 presidential campaign, 83; during Johnson administration, 117–18; and Nixon administration, 135
Committee of One Million, 13, 114, 145 (n. 21)
Congress on Racial Equality, 83
Conservative Party of New York, 64, 113
Conservatives, 3, 8–9; and the press, 2, 11, 24, 29; coalition of, 2, 139–40; and traditionalism, 9–10; and classical liberalism, 10; and youths, 12, 64–65, 115–16, 162 (n. 15); and citizens' groups, 12–13; political activity, 14, 18, 23–25, 31–32, 35, 36, 37, 38, 39, 41, 44, 53, 60–62, 63–64, 66–70, 72, 93–94, 99, 100, 102–4, 110, 111–14, 116, 119, 125–29, 133, 139–42; diversity of, 15; definition, 17; as critics of Eisenhower, 23–25; views on Nixon, 28–29, 39, 122; and Rockefeller,

34–35, 52–53, 55, 77, 123–24; views on 1960 presidential campaign, 37; views on civil rights, 47–48, 54; views on Kennedy's foreign policy, 49; and John Birch Society, 55, 62–63, 110; and changing political atmosphere, 58–59, 60–61, 130–31; relationship with GOP, 63, 64, 66–69, 77, 80–81, 82, 107–8, 111–12, 140, 153 (n. 14), 160 (n. 4); and 1964 presidential race, 72, 77, 82, 95, 99; and results of 1964 campaign, 100–103; and Burch's resignation as RNC chair, 105–6; evolution of conservative movement, 116, 127–28, 139–42; and Vietnam, 117, 129, 136; and 1966 elections, 119; and 1968 campaign, 122–23, 127–28; and Reagan, 124–26; and Wallace, 132–33; victory, 133–34; reaction to Nixon administration, 135–37

Democratic Party, 4, 14, 43, 184 (n. 30); and 1960 presidential campaign, 27; as coalition, 27, 131; and civil rights movement, 42, 70, 83, 126; and the Right, 50–51, 64; and 1964 presidential race, 70, 76, 78, 81, 86, 94, 98; and Johnson administration, 84, 131; Goldwater's reactions to programs of, 84–87; campaign against Goldwater, 94–95; and 1965 elections, 118; and 1966 elections, 118–19; and 1968 campaign, 124, 131; 1968 Democratic National Convention, 131–32; and Nixon administration, 137
Dirksen, Everett, 54, 77, 158 (n. 43)
Douglas, Helen Gahagan, 29
Doyle, Dane, and Bernbach advertising firm, 94
Draft Goldwater Committee. *See* National Draft Goldwater Committee
Dulles, John Foster, 22

"Eastern Establishment": definition, 7–8, 143 (n. 2); and conservatives, 18; and Republican Party, 20; Eisenhower as member of, 21; Rockefeller as member of, 34
Eastman, Max, 15, 24
Eisenhower, Dwight D., 7, 10, 34, 38, 54, 85, 86, 88, 107, 168 (n. 46); administration, 20, 21–22, 27; relationship with conservatives, 22–24; budget, 23; foreign policy, 23, 26; and Cuba, 26; U-2 incident, 26; and 1960 presidential campaign, 35, 40, 152 (n. 3); relationship with Nixon, 40, 51, 122–23, 157 (n. 36); and Republican Citizens' Committee, 56–57; and John Birch Society, 62, 94; and 1964 presidential race, 73, 74–75, 76, 78–80, 97–98; and Goldwater, 73, 78–79, 97; and GOP's future, 104–6, 108, 121
Eisenhower, Milton, 34, 58, 152 (n. 2)
Estes, Billie Sol, 89–90, 99
Evans, M. Stanton, 12, 102
Extremism: associated with conservatism, 16–17, 50–51, 54, 62, 140; John Birch Society and, 52, 55, 62, 110; Goldwater and, 71, 76, 78, 79–80; and 1964 campaign, 93–96; GOP and, 109–10; Wallace and, 132

Federation of Republican Women, 66, 112
Ford, Gerald, 54, 107, 109, 110, 117, 121
Formosa, 26, 95, 135
Free Society Association, 114, 186 (n. 38)

Galbraith, John Kenneth, 44, 84, 90
Goldwater, Barry, 2, 8, 14, 16, 19, 28, 38, 51, 107; as critic of Eisenhower, 23, 24; background, 29–30; views on conservatism, 30–31, 147

(n. 5); compared to Taft, 31–32, 109; as candidate in 1960, 32–33, 36–37, 150 (n. 36); and youths, 32–33, 64–65, 113, 123; reaction to Rockefeller-Nixon pact, 36; views on Kennedy, 49, 68; views on Nixon, 52, 122, 132; and Rockefeller, 52–53; as potential party leader, 53, 67; and John Birch Society, 55, 62; and Republican Citizens' Committee, 56, 57; and White's committee, 67–68, 164 (n. 25); decision to run, 68–71; campaign financing, 71–72, 87–88; and 1964 primary race, 71–77, 157 (n. 41); associated with extremism, 76–78, 93–96, 176 (n. 47); acceptance speech, 78–79; and unity conference, 79–80; and 1964 presidential race, 82–103, 167 (n. 43); views on issues, 84–87, 93; Democrats' campaign against, 89, 94–95; campaign staff, 90–93, 98–99, 172–73 (n. 24); and the press, 95–96, 175 (n. 42); and the Republican Party, 96–98, 100–101, 109; flaws of campaign, 98–99; defeat, 99–100; and results of 1964 campaign, 100–103; and Burch's resignation as RNC chair, 105–6, 181 (n. 7); and GOP's future, 110; and Free Society Association, 114; reassessment of, 118, 130; and 1968 campaign, 121; and Reagan, 124–25, 170 (n. 10); legacy, 127–28; return to Senate, 133; and evolution of conservative movement, 139–42
Goldwater for President Committee, 71, 72, 167 (n. 43)
Grass roots: organization, 3, 63–64, 139; support for Goldwater, 33, 66, 67, 71, 82, 87, 90, 107, 150 (n. 36), 171 (n. 13); problems with 1964 campaign, 93, 99, 103; and GOP, 112, 128; fund-raising, 115, 116

Great Society, 83–84, 116–17, 130–31
Grenier, John, 91–92, 98, 101

Hall, Leonard, 57
Halleck, Charles, 54, 104, 109, 158 (n. 43)
Harrington, Ione, 91
Hartz, Louis, 20
Hatfield, Mark, 105, 127
Hershey, Pennsylvania, unity conference, 79–80
Hess, Karl, 91, 173 (n. 25)
Hiss, Alger, 28, 29
Hofstadter, Richard, 2, 20
Hoover, Herbert, 24, 101
Humphrey, Hubert, 27, 131–32, 133
Hunt, H. L., 61, 95

Intercollegiate Society of Individualists, 12, 14, 64

Jaquith, David, 64, 113
Javits, Jacob, 47
Jenkins, Walter, 90, 172 (n. 22)
John Birch Society, 17, 51, 52, 91, 129; ideology, 13–14; associated with extremism, 54–55, 77, 80, 94, 109–10; and 1964 Republican platform, 77; and conservatives, 114–15; and Nixon administration, 136
Johnson, Lyndon B., 2; and 1960 presidential campaign, 27; and 1964 presidential race, 70, 76, 82–83, 88–90, 94–96, 98, 176 (n. 47); administration, 83–84, 108, 116–18, 130–31, 190 (n. 10); and results of 1964 campaign, 100–102

Keating, Kenneth, 47, 57, 145 (n. 21)
Kennedy, John F.: and 1960 presidential campaign, 27, 36, 37; administration, 44–50, 53; views on civil rights, 46–47; foreign policy, 48–49, 52; and Radical Right, 50–51,

156 (n. 31); and 1964 presidential race, 68, 70, 73, 78, 100
Kennedy, Robert, 70, 95, 129
Keynesian economics, 7, 44, 86
Khrushchev, Nikita, 26, 28, 48, 90, 135
King, Martin Luther, Jr., 123, 127, 129
Kirk, Russell, 10, 18
Kissinger, Henry, 134
Kitchel, Denison, 69, 71, 91–92, 98–99, 110, 111, 173 (n. 5)
Kleindienst, Richard, 71, 91, 128, 167 (n. 43), 173 (n. 5)
Knowland, William, 15, 23, 92, 144 (n. 6)
Kohlberg, Alfred, 28
Kuchel, Thomas, 43, 47

Laird, Melvin, 36, 109, 120–21
Landon, Alf, 108
Larson, Arthur, 21, 43, 96
Left, the, 4, 49, 61, 112, 122
Liberty Lobby, 61
Lichenstein, Charles, 40, 95
Liebman, Marvin, 62, 63, 115, 133
Life Line Foundation, 61
Lodge, Henry Cabot, 72–73
Luce, Clare Booth, 77, 133
Lukens, Donald, 65, 111, 112, 128, 179 (n. 61)

MacArthur, Douglas, 53
McCabe, Edward, 69
McCarthy, Joseph, 10, 16, 44
McGee, Gale, 50
Manion, Clarence, 14, 62
Meyer, Frank, 14, 18, 112, 116, 122, 125, 131, 132
Miller, William, 41, 44, 56, 57; and 1964 presidential campaign, 77, 79–80; and GOP's future, 111
Milliken, Roger, 31, 62
Modern Republicanism: definition, 22; and 1958 election, 24

Morton, Thruston, 40–41, 107
Moynihan, Daniel Patrick, 134

National Draft Goldwater Committee, 65, 69–71, 72, 114
Nationalism: during Eisenhower administration, 26
National Republican Citizens' Committee. See Republican Citizens' Committee
National Student Association, 65
National Student Committee for the Loyalty Oath, 12, 145 (n. 14)
New Right, the, 142
Nixon, Richard M., 11, 15, 33, 34, 88, 107, 147 (n. 5), 190 (n. 10); 1958 South American trip, 26; and conservatives, 28, 29, 122, 133; and 1960 presidential campaign, 28–29, 34–37, 152 (n. 3); as centrist, 29; relationship with Rockefeller, 35, 150 (n. 41); post-1960 election, 39–41, 43, 152 (n. 2); and California gubernatorial race, 51–52, 156 (n. 36), 157 (n. 37); and John Birch Society, 54–55; and 1964 presidential race, 71, 73, 74, 76–79, 97–98; relationship with Goldwater, 73, 76, 78, 122; and GOP's future, 104; and 1968 campaign, 121–28, 138; as heir to Goldwater, 127–28; and Wallace, 132–33; victory, 133; administration, 134–37

O'Donnell, Peter, 69, 91, 105, 128, 163 (n. 21)

Patman, Wright, 50
People's Republic of China, 26, 135
Percy, Charles, 36

Radical Right, the, 50, 53
Reagan, Ronald, 28, 33, 157 (n. 37); and John Birch Society, 62; and 1964 campaign, 102; and GOP's

future, 112; as governor, 119; and youths, 123; and 1968 campaign, 124–26, 133, 134, 138, 191 (n. 13); and the South, 125–27; as heir to Goldwater, 127–28, 141–42, 170 (n. 13)

Republican Citizens' Committee, 56–58, 111, 159 (n. 48)

Republican Coordinating Committee, 108–10

Republican Governors' Association, 69, 105, 119; formation of, 108

Republican National Committee, 33, 55, 66, 79, 91, 92, 100–101, 106, 108, 158 (n. 43)

Republican Party, 1, 33, 91, 184 (n. 30); liberals in, 4, 8, 14, 17, 34, 36, 40, 43, 46, 49, 53, 55, 73–74, 77, 108, 110–11, 113, 136, 141, 147 (n. 5); history of, 6–8; divisions within, 7–9, 22–23, 43–44; conservatives in, 14, 35, 38, 44, 51, 77, 81, 82, 127–28, 153 (n. 14); and 1958 election, 24; and 1960 presidential campaign, 27–28; and the South, 41–43, 101, 125–27; relationship with Kennedy administration, 44–50; image, 54; and extremism, 54–55; building support, 56–57; and 1964 campaign, 71, 74–75; support for Goldwater, 72; opposition to Goldwater, 73–74, 77, 80, 87, 96–97; and Johnson administration, 84; support for Johnson's campaign, 89, 96; and results of 1964 campaign, 102, 104; unity, 105, 107–8, 110, 120–21; future of, 107–9, 120–21; extraparty organizations, 110–11; response to Johnson, 116–18; and 1965 elections, 118; and 1966 elections, 118–19; and 1968 campaign, 121, 133; as conservative party, 133–34, 137–42

Right, the, 1, 23, 40, 50, 55, 116, 122; and Republican Party, 9, 110–11,

112, 122, 133–34; and Rockefeller, 34, 52; and 1964 presidential race, 70, 101–2; and 1968 campaign, 127–28, 133, 138; reactions to Nixon administration, 135–37; evolution of conservative movement, 139–42. See also Conservatives

Ripon Society, 111, 119

Rockefeller, Nelson, 43, 51, 64, 94, 147 (n. 5); background, 34–35; and 1960 presidential campaign, 35–36, 40, 150 (n. 41); relationship with Goldwater, 52; as potential party leader, 52–53; and 1964 presidential race, 73, 76–80, 97, 109, 167 (n. 43), 169 (n. 52), 176 (n. 47); and 1968 campaign, 121, 123–25, 127–28

Rockefeller-Nixon pact, 35–36, 150 (n. 41)

Rockwell, George Lincoln, 17

Romney, George, 53; and John Birch Society, 55; and 1964 presidential race, 72–73, 74, 77, 79, 93, 97; and GOP's future, 104, 105, 107; and 1968 campaign, 121, 123

Roosevelt, Franklin D., 7, 42, 46, 65, 88, 101

Rusher, William, 2, 11–12, 37, 156 (n. 31), 160 (n. 3); and White's committee, 66–67, 162 (n. 17); and 1964 presidential campaign, 92, 172 (n. 24); and GOP's future, 112, 116, 193 (n. 3); and Nixon, 123, 133; and Reagan, 124

Schlamm, Willi, 11

Schlesinger, Arthur M., Jr., 2, 16, 44, 70, 95

Schwarz, Fred C., 13

Scranton, William: and 1964 presidential race, 75–76, 97; and Burch's resignation as RNC chair, 105

Shadegg, Stephen, 41, 91, 99, 163 (n. 21), 169 (n. 52), 173 (n. 24)

Smylie, Robert, 97, 105, 107
Sokolsky, George, 14, 153 (n. 14)
South, the: and conservatives, 8, 43, 134, 152–53 (n. 6); and Democratic Party, 27, 42–43, 70; Republican Party in, 41–43, 101, 118, 125–27; associated with extremism, 54; and 1964 presidential race, 70, 101; and Reagan, 125–27; and 1968 campaign, 125–28, 132; and Nixon administration, 135
Soviet Union: and Eisenhower administration, 23, 25; *Sputnik I*, 26; and Kennedy administration, 48, 85; and Nixon administration, 135–36; and Carter administration, 141
Student movement, 64, 118, 129–30
Student Nonviolent Coordinating Committee, 83, 117–18

Taft, Robert A., 9, 18, 69, 107, 109, 144 (n. 6); relationship with Eisenhower, 22; compared to Goldwater, 31–32, 38; views on education and housing, 31–32; views on foreign policy, 32
Thurmond, Strom, 126–27, 132, 162 (n. 14)
Tower, John, 43, 44, 62, 132, 153 (n. 10)

Vietnam War, 84, 102, 115, 116–18, 121, 122, 128–29, 130, 131–32, 136, 142

Viguerie, Richard, 114

Wallace, George: and 1964 presidential campaign, 72–73, 83; and 1968 presidential campaign, 132–33
Watergate, 136–37, 142
Weaver, Richard, 14
Welch, Robert, 13, 17, 54, 62, 63, 95
White, F. Clifton, 2, 33, 37, 57; background, 66, 162 (n. 17); and "Chicago group," 66–68, 163 (n. 22), 164 (n. 25); and development of conservative movement, 69, 163 (n. 21); and 1964 campaign, 71, 72, 78, 79, 87–88, 91–92, 99, 103, 172–73 (n. 24), 179 (n. 61); and GOP's future, 111; and 1968 campaign, 124, 128
White, Theodore, 39, 78
"White backlash," 83, 119, 155 (n. 25)
World Youth Crusade for Freedom, 115

Young Americans for Freedom, 12, 14, 51, 64, 114, 115, 161–62 (n. 14)
Young Republican National Federation, 12, 14, 33, 38, 64, 161–62 (n. 14); in Goldwater's 1964 campaign, 65, 66, 69, 162 (n. 17); and GOP's future, 112, 113; and Nixon, 123